THE CAMBRIDGE COMPANION TO
HENRY FIELDING

Now best known for three great novels – *Tom Jones*, *Joseph Andrews* and *Amelia* – Henry Fielding (1707–1754) was one of the most controversial figures of his time. Prominent first as a playwright, then as a novelist and political journalist, and finally as a justice of the peace, Fielding made a substantial contribution to eighteenth-century culture, and was hugely influential in the development of the novel as a form, both in Britain and more widely in Europe. This collection of specially commissioned essays by leading scholars describes and analyses the many facets of Fielding's work in theatre, fiction, journalism and politics. In addition it assesses his unique contribution to the rise of the novel as the dominant literary form, the development of the law, and the political and literary culture of eighteenth-century Britain. Including a Chronology and Guide to Further Reading, this volume offers a comprehensive account of Fielding's life and work.

# THE CAMBRIDGE
## COMPANION TO
# HENRY FIELDING

EDITED BY
CLAUDE RAWSON

 CAMBRIDGE
UNIVERSITY PRESS

CAMBRIDGE UNIVERSITY PRESS
Cambridge, New York, Melbourne, Madrid, Cape Town, Singapore, São Paulo

Cambridge University Press
The Edinburgh Building, Cambridge CB2 2RU, UK

Published in the United States of America by Cambridge University Press, New York

www.cambridge.org
Information on this title: www.cambridge.org/9780521670920

First published 2007

Printed in the United Kingdom at the University Press, Cambridge

*A catalogue record for this publication is available from the British Library*

ISBN 978-0-521-85451-1 hardback
ISBN 978-0-521-67092-0 paperback

# CONTENTS

# NOTES ON CONTRIBUTORS

PAUL BAINES is a Professor in the School of English, University of Liverpool. He has published *The House of Forgery in Eighteenth-Century Britain* (1999), *The Complete Critical Guide to Alexander Pope* (2000), an edition of romantic-period plays (2000), *The Long Eighteenth Century* (2004), and articles on several eighteenth-century figures in the *Oxford Dictionary of National Biography*. His biography of Edmund Curll, *Edmund Curll, Bookseller*, co-written with Pat Rogers, will appear in 2007.

LINDA BREE is the Literature Publisher at Cambridge University Press. She is the author of *Sarah Fielding* (1996) and editor of Sarah Fielding's *The Adventures of David Simple* (2002) and (with Claude Rawson) of Henry Fielding's *Jonathan Wild* (2004), as well as of Jane Austen's *Persuasion* (2000).

JENNY DAVIDSON teaches in the Department of English and Comparative Literature at Columbia University. She is the author of two books: *Hypocrisy and the Politics of Politeness: Manners and Morals from Locke to Austen* (2004), and *Heredity* (2003), a novel about Jonathan Wild.

BERTRAND A. GOLDGAR, Professor of English at Lawrence University, is the author of *The Curse of Party: Swift's Relations with Addison and Steele* and *Walpole and the Wits: The Relation of Politics to Literature, 1722–1742*. For the Wesleyan Edition of Fielding's Works he has edited *The Covent-Garden Journal* (1988) and co-edited (with Hugh Amory) *Miscellanies*, vol. II (1993) and *Miscellanies*, vol. III (*Jonathan Wild*) (1997). Currently he is preparing the volume *English Political Writings 1711–1714* for the forthcoming *Cambridge Edition of the Works of Jonathan Swift*.

NICHOLAS HUDSON, Professor of English at the University of British Columbia, is the author of *Samuel Johnson and Eighteenth-Century Thought* (1988), *Writing and European Thought, 1600–1830* (1994), *Samuel Johnson and the Making of Modern England* (2003), and of numerous essays on eighteenth-century literature, thought, and culture.

THOMAS KEYMER is Chancellor Jackman Professor of English at the University of Toronto and a Supernumerary Fellow of St Anne's College, Oxford. His books include *Richardson's 'Clarissa' and the Eighteenth-Century Reader* (Cambridge University Press, 1992, 2004), *Sterne, the Moderns, and the Novel* (2002), and the Penguin Classics editions of Fielding's *Journal of a Voyage to Lisbon* (1996) and *Tom Jones* (2005).

CHARLES A. KNIGHT is Emeritus Professor of English at the University of Massachusetts, Boston. He has written *The Literature of Satire* (Cambridge University Press, 2004) and *Joseph Addison and Richard Steele: A Reference Guide* (New York, 1994), as well as numerous articles on literary periodicals, on satire, and on Fielding and other eighteenth-century novelists.

THOMAS LOCKWOOD is Professor and former Chair of the Department of English at the University of Washington, Seattle. He has published widely on Fielding and other eighteenth-century subjects and is editor of the drama volumes of the Oxford 'Wesleyan' edition of the works of Fielding: *Plays*, vol. I (2004), vol. II (2007), and vol. III (in progress).

CLAUDE RAWSON is Maynard Mack Professor of English at Yale University. His publications on Fielding include *Henry Fielding* (1968); *Henry Fielding and the Augustan Ideal under Stress* (1972); *Henry Fielding: A Critical Anthology* (1973); *Order from Confusion Sprung* (1985); and *Satire and Sentiment 1660–1830* (1994). He contributed the chapter on Fielding in the *Cambridge Companion to the Eighteenth-Century Novel* (1996). His most recent book is *God, Gulliver, and Genocide: Barbarism and the European Imagination 1492–1945* (2001).

PAT ROGERS, DeBartolo Chair in the Liberal Arts at the University of South Florida, is the author of numerous books and articles on all aspects of eighteenth-century literature and culture, of which the most recent are *Pope and the Destiny of the Stuarts* (2005) and, with Paul Baines, *Edmund Curll, Bookseller* (2007). He is the editor of *The Cambridge Companion to Alexander Pope* (2007).

PETER SABOR is Canada Research Chair in Eighteenth-Century Studies and Director of the Burney Centre at McGill University. His work includes (with Thomas Keymer) *'Pamela' in the Marketplace: Literary Controversy and Print Culture in Eighteenth-Century Britain and Ireland* (Cambridge University Press, 2005), and the *Juvenilia* volume in The Cambridge Edition of the Works of Jane Austen (2006).

JANE SPENCER is Professor of English at the University of Exeter. She has published widely on the eighteenth-century novel and women's literary history from the Restoration to the nineteenth century. Her latest book is *Literary Relations: Kinship and the Canon, 1660–1830* (2005). She is currently working on animals in eighteenth-century writing.

Unless otherwise noted, all quotations from Fielding will be from the Wesleyan Edition of the Works of Henry Fielding, Executive Editor W. B. Coley (Oxford: Clarendon Press, 1967–), and page references will be to the relevant volumes of that edition. Sectional references to book, chapter, act, or scene will be provided for readers using other editions. Parenthetical references in the text will therefore give page numbers in the Wesleyan Edition, followed by book and chapter (or act and scene) numbers, e.g. 96; II. iv. The Wesleyan Edition to date includes (for full publication details, see Guide to Further Reading):

The Adventures of Joseph Andrews, ed. Martin C. Battestin
Amelia, ed. Martin C. Battestin
Contributions to the Champion, ed. W. B. Coley
Covent-Garden Journal, ed. Bertrand A. Goldgar
'An Enquiry into the Causes of the Late Increase of Robbers' and Related Writings, ed. Malvin R. Zirker
The History of Tom Jones, ed. Martin C. Battestin
The Jacobite's Journal, ed. W. B. Coley
Miscellanies, vol. I, ed. Henry Knight Miller
Miscellanies, vol. II, ed. Bertrand A. Goldgar and Hugh Amory
Miscellanies, vol. III, ed. Bertrand A. Goldgar and Hugh Amory (includes Jonathan Wild)
Plays, vol. I, 1728–31, ed. Thomas Lockwood
The True Patriot and Related Writings, ed. W. B. Coley

For the Journal of a Voyage to Lisbon, not yet included in the Wesleyan Edition, the edition used is that of Thomas Keymer (London: Penguin, 1996). For Fielding's letters, the edition used is The Correspondence of Henry and Sarah Fielding, ed. Martin C. Battestin and Clive T. Probyn (Oxford: Clarendon Press, 1993).

# CHRONOLOGY

| | |
|---|---|
| 1707 | 22 April, HF born at his maternal grandfather's house, Sharpham Park, near Glastonbury, Somerset |
| 1710 | November, Sarah, the third of HF's four sisters, born at the family estate at East Stour, Dorset |
| 1714 | Death of Queen Anne, accession of George I. Alexander Pope, *The Rape of the Lock*, published |
| 1715–20 | Pope, *The Iliad of Homer* (translation), published |
| 1718 | April, death of HF's mother, Sarah Gould Fielding. Within a year HF's father Edmund Fielding remarries and an acrimonious battle with Lady Gould, the children's maternal grandmother, for the custody of the children begins |
| 1719 | Daniel Defoe, *Robinson Crusoe*, and Eliza Haywood, *Love in Excess*, published |
| 1719–24 | Education at Eton. Among his fellow students is George Lyttelton, a friend and patron in HF's later life |
| 1721 | September, birth of HF's half-brother John, who later worked with HF and succeeded him as magistrate at Bow Street |
| 1722 | Lady Gould wins the court case for custody of the Fielding children. Robert Walpole (1676–1745), having already held various offices of state, comes to power as head of government. Defoe, *Colonel Jack*, *Journal of the Plague Year*, *Moll Flanders* published |
| 1724 | Defoe, *Roxana*, published |
| 1724–6 | Defoe, *Tour through the Whole Island of Great Britain*, published |

| | |
|---|---|
| 1725 | May, Jonathan Wild hanged at Tyburn |
| 1725–6 | Pope, *The Odyssey of Homer* (translation), published |
| 1726 | Jonathan Swift, *Gulliver's Travels*, published |
| 1727 | Death of George I, accession of George II |
| 1728 | January, *The Masquerade* (HF's first published poem) published. John Gay's *The Beggar's Opera* performed, breaking all box-office records in London. February, *Love in Several Masques* (first play) performed. March, HF registers as a student of humane letters at the University of Leiden. May, first version of Pope, *The Dunciad*, published |
| 1729 | Return to London from Leiden. April, Pope, *Dunciad, Variorum*, published |
| 1730 | *The Temple Beau* (January), *The Author's Farce* (March), *Tom Thumb* (April), *Rape upon Rape* (later known as *The Coffee-House Politician*) (June) performed |
| 1731 | *The Tragedy of Tragedies: Or, the Life and Death of Tom Thumb the Great* (March), *The Letter-Writers* (March), *The Welsh Opera* (April) performed; *The Grub-Street Opera* rehearsed but not performed |
| 1732 | *The Lottery* (January), *The Modern Husband* (February), *The Covent-Garden Tragedy* (June), *The Old Debauchees* (June), *The Mock-Doctor* (from Molière, June) performed |
| 1733 | February, *The Miser* (from Molière) performed |
| 1734 | *The Intriguing Chambermaid* (January), *Don Quixote in England* (April) performed. November, marriage to Charlotte Cradock at Charlcombe, just outside Bath |
| 1735 | *An Old Man Taught Wisdom* (January), *The Universal Gallant* (February) performed |
| 1736 | *Pasquin* (March), *Tumble-down Dick* (April) performed. Eliza Haywood, *Adventures of Eovaii* (satirical novel about Walpole), published |
| 1737 | *Eurydice* (February), *The Historical Register for the Year 1736* (March), *Eurydice Hiss'd* (April) performed. Passing of Licensing Act, effectively ending HF's career as a playwright. HF becomes a law student in the Middle Temple |

| | |
|---|---|
| 1739–41 | Edits the *Champion*, a paper politically opposed to Walpole |
| 1740 | June, called to the Bar. *The Military History of Charles XII, King of Sweden*, by M. Gustavus Adlerfeld (HF translation) published. Colley Cibber, *An Apology for the Life of Mr. Colley Cibber, Comedian*, and Samuel Richardson's novel *Pamela* published. December, beginning of the War of Austrian Succession, which continues until 1748 |
| 1741 | April, *An Apology for the Life of Mrs. Shamela Andrews*, HF's parody of Cibber's *Apology* and especially Richardson's *Pamela*, published anonymously. December, sequel to *Pamela* (vols. III and IV), published. HF seems to break with Opposition and to side with Walpole's government |
| 1742 | Walpole forced out of office, retires from politics and is created Earl of Orford. February, *The History of the Adventures of Joseph Andrews, and of his Friend Mr Abraham Adams; Written in Imitation of the Manner of Cervantes* published. March, Pope, *The New Dunciad* (i.e. Book IV), published. May, *Miss Lucy in Town* performed. Death of HF's daughter Charlotte and severe illness of HF's wife |
| 1743 | February, *The Wedding-Day* performed. April, *Miscellanies* published in three volumes, including poems, plays, essays, the otherworldly fiction *A Journey from this World to the Next*, and, occupying the whole of the third volume, *The History of the Life of the Late Mr. Jonathan Wild the Great*. October, Pope, *The Dunciad, in Four Books* (final version), published |
| 1744 | May, Sarah Fielding's *The Adventures of David Simple* published. Second edition published in July, including HF's Preface and revisions. November, death of HF's wife Charlotte. December, several of his patrons including Lyttelton receive appointments in the new government |
| 1745 | The 'Forty Five', the invasion by the 'Young Pretender' Prince Charles Edward Stuart attempting to restore the long-exiled Stuart monarchy with the aid of Jacobite supporters in Britain. November 1745 to June 1746, HF edits *The True Patriot*, a pro-Hanoverian paper opposing the rebellion |
| 1746 | April, final defeat of the Jacobites at Culloden |

1747 April, Sarah Fielding's *Familiar Letters between the Principal Characters in 'David Simple' and Some Others* published, with a Preface and some other contributions from HF. November, marries Mary Daniel, formerly his first wife's maid, now pregnant with his child. December 1747–November 1748, HF edits *The Jacobite's Journal*. December 1747, the first part of Richardson's novel *Clarissa* published

1748 January, HF reviews *Clarissa* favourably in *The Jacobite's Journal*. January, Tobias Smollett's *The Adventures of Roderick Random* published. April and December, the remaining part of *Clarissa* published. Autumn, HF privately circulates copies of Books I–VI of *The History of Tom Jones: A Foundling*. October, becomes Justice of the Peace for Westminster (jurisdiction later extended to cover Middlesex), appointment owing largely to Lyttelton and also to John Russell, Duke of Bedford. November, John Cleland, *Memoirs of a Woman of Pleasure*, published (second volume in February 1749)

1749 February, *The History of Tom Jones: A Foundling* published. A second edition published before the end of February, a third in April and a fourth revised edition in December

1750 February, the opening of the Universal Register Office, a clearing house for employment, sales, exchange and property transactions, managed by HF and his half-brother John. July 1750–January 1751, three of HF's four sisters die in London. 1750–2, Samuel Johnson's *The Rambler* published

1751 January, *An Enquiry into the Causes of the Late Increase of Robbers*, an important legal-sociological work reflecting HF's views on crime and the ways in which it could be controlled, published. February, Tobias Smollett's *The Adventures of Peregrine Pickle* published. Eliza Haywood, *The History of Miss Betsy Thoughtless*, published. December, *Amelia* published (dated 1752)

1752 January–November, edits *Covent-Garden Journal*

1753 January, *A Proposal for Making an Effectual Provision for the Poor, for Amending their Morals, and for Rendering them Useful Members of the Society* published; February, Sarah Fielding, *David Simple: Volume the Last*, published

| | |
|---|---|
| 1754 | March, revised edition of *Jonathan Wild* published. HF's health, poor for several years, deteriorates to the extent that he has to resign his office as magistrate. June–August, HF travels to Lisbon in hopes the Portuguese air would improve his health. 8 October, dies at Junqueira near Lisbon |
| 1755 | February, the *Journal of a Voyage to Lisbon* published |

CLAUDE RAWSON

# Introduction

Henry Fielding was born on 22 April 1707 and this *Companion* thus appears in his tercentenary year. He died on 8 October 1754. In a life of less than fifty years he became the most important English playwright of his time, whom Shaw thought the 'greatest practising dramatist . . . between the Middle Ages and the nineteenth century'[1] apart from Shakespeare. He is also one of the great inaugural figures of the history of the novel, admired and imitated by Stendhal, Dickens, Thackeray, and other masters of the particular species of fiction that uses a strong controlling narrator. His novels were from the start written in self-conscious opposition to those of his rival Samuel Richardson (1689–1761), who represents an equally foundational but more self-effacing mode, in which the author purports to be invisible, and which aims at creating a feeling that the reader is witnessing real events rather than reading a story. Though not the only or the first important early novelists in Western literature, both writers represent, and helped decisively to shape, alternative styles of what was to become the dominant literary form of the modern world.

Fielding had aristocratic lineage and was educated at Eton. He was also continuously short of money, and experienced debt and various forms of low life as a penniless author and frequenter of taverns. His novels are laced with a lightly worn classical erudition, and have an ironic urbanity, partly worn as a badge of caste, but they also show a not wholly incompatible fondness for coarse popular entertainments. His manner derives to some extent from the satirical writers of the preceding generation, themselves spokesmen for a quasi-aristocratic ethos and a deep cultural loyalty to the ancient classics, who, while themselves mostly non-patrician, knew how to combine lordly hauteur with touches of demotic vulgarity. Fielding formed his oblique, ironic style, and his thrusting satirical energy, partly from Jonathan Swift (1667–1745), whom he venerated as a satiric master. But his writings are marked with his own individual stamp, warmer, more generous, and (except in some later works) less pessimistic. The Scriblerus Club, the coterie led by Swift and the poet Alexander Pope (1688–1744), was the source of the pseudonym Scriblerus Secundus, which Fielding used in his early plays. In this too he differed from Richardson, a more bourgeois figure, equally suspicious of the lordly and the low, and not naturally given to urbanity or ironic finesse.

Fielding wrote over two dozen plays between 1728 and 1737, when his outspoken criticism of Sir Robert Walpole's government helped to bring about the Licensing Act. This legislation imposed pre-production censorship on the English stage and lasted until 1968, though latterly exercised over moral rather than political issues. Fielding had engaged in political controversy in the 1730s, and continued throughout his life as a pamphleteer and journalist, editing several important journals from the *Champion* (1739–40) to the *Covent-Garden Journal* (1752). He also began to practise law, eventually becoming Justice of the Peace for Westminster and Middlesex, and writing several works on social and political issues, of which the best known are the *Enquiry into the Causes of the Late Increase of Robbers* (1751) and *A Proposal for Making an Effectual Provision for the Poor* (1753). He played a role in the shaping of what eventually became the Metropolitan Police.

This *Companion* considers Fielding's achievements as a dramatist, journalist, political writer, and socio-legal thinker. But he is principally celebrated for his fiction, which effectively began with *An Apology for the Life of Mrs Shamela Andrews* (1741), a parody of Richardson's first novel, *Pamela* (1740). Most of his subsequent fictions, *Joseph Andrews* (1742), *Tom Jones* (1749), and *Amelia* (1751), pointedly define themselves in relation to Richardson's work and personality, which stood as a lifelong shadow over Fielding's shoulder. His feelings for Richardson, unlike Richardson's for him, were not wholly negative, and included a warm admiration for Richardson's second novel, *Clarissa* (1747–8). There was personal antagonism between the two writers, but it helped to establish and refine two rival models of the novel, and the effect of Fielding's almost obsessive concern with Richardson was to develop and sharpen a mode of fiction-writing whose life and afterlife continue strong.

## NOTES

1. George Bernard Shaw, Preface to *Plays Unpleasant* (1898; Harmondsworth: Penguin, 1951), xii.

# I

LINDA BREE

# Henry Fielding's life

Henry Fielding was born on 22 April 1707. His father, Edmund Fielding, was the son of a younger son of a seventeenth-century Earl of Desmond, whose family claimed kin (erroneously as it later turned out) with the imperial Habsburg dynasty. In 1707, at the age of twenty-seven, Edmund was a Lieutenant Colonel in Queen Anne's army, and had served with distinction in the wars against France, including the Duke of Marlborough's great victory at Blenheim (1704). Henry's mother, Sarah, was daughter of Sir Henry Gould, who had succeeded in a more prosaic but no less powerful profession, rising to be one of the most distinguished lawyers of his time. It was at Sir Henry's estate, Sharpham Park in Somerset, that Edmund and Sarah's first child, named for his grandfather, was born. The match was a fruitful one, producing seven children in nine years: Henry was followed by Catherine, Ursula, Anne (who died in 1715 at the age of three), Sarah, Beatrice, and Edmund. Shortly before his death in 1710 Sir Henry Gould arranged the purchase of a substantial farm for them in the village of East Stour in Dorset. Here, in a rich rural setting later celebrated by the novelist Thomas Hardy, the Fielding children spent their early childhood, mostly in the care of their mother, since Edmund, who clearly found the idea of being a country squire unappealing, was often away on active service, or on pleasure trips in Ireland or London.

In 1718, just before Henry's eleventh birthday, his mother died, and this led to a series of upheavals which transformed the children's lives. Their father, still only in his late thirties, remarried within a year; his return to East Stour from London with his new wife, who was already pregnant, initiated a new regime, in which, it was rumoured, the children of Edmund's first marriage were at best neglected and at worst abused. Moreover, the new Mrs Fielding was said to be a practising Catholic – a serious charge in the early years of the first Hanoverian king, George I, amid continuing fears of an attempt to restore the Catholic Stuarts to the throne. All this stirred Sir Henry's widow, the children's formidable grandmother, Lady Gould, to action. Sir Henry had not completed the purchase of the East Stour farm before his death, leading to legal confusion about its ownership; moreover, clearly doubtful of his son-in-law's ability to handle money or domestic responsibility, he had left the farm for the benefit of his daughter and her children only. Now Lady Gould sued Edmund both for the farm's income, which, she said, he had appropriated to himself rather than spending it on his children, and for custody of the children themselves because of the neglect and abuse they were suffering.

Court records document the charges and counter-charges that followed, as Edmund tried to assert his rights to his children on the one hand, and to the farm and its income on the other. Perhaps he was never likely to succeed, with the legal skill and knowledge of the Goulds ranged against him. After two years and a series of bruising encounters during which family members and servants took partisan positions, revealing intimate and embarrassing details of the Fieldings' life in open court, Lady Gould gained custody of the children, and obtained legal guarantees that the income from East Stour would be used for their benefit. It was determined that Henry, who was by now at school at Eton, would spend his school holidays with his grandmother.

It is easy to imagine how distressing and disruptive all this must have been to Henry, a boy who already, according to evidence given in court, was passionate, headstrong, and unruly. He had, with his siblings, been publicly wrangled over; he must have been aware of the accusations of abuse and bad behaviour on all sides; he was now to be deprived of the control which might be exercised by his father, in favour of occasional attendance in a household dominated by two elderly women – his grandmother and her sister – and containing five younger siblings, four of them girls.

Lady Gould had recently moved to Salisbury, and the Fielding girls had been placed in a school there. On at least one occasion Henry apparently ran away from Eton to the sanctuary of his grandmother; certainly he seems not to have defied the courts to be with his father. But in fact, during his adolescent years, he seems to have been content enough at school. Eton was one of the leading schools in the country, the first choice for the sons of many of the aristocracy and gentry. Along with the harsh regime of bullying and beating which afflicted most boys' schools in the eighteenth century, Eton offered a curriculum, based on thorough knowledge of classical literature in the original Latin and Greek together with a close familiarity with the Bible, which was felt to equip a gentleman's son to make his way in any of the leading professions, as well as to provide him with superior social and intellectual resources. The extent to which Fielding enjoyed, and was influenced by, a wide range of classical writers first encountered at Eton is evident from his later work (although projects to translate the works of Aristophanes and Lucian never reached fruition). Eton's other major attraction was extra-curricular: it enabled the sons of aristocrats and gentry to make friendships which were intended to serve them well in adult life. Again Fielding benefited: the friendships he made at Eton – with George, later Lord, Lyttelton, and with Charles Hanbury Williams and William Pitt, later Lord Chatham, all of them powerful in government in the mid-century – created loyalties which lasted for the rest of his life.

During school holidays, and frequently afterwards, he made his home with his grandmother and sisters in Salisbury. Visiting Salisbury around this time, as part of his 'tour through the whole island of Great Britain', Daniel Defoe described 'a large and pleasant city' – in fact, with 8,000 inhabitants, one of the ten largest cities in England – driven by prosperous mercantile activity and only slightly marred by its perennially wet and dirty streets. At the heart of the city was the magnificent cathedral, with its surrounding 'close' of substantial houses; here the Fielding sisters went to school, and here prominent local gentry – including Lady Gould – lived. 'The people of Salisbury are gay and rich . . . and there is a great deal of good manners and good company among them', wrote Defoe.[1] The local gentry included several with children around the same age as the Fieldings, and more friendships were formed. James Harris, whose family was related to the Earls of Shaftesbury, and who was later the author of the grammatical treatise *Hermes* and later still a prominent politician, became Fielding's closest friend. The later history of the Collier siblings would also be bound up with that of the Fieldings, for good and ill: Arthur Collier would involve Fielding in financial difficulties; Jane, who lodged with Sarah Fielding and collaborated with her on *The Cry* (1754), was one of the few close friends who saw Henry and his family off on his final voyage to Lisbon in 1754; while Margaret travelled to Portugal as part of Fielding's household.

Despite making friends there, however, Fielding seems to have had no intention of settling in Salisbury. Indeed, immediately after Eton he did not seem to be settling at all. In Lyme Regis in the summer of 1725 he caused mayhem when he attempted to elope with his cousin Sarah Andrew; in London in 1726 he was accused of assaulting one of his father's servants.

However, it must always have been clear that Fielding would need, sooner rather than later, to undertake a profession. The Goulds were fond of the Fielding children, but the Gould fortune was comfortable rather than opulent, and would descend not to the Fieldings but to Lady Gould's son and his children. Edmund Fielding had paid for his son's schooling, and allowed him a modest maintenance for a while afterwards, but Sir Henry's earlier caution seems to have been well justified: though Edmund continued to rise in the army, he was never able to hold on to money he earned: he lost one large sum at the gaming tables, and another in the South Sea Bubble. His second wife having died after giving him six sons, he married a third, and though her wealth was said to be significant it was still unequal to his expenses.

Fielding once said that he had a choice between becoming a hackney writer or a hackney coachman.[2] The word 'hackney' – from which the modern term 'hack' derives – is telling, since throughout his life Fielding felt ambivalent, at best, about the dignity of writing for a living. He was very conscious of his aristocratic connections, and he had been brought up with boys whose futures as gentlemen, with the financial resources to exercise what political or intellectual interests they chose, were assured; if they indulged in literature it would be as amateur authors. But Fielding's own family and background was not unlike theirs, and a more realistic choice for a career was not between being a hackney writer or a hackney coachman, but between the army, the profession of his father and paternal uncle (and eventually of his younger brother), and the law, which had been the choice not only of his grandfather, but also of his maternal uncle, and more than one of his cousins on his mother's side. Whichever of these he chose, family 'interest' would have helped him – a very important consideration in a society which largely operated through patronage. In the face of this Fielding's decision to make his income from the highly precarious profession of writing looks like an act of rebellion against both sides of the family.

He began where he clearly meant to continue, at the centre of things in London, in the momentous year of 1727, as George II acceded to the throne on the death of his father, and the first minister Sir Robert Walpole confounded his rivals by hanging on to office despite the change of regime. Fielding's first known attempt at authorship was a pamphlet containing two poems, *The Coronation, A Poem, and an Ode on the Birthday* – which is ironic on two counts, since Fielding would later become notorious for his writings against the government (though not against the king), and he wrote of poetry as a 'Branch of writing [that] I very little pretend to, and ... very little my Pursuit'.[3]

London in the early eighteenth century, with a population of around 600,000, was the largest city in Europe and ten times bigger than any other city in Britain; and it was still growing fast. It was essentially two cities, now merging into one as it grew: the City of London, national and international centre of trade and commerce, at the height of its prosperity before the Industrial Revolution diverted investment further north; and Westminster, centred on Parliament, and the king's court. Everywhere aristocracy and gentry, expanding with wealth and confidence, lived their lives in close proximity to abject poverty, misery, violence, and crime.

People of all kinds and intentions were drawn to London as by a magnet, and once there they formed a noisy, boisterous, self-confident, and self-centred population. They kept up with the news of the day through a vast range of newspapers and pamphlets, and through discussion and debate at taverns, coffee houses, and drinking clubs. Inhabitants of London loved to see and be seen, whether promenading in the pleasure gardens of Vauxhall and Ranelagh or crowding through the main streets of the city. London was a place of spectacle and public display, from the hangings at Tyburn to the puppet-drolls of Bartholomew Fair, from the playful and dangerous 'anonymity' of masquerades to the formal performances of the London theatre, where – partly because the theatres were lit throughout the performance – the audience was as much a centre of attention as the actors or musicians. Only two theatres, Covent Garden and Drury Lane, were officially licensed, though other theatres successfully skirted the law from time to time. During the long theatrical 'season' from autumn to midsummer operas were performed, both Italian and English, and 'the back of Mr Handel' could frequently be seen in the orchestra pit. And plays were presented, often in very short runs if audiences failed: they included work by Shakespeare and his adaptors, and the still popular playwrights of the late seventeenth century, Dryden, Congreve, and Vanbrugh. New plays had to earn their place in this repertoire, and not many succeeded.

It has been said that of all the Hanoverian kings George II was the least interested in literature or the arts.[4] Certainly the most prominent writers of the day were out of favour both with the king and with Walpole's government. And while Jonathan Swift's *Gulliver's Travels* (1726) and Alexander Pope's *Dunciad* (1728) were offering young writers examples to follow in fiction and poetry, the most spectacular success of the late 1720s was a play – not only a new play, but a new dramatic form: in 1728 John Gay's popular, radical *Beggar's Opera* astonished everyone with an unprecedented run of sixty-three consecutive performances.

It was into this world that Fielding stepped, and his beginning was auspicious: his first play, *Love in Several Masques*, was performed at Drury Lane in February 1728. Fielding had the support of his cousin Lady Mary Wortley Montagu, but even so, for a twenty-year-old to have his first play produced under the direction of Colley Cibber, the most powerful figure in the London theatre, was an extraordinary achievement. *Love in Several Masques* was not a spectacular success: it ran for only four nights (though it did play past the all-important third night, from which the playwright took the profits, and the playscript was published). Still, Fielding evidently found the dramatic medium congenial, and – after a short break studying at the University of Leiden – he returned to the London stage. For the moment his links with established theatre were broken. His second play, *The Temple Beau* (1730), was performed at the new, small Goodman's Fields venue. And with his third play, *The Author's Farce* (also 1730), not only did he change theatres yet again – this time to the Little Theatre, Haymarket – but he turned to a new kind of writing: under the significant signature of 'Scriblerus Secundus' (thus allying himself with the 'Scriblerian' satirists Swift, Pope, and Gay) Fielding now offered an anarchical mix of ballad opera, gossip, satire, and farce which proved enormously popular. From now onwards, while he continued to write conventional five-act plays, and pleased audiences with his adaptations from Molière, *The Mock-Doctor* and *The Miser*, it was with clever comic-satiric burlesques of various kinds that he had his greatest triumphs, most notably perhaps *Tom Thumb* (1730), particularly in its revised version, *The Tragedy of Tragedies* (1731). For several heady years Fielding was the most successful playwright in the British theatre. Not only were his plays and shorter afterpieces widely performed in the London playhouses, but they were also seen, performed by actors or puppets, at the London fairs.

During these years Fielding collaborated with a new group of London people, not just the famous actors of his day – Charles Macklin, James Quinn, Kitty Clive – but also the American-born writer and critic James Ralph, and the artist William Hogarth, who, Fielding wrote in *Amelia*, painted to 'perfection' (Book I, ch. vi), and whose views on the twin realistic and moral purpose of art and literature were very much in harmony with Fielding's. At the same time Fielding was making his mark not only as a playwright but as a personality, and a controversial one at that.

> Bedaub'd o'er with Snuff, and as drunk as a Drum,
> And mad as a *March* Hare Beau F[ielding] does come;
> He staggers, and swears he will never submit
> To correction of (*a*) Friends, or the Censure of *Pit* ...

(*a*) This Gentleman is so self-conceited that he quarrels with every one that shews him a Fault.

wrote a waspish commentator in 1730:[5] a vivid example not only of the speed with which Fielding achieved prominence in the small-town city of London, but also of the extreme responses he attracted throughout his life. Throughout his career he had what his most sensitive recent biographer has described as 'an incapacity to go about the world unobserved'.[6]

There is, alas, no contemporary portrait of Fielding. The most sympathetic description was given by his friend the mild-mannered James Harris, in a biographical essay written in the late 1750s but not published. Harris wrote that Fielding's 'Genius was acute, lively, docile, capable equally both of the Serious and Ridiculous; his Passions vehement & easily passing into Excess;

his Person strong, large, and capable of great Fatigues; his Face not hand-some, but with an Eye peculiarly penetrating, & which during the sallies of wit or anger never failed to distinguish it self'.[7] Fielding's first official biographer, Arthur Murphy, while also recording Fielding's imposing phy-sical presence – he was over six feet tall, with a 'frame of body large, and remarkably robust'[8] – was more censorious, at least about Fielding's early activities in London: with a temper 'for the most part overflowing into wit, mirth, and good humour' and 'formed … for enjoyment', Murphy opines that the young Fielding 'launched wildly into a career of dissipation' (10, 9).

Clearly Fielding indulged to excess in alcohol and tobacco, and he relished the rich diet of the time – his writings are remarkable for their appreciative references to food, and it is no coincidence that one of his greatest successes was with the song 'The Roast Beef of Old England' (1736). It seems very likely that his dissipations also involved sexual escapades. However, as early as the late 1720s he had been writing sentimental poems to 'Celia', a Salisbury beauty, probably Charlotte Cradock, daughter of one of Lady Gould's neighbours; and in 1734 he married her. Contemporaries acknowl-edged that he loved her dearly; he later called her 'one from whom I draw all the solid Comfort of my life'.[9]

According to Murphy Charlotte had a dowry of £1,500 on her marriage, and a larger inheritance when her mother died in 1735. And Fielding had accumulated large sums of money from his plays – money relatively easily earned, since he may not have laboured too hard over the playscripts if the story is true that he 'would go home rather late from a tavern, and would, the next morning, deliver a scene to the players written upon the papers which had wrapped the tobacco in which he so much delighted' (27). Nevertheless, whatever else Fielding was accused of, no-one ever alleged that he was mean with his money: as large sums came in, even larger sums slipped away. In the mid-1730s, it was widely believed, when the new-married couple set up home at East Stour Fielding spent his wife's fortune in expansive country living and hospitality.

This left them with the small income from his share of the farm (which was finally sold when the last of the Fielding children, Edmund, reached the age of twenty-one in 1738), and a tiny annuity from an uncle, as all he could hope for from his family. Edmund senior had never been able to hang on to the money he had received; although he had occupied the remunerative office of Acting Governor of Jersey in the late 1730s he became caught up in another financial disaster in London, was reduced to debtors' prison, and when he died in 1742 was said to be worth less than £5. As Fielding's own family began to increase – his first child Charlotte was born in 1736 – his assets diminished, and poverty stared him in the face.

And in 1737 the Stage Licensing Act ended Fielding's career as a dramatist. In the 1730s Fielding wrote a series of very funny plays, several of which were seen, at least in part, as satires on the shortcomings of Walpole and his government. Walpole had now been first minister for more than twenty years, and was the most powerful politician England had seen for a long time. His professional relationship with Fielding is murky. Through his friendship with George Lyttelton, Fielding was naturally associated with Opposition politicians, and his hits at political corruption inevitably had Walpole in their sights. However, in 1731 *The Grub-Street Opera*, which was known to ridicule Walpole as Robin the butler, somehow never appeared: had the government exerted pressure to stop it, or had Fielding done a deal with Walpole? Such an accommodation might explain Fielding's startling decision to dedicate to Walpole his play *The Modern Husband* (1732, and a most unsuitable title with which to compliment a man with known marital difficulties). Whatever had happened, it did not prevent Fielding from lampooning Walpole again and again. In 1736, he took on a new role as director of 'The Great Mogul's Company of Comedians' (an ungrateful Eliza Haywood, a member of the company, later referred to it as 'F——g's Scandal Shop'[10]) and in a series of entertainments – *Pasquin*, *The Historical Register for the Year 1736*, *Eurydice Hiss'd* – Walpole was again a target for ridicule. Judged by present-day standards the satire, though pointed and witty, seems mild – the conventions of the day led to a scatter-gun approach rather than a consistent attack – but although Walpole must have been well used to being pilloried in the press and on stage, by the late 1730s opposition to his authority was becoming more serious, and he was feeling under threat. In these circumstances he moved against the theatres, and a law was passed requiring all new plays to be licensed by the Lord Chamberlain before they could be performed. The ostensible provocation was an anonymous play, *The Golden Rump*, which was said to promise unprecedented hostility to Walpole (though since it was never performed it is impossible to prove this; and some suspected it was a figment created by pro-government interests). It was however widely felt that, whatever justification might be claimed, the legislation was in fact a direct response to Fielding: James Harris declared, loyally and memorably, that 'The Legislature made a law, in order to curb one private man' (fos. 5–6).

Fielding's years as Britain's most popular contemporary dramatist were over as suddenly as they had begun. His income dried up, and the professional skills he had developed were useless to him. In these circumstances he took a decision which was at the same time extraordinary and utterly predictable: at the age of thirty he changed direction completely and decided to train to be a lawyer. Harris recorded that he toiled like a drudge to master the necessary laws and precedents, although – with Charlotte temporarily back in Salisbury – he seems in true student fashion to have combined intense study with equally intense social evenings in local taverns. His maternal relatives helped fast-track him through the training process, and Fielding qualified as a lawyer in 1740. The next step was to begin a routine which would last for the best part of a decade, working on the Western Circuit: that is, visiting the main population centres of the Western counties of England – including Salisbury, along with Winchester, Exeter, and Bristol – when the court assizes were sitting, hoping to obtain work on local cases as he went along. He included the popular spa town of Bath in his journeys, and it may well have been now that he made the acquaintance of the self-made man and philanthropist Ralph Allen, who quickly became a close friend: Fielding was often to be seen at Allen's newly built mansion of Prior Park, along with other notable gentry and intellectual figures.

Fielding may have been expanding his circle of friends and acquaintances, but he did not achieve immediate professional success, and in the early years of his legal career he only kept himself and his family from destitution by his political journalism, chiefly the successful Opposition journal *The Champion*, which he managed and wrote for between 1739 and 1742, excoriating Walpole in this medium quite as keenly as he had in his dramas. In addition he undertook a range of literary projects including not only political pamphlets but also a translation of a biography of the early-eighteenth-century Swedish conqueror-king Charles XII, and he even made a brief return to the stage with *Miss Lucy in Town* (his first collaboration with the new theatrical star David Garrick).

Around 1740 he began experimenting with prose fiction. Prompted by the huge success of Samuel Richardson's novel *Pamela* (1740–1), he wrote first the witty and scurrilous satire *Shamela* (1741), and then the much more independent narrative of *The History of the Adventures of Joseph Andrews, and of his Friend Mr Abraham Adams; Written in Imitation of the Manner of Cervantes* (1742); at around the same time came the black comedy *The History of the Life of the Late Mr Jonathan Wild the Great*, which appeared alongside a selection of his earlier poems, plays, and essays in the three-volumed *Miscellanies*, published by subscription in 1743.

In the Preface to the *Miscellanies* Fielding revealed the 'Distresses I have waded through whilst I have been engaged in these Works', referring particularly to the winter of 1741–2 when he had been 'laid up in the Gout, with a favourite Child dying in one Bed, and my Wife in a Condition very little better, on another', accompanied by acute financial problems 'which served as very proper Decorations to such a Scene'.[11]

Things did not ease. A second daughter, Harriot, had been born in 1738, but little Charlotte had indeed died in 1742, just before the birth of Fielding's first son, Henry. Then in November 1744 Fielding's beloved wife Charlotte died. Friends feared for his sanity. By then his four sisters were in London and able to give some support to the widower and his small son and daughter. And it was in the early and mid-1740s that he was closest to his third sister Sarah, whose first novel *David Simple* had been published earlier in 1744 with his help, and whose second literary venture, *Familiar Letters between the Principal Characters in 'David Simple' and Some Others* appeared in 1747 with contributions, and a Preface, by Henry. James Harris kept in close touch with his friend. Otherwise in the mid-1740s Fielding doggedly pursued his legal career on the one hand, and his political journalism on the other.

Even more than the late 1720s, the mid-1740s were unstable times. After decades of peaceful rule by the first two Hanoverian kings, the heir of the ousted House of Stuart – the romantic figure of Charles Edward, 'Bonnie Prince Charlie' – landed in Scotland in 1745 in an attempt, aided by the French, to seize the throne for his father. Though in retrospect his attempt seems to have been doomed from the outset, this was certainly not how it was perceived at the time. Charles's army, attracting new recruits as it marched, aimed south, and reached Derby, deep in the Midland counties of England and only 200 miles from London, before it was halted. At a time of national threat every loyal subject supported the government: in Fielding's case this was chiefly through two journals, *The True Patriot* (1745–6) and *The Jacobite's Journal* (1747–8), which covered arts and intellectual matters as well as contemporary politics, and were conspicuously pro-government throughout. This position was now much easier for Fielding. Though he may have had a rapprochement with Walpole in the early 1740s (the most plausible explanation for *The Opposition*, a pamphlet in which Fielding praised Walpole at his opponents' expense), by 1745 the Great Man had retired and died, and Fielding's own friends were in government.

His private life however continued turbulent a while longer. In November 1747 he married Mary Daniel, his first wife's maid, who was six months pregnant at the time of the wedding. Fielding later referred to Mary in affectionate terms,[12] and she bore him five children in the six years of their marriage. However, in 1747 the marriage was a public embarrassment. Horace Walpole, who loved gossip and did not like Fielding, reported that 'Fielding, hearing Lyttelton praised for his virtue, started up, & striking his Breast, cried, If you talk of Virtue, here's a Virtue! I married my Whore yesterday. – He had; Lyttelton made him.'[13] Lyttelton and Fielding had been friends since they had been at Eton together. By 1748 Lyttelton was finally able to offer Fielding material help: through his interest, and that of the Duke of Bedford, Fielding – who was now supplementing his income by managing a satirical puppet show – was appointed to the positions of Justice of the Peace, first for Westminster and later for Middlesex. At about the same time, Fielding dedicated his new novel, *The History of Tom Jones: A Foundling*, begun in the mid-1740s and finally published early in 1749, with fulsome thanks, to his old school friend.

Fielding had remained a high-profile figure in the small world of London politics and journalism, and his many enemies leapt on these events with glee. The huge success of *Tom Jones* only roused further jealousies. The young Tobias Smollett, in *Peregrine Pickle* (1751), distilled the torrent of criticism, writing that if Mr Spondy the poet shows enough humility to the idiot patron Sir Gosling Scrag [a transparent attack on Lyttelton], 'when he is inclined to marry his own cook-wench, his gracious patron may condescend to give the bride away; and finally settle him in his old age, as a trading Westminster-justice' (Chapter 102).

Justices of the Peace then had responsibility not only for administering the law, but also for the detection of crime, and for maintaining public order, and so the position was an important one, particularly in London; and since Middlesex and Westminster were adjacent areas it was highly beneficial for a single Justice to have jurisdiction over both. However, to say the least, the offices were not much admired: Murphy wrote of Middlesex as 'an office, which seldom fails of being hateful to the populace, and of course liable to many injurious imputations' (38). The position was unpaid: income accrued from the 'trade' undertaken in the position, that is, officially from fees of various kinds and unofficially from bribes. Previous Justices, notoriously including Fielding's immediate predecessor Thomas de Veil, had grown rich in the job.

However, Smollett's hit could not have been more unjust in its major accusation that Fielding was set to line his pockets 'as a trading Westminster justice'. Fielding, once he took over in de Veil's old premises in Bow Street, just off Covent Garden, was notable for refusing the more lucrative possibilities of his office. Leading a tight-knit team of his half-brother John, assistant Saunders Welch, and clerk Joshua Brogden, he tried to keep the peace, reduce crime, and operate justice in a relatively fair way. In addition to this, he wrote pamphlets urging legal reform, including the influential *Enquiry into the Causes of the Late Increase of Robbers* (1751); recommendations in his *Proposal for Making an Effectual Provision for the Poor* (1753) might have had beneficial impact on an intractable eighteenth-century problem if the government had not fallen before they could be implemented. Fielding's principles were not necessarily as humane as his novels might suggest, his judgement was not infallible, and his legal interventions – including, in one of the most high-profile events of the time, a riot after which a sailor, Bosavern Penlez, was controversially executed – often attracted criticism, partly because he was now closely associated with politicians in power. However, it is generally agreed that his influence, both on the immediate operation of the laws under his jurisdiction, and on broader questions of reform, was powerful and positive. One of his achievements was the establishment of the prototype of the 'Bow-Street-runners', an organized police force with a salary, and so in its turn independent of the bribery of the rich or clever, which eventually transformed the processes of detection of crime.

He did not entirely give up money-making ideas. In 1749, with John, he opened the Universal Register Office, which offered an ingenious mix of services, including employment, housing, financial advice, and product placement. And he set up one more periodical venture, *The Covent-Garden Journal*, which was published through most of 1752. He used this journal as a vehicle for his ideas, including defending his new novel, *Amelia* (1751), which had been much attacked by the critics. However, he was clearly disillusioned with the response *Amelia* received, and that deterred him from thoughts of writing another novel: there is a convincing seriousness and sadness about his *Covent-Garden Journal* declaration that 'I will trouble the World no more with any Children of mine by the same Muse'.[14]

Partly this was because he was increasingly absorbed in the serious legal and social matters related to his work with the poor, the dispossessed, and the criminal. Partly he had been rocked by further family bereavements, including the deaths of his son Henry, a daughter by Mary Daniel, and three of his own four sisters. But partly this man of huge energy was finally reaching the end of his capacities. At the time when Smollett wrote jeeringly of his 'old age' Fielding was just forty-three years old. But he was 'Beau Fielding' no longer. His health had been badly damaged by his early excesses: Murphy saw him at this point as 'a melancholy repentant for the free indulgencies of his youth' (9). He had been afflicted with severe gout since the early 1740s, and by the early 1750s he suffered from a dismayingly wide range of other diseases including dropsy. His conscientious work as Westminster justice, which involved close contact with the dirtiest and most diseased inhabitants of the city, completed the demolition of his health. By 1753 he was hardly able to continue his work, and by early in 1754, after one of the hardest winters in living memory, it was made clear to him that another winter in Britain would kill him. Reluctantly he handed over responsibility in Bow Street to John, and set off, with his wife and daughter and Margaret Collier, for the milder air of Lisbon.

Fielding described his desperate physical condition in the poignant gallows-humour of his *Journal of a Voyage to Lisbon*. Having to be 'tapped' at increasingly frequent intervals of pints of fluid which grossly distended his otherwise scrawny frame, and having to be lifted on and off the ship by means of a hoist, Fielding was stripped of his personal dignity. As the *Journal* shows, he was reduced to creating waspish pen-portraits of his captain and his landlady in order to maintain some pretence of personal power and authority. The journey was clearly a nightmare for him, and in any case it was far too late to do any good. He died in Lisbon on 14 October 1754.

Murphy, in summarizing the talents of his subject through the famous novels, makes an analogy with the movement of the sun through the day, with *Joseph Andrews* its 'morning glory', *Tom Jones* its 'meridian majesty', and *Amelia* 'gilding the western hemisphere' (35). This gives an orderly trajectory to a life and career that was far from orderly, and that had no stately sunset about it. When Lady Mary Wortley Montagu heard of his death she offered a very different account: 'no man enjoy'd life more than he did ... His happy Constitution (even when he had, with great pains, half-demolish'd it) made him forget every thing when he was before a venison Pasty or over a Flask of Champaign, and I am perswaded he has known more happy moments than any Prince upon Earth.'[15] But this too only catches one of the many facets of Henry Fielding: playwright and lawyer, polemical journalist and moral novelist, storyteller and scholar, entrepreneur and intellectual, he was a man with the contradictory distinctions of being instrumental in creating the modern police force, of provoking stage censorship legislation through his political satire, and of being claimed by his literary successors as 'the father of the English Novel'.[16]

## NOTES

1. Daniel Defoe, *Tour through the Whole Island of Great Britain* (1724), ed. Pat Rogers (Harmondsworth: Penguin, 1971), Letter 3, 194.
2. Lady Mary Wortley Montagu to Lady Bute, 23 July 1754, in *Lady Mary Wortley Montagu: Selected Letters*, ed. Isobel Grundy (Harmondsworth: Penguin, 1970), 402.
3. Henry Fielding, *Miscellanies* (London, 1743), vol. I, ii.
4. John Brewer, *Pleasures of the Imagination* (London: HarperCollins, 1997), 19.
5. 'Scriblerus Tertius' [Thomas Cooke], *The Candidates for the Bays* (London, 1730), 9.
6. Pat Rogers, *Henry Fielding: A Biography* (London: Paul Elek, 1979), 14.
7. James Harris, 'An Essay on the Life and Genius of Henry Fielding', fo. 4, draft papers held at Wiltshire Record Office. Future reference by folio number in the text.
8. Arthur Murphy, 'Essay on the Life and Genius of Henry Fielding, Esq.', included in Fielding, *Works* (London, 1762), vol. I, 47. Future reference by page number in the text.

# 2

THOMAS KEYMER

# Fielding's theatrical career

It is hard to avoid the teleological fallacy when considering Fielding's plays: the fallacy, that is, of viewing his theatrical career entirely through the lens of later events, and of allowing these events to limit our sense of its scope, direction, and meaning. Two particular developments have dominated thinking about Fielding's output as a dramatist, though neither of them fully explains it. The first came with the passage and implementation in June 1737 of the Stage Licensing Act, a stringent piece of antitheatrical legislation that limited to two the number of playhouses authorized to operate in London and subjected new drama to advance censorship by the Lord Chamberlain, especially on political grounds. Fielding was put out of business as a playwright, and theatre was stunted for decades. The second key event was more gradual and protracted: Fielding's reinvention of himself as a novelist in the 1740s, and the steady elevation of his fiction to a canonical status that seemed to efface the plays or identify them as creative false starts.

For many of Fielding's contemporaries, and in later accounts of his career, the Licensing Act was an *ad hominem* measure targeted by a wounded ministry against a single theatrical bugbear. 'The Legislature made a Law, in order merely to curb one private man', as James Harris bluntly put it in 1758. The truth is rather more complex, but Fielding was certainly a prime contributor to ministerial anxieties about the theatre, and the retaliatory clampdown his plays provoked conferred on them a lasting reputation as works defined and dominated by a specific political campaign. In Harris's own brief sketch, there is a genuinely Aristophanic amplitude to his old friend's work for the stage: 'scenes of fancy and allegoric humour, pictures of human Life Extravagance and Nature, ye highest humour imaginable occasionally interspersed with a large mixture of bitter sarcasm and personal Satire, respecting ye leading Persons and measures of the times'.[1] In many subsequent accounts, however, these political 'interspersions' have consumed attention to the exclusion of everything else, and not only in the case of *Pasquin* (March 1736) and *The Historical Register for the Year 1736* (March 1737), the incendiary later plays that Harris has in mind at this point. Even some of Fielding's most innocuous early comedies and farces have been ingeniously decoded as partisan interventions, their texts combed for lurking signs of antiministerial innuendo. Cumulatively, a picture has emerged of a writer dedicated to political satire not only in the closing phase of his career as a dramatist but almost from his precocious start. The most rigorous recent scholarship presents an alternative view of Fielding's allegiances as pragmatic and mobile for most of his playwriting years, and as irrelevant to the many plays in which political allusion is lacking in partisan spin or simply absent. But the myth endures of Fielding as a theatrical version of Alexander Pope, a satirist fixed and indefatigable in his oppositional posture throughout the period, and a writer whose last stage works in 1736–7 only distil and intensify the animus of his drama from the start.

Where one tradition of criticism finds in the Licensing Act the interpretative key to Fielding's plays, a second sees the Act as his means of escape: a Fortunate Fall that released him to find his true metier, and his appropriate form, as a writer of prose fiction. For another early memoirist, Arthur Murphy, Fielding had launched his literary career in the wrong genre, writing plays that were too elaborate in their plotting for the economy of theatre, too reliant on modes of humour that could only work on the page. The strictures of 1737 were deplorable in their wider effects, but sprang Fielding from a generic dead end. A similar sense of mismatch between creative impulse and constraining medium survives in J. Paul Hunter's comment, in an influential modern study of Fielding's career, that his 'separation from the theatre was a forced one, but the expulsion was fortunate, freeing him from a relationship and commitment that had always been in some sense against the grain'.[2] This was not a separation that Fielding accepted himself, and even as he took to the novel he made sporadic efforts to return to the stage. In 1742–3, shortly after publishing *Joseph Andrews*, he dusted off two previously unperformed comedies for production at Drury Lane, only to fall foul of obscenity allegations; in 1748, as *Tom Jones* neared completion, he ran a series of crowd-pulling puppet shows, brazenly mixing social satire with 'all the Original Jokes, F–rts, Songs, Battles, Kickings' of the Punch tradition.[3] But Fielding's ongoing need for the energies of performance has done little to dislodge his reputation as always somehow a novelist at heart, a writer who found his creative feet only when forced from the stage. His plays, in this tradition of criticism, were works of literary apprenticeship, thwarted by the conditions of their own mode, and of little significance beyond their capacity to explain the residual theatricality of his fiction. They could be read as expressions of potential achievement, but always for the sake of the novels: as sources for the persistence of stage types, farce devices, and dramatic conventions in Fielding's fictional plots; as early instances of the self-consciousness about literary framing that marks his narrative technique; as proto-novelistic experiments in the construction of authorial voices.

Yet to read Fielding's drama as a single-minded exercise in Opposition propaganda, or as a repertoire of creative possibilities that could only be fulfilled in another genre, is to distort and diminish a vital category of his output. Fielding the playwright was not only, and often not even, a political satirist, and his stage comedies were much more than botched rehearsals for his novels. Aspects of the plays that resist interpretation as partisan politics or proto-novelistic experiments have begun to climb the critical agenda in recent decades. More fundamentally, historical scholarship by Robert D. Hume, Thomas Lockwood and others has retrieved a full sense of Fielding's cultural impact in his early career, an impact achieved solely by virtue of his work as a dramatist, irrespective of later achievements.

If the plays strike modern readers of his fiction as archaeological items, to theatre-goers in the years before the Licensing Act they were inescapably alive. Fielding was the most conspicuous and influential force in the London theatre in one of its most vigorous and innovative decades, and something of his prominence can be seen in the bald statistics. In 1727 he placed his first comedy (performed 1728) at Drury Lane, the most prestigious theatre of the day, while still aged twenty, and at the peak of his Drury Lane association in 1732–3 he saw seven new plays produced in the space of eighteen months. By mid-1737 he had written more than two dozen plays, using almost every available dramatic genre and some ingenious hybridized modes: traditional comedy, burlesque tragedy, social satire, afterpiece farce, ballad opera, mock pantomime, the self-reflexive form of the 'rehearsal' play. Including the three works first performed after 1737, and double-counting three others that Fielding rewrote and restaged in thoroughly overhauled versions, his total output extends to twenty-nine plays: a record that is, Lockwood observes, 'unlike any other in the period and almost without parallel from the Restoration to the nineteenth century'. (The famously prolific Tom D'Urfey is the nearest aggregate competitor between 1660 and 1737, Lockwood adds, but took thirty years – three times as long as Fielding – to produce roughly the same number of plays.)[4] It is a measure of the long runs and frequent revivals enjoyed by many Fielding plays that within a mere three nights in 1736, from 27 to 29 April, seven of them could be seen, across four venues, in a total of nine stagings. Comparable patterns can be found as early as 1732, when Fielding was entrenched at Drury Lane and had already made himself, in Hume's words, 'the most dominant professional playwright in London since Dryden'.[5]

Part of this dominance resulted from Fielding's legendary workrate. Murphy describes the late-night, nicotine-fuelled bursts of creativity from which new plays would spring after idle months, and later biographers have rightly associated with Fielding the 'vigorous fancy' of the playwright Pillage in *Eurydice Hiss'd* (April 1737), who could 'write nine scenes with spirit in one day'. (Murphy adds that Fielding's scripts would sometimes reach the playhouse on used tobacco wrappers, deploring the glitches in the textual record 'which have arisen from this method of proceeding'.)[6] The same energy allowed Fielding to thrive in the shark-infested theatre world of the day, when the many hazards ranged against aspiring authors included monopolistic collusion between playhouses, arbitrary and exploitative management regimes, inadequate and unpredictable remuneration, fickle and sometimes riotous audiences, an acrimonious labour dispute and lock-out, and Opposition as well as ministerial campaigns to subordinate the stage to regulation. Fielding suffered inevitable setbacks in this environment, and was more than once driven from mainstream venues to the fringe. But for the most part he played the weak hand of a working playwright with great adroitness, turning his professional tribulations to creative account in satires like *The Author's Farce* (March 1730), and eventually breaking the stranglehold of the managers by establishing a company of his own.

Fielding's professionalism is also apparent in his expert maximization of practical theatre resources. Shaw's provocative view of him as (excepting only Shakespeare) 'the greatest practising dramatist ... produced by England between the Middle Ages and the nineteenth century' stresses this command of theatricality,[7] and Fielding attracted praise from contemporaries for compelling audience attention even when confined, as in his Little Haymarket plays, to the most basic stage facilities. He skilfully exploited the talents of the star actors such as Kitty (Raftor) Clive, a specialist in foxy comic roles for whom he tailored no fewer than ten vehicles between *The Lottery* (January 1732) and *Miss Lucy in Town* (May 1742). He monitored and absorbed emerging fashions in dramatic form and staging technique, notably the vogue for spectacular pantomime, and repeatedly pulled off the trick of catering to the latest tastes in a manner that also suggested parodic detachment. He made particularly creative use of afterpieces: supplementary entertainments that were frequently added to theatrical productions after about 1715, and most effective when placed in meaningful (sometimes ironic) relation to the 'mainpiece'. Versatile, innovative, and pragmatic, he modified his modes of writing in light of audience response, moving away from traditional models of comedy to the madcap forms of burlesque and farce that released his most exuberant satire. Individual plays such as *The Author's Farce* were treated not as stable artefacts but as living theatre, malleable scripts to be fleshed out in rehearsal and then adapted and revived as circumstances changed in theatrical culture, or as new targets emerged for mockery or attack.

For all this flexibility and readiness to improvise in response to chance and change, Fielding's drama also revolves around a stable thematic core. The plays represent an ongoing negotiation between a coherent authorial vision of modern England – a vision hovering between satirical rigour and comic relish – and the material and institutional conditions of theatre at the time, which exerted constant pressures and constraints on the creative agency of writers. Throughout this process, Fielding's plays satirize a world in which all human transactions amount to commercial propositions, from courtship and marriage to politics and theatre, and a distinctive feature of the plays is to represent the playwright himself as implicated, and knowingly so, in the commercial world he describes. Part of the insistent self-consciousness of Fielding's drama flows from his sense of himself as an exponent of what he elsewhere calls the 'Trade . . . of *Authoring*.'[8] Across successive phases of his playwriting career, he turned his prosecution of this trade into a performance itself, involving several ingenious and calculated shifts of public identity and posture.

In *Love in Several Masques*, Fielding's precocious theatrical debut of 16 February 1728, he began with a play about poses. A comedy of intrigue that hinges on the romantic ruses and mercenary subterfuges of three pairs of lovers, it exhibits many further modes of hypocrisy and disguise in its fashionable town milieu. With their affectations of gallantry or virtue, their pretensions to wisdom or wit, all the play's characters perform identities for public consumption, the nature of the activity differing only in the degree of sincerity involved. The pattern affects even the commentating figure of Wisemore, a former actor turned Man of the Hill-like misanthrope, who feigns aloofness from a society he condemns as a realm of Proteus, a hazardous theatre of false and changeable forms. With this somewhat insistent theme, *Love in Several Masques* resumes the interest of Fielding's earliest surviving publication, his satirical poem *The Masquerade* (January 1728), and looks forward to a key concern of his later work, in which the world 'becomes a vast Masquerade, where the greatest Part appear disguised under false Vizors and Habits.'[9]

Yet easily the most interesting identity in performance here is that of the playwright himself. In the print version of *Love in Several Masques*, published a few days after the play's fourth and final night, the author's name is announced in the style of a gentleman amateur ('Written by Mr *FIELDING*') and adorned with a showy dedication to his noble cousin, Lady Mary Wortley Montagu. In the Preface, he modestly presents himself as 'a raw and unexperienced Pen', only to overturn the modesty with a sly parenthetical addition: '(for I believe I may boast that none ever appeared so early on the Stage)' (*Plays*, vol. I, 20). Here, and in other paratextual features of the published edition, Fielding firmly positions himself as the coming man in his field: an ambitious tyro aware of the stature of key precursor playwrights (Wycherley, Congreve) and the popularity of his contemporaries (Gay, Cibber), but eager to take them all on. It is the bullish self-presentation of an aspirant to pure fame, with no hint of Fielding's private, though no less carefully fashioned, account to Montagu of the primary financial need that fuelled his efforts. As Montagu recalled decades later, Fielding 'was to be pity'd at his first entrance into the World, having no choice (as he said himself) but to be a Hackney Writer or a Hackney Coachman'.[10]

A few years before this 'first entrance', when Defoe's *Robinson Crusoe* (1719) and Haywood's *Love in Excess* (1719–20) seemed to have created a large new market for prose fiction, the novel might have been the appropriate choice for a would-be professional author. But the moment had passed, and was not to return until the *Pamela* controversy of 1740–1 (at which point Fielding was quick to cash in, with lasting consequences for the genre). Theatre was the more promising medium in the later 1720s, but still far from easy. A fashionable opera company performed in the King's Theatre, Haymarket, and a venue for visiting entertainers was provided by the Little Haymarket, an unlicensed playhouse where facilities were rudimentary. Otherwise London theatre was still restricted by the patent monopoly system established at the Restoration, and only two repertory playhouses existed. The Theatre Royal at Drury Lane was the larger and more prestigious playhouse, run by a formidable 'triumvirate' of actor-managers (Colley Cibber, Robert Wilks, and Barton Booth) who were notorious for exploiting, stifling, or blocking new talent. Lincoln's Inn Fields had a reputation for lowbrow spectacle and extravagant theatrical machinery, especially in the pantomime afterpieces favoured by its manager, John Rich: exuberant fusions of commedia dell'arte traditions with opera, farce, acrobatics, and dance, typically with Rich himself in the Harlequin role. In this restricted environment, lack of competition, managerial conservatism, and the tempting cheapness and ease of revivals meant that new drama rarely came to performance. As late as 1743, Fielding comments sourly on 'the Theatrical Politics, of never introducing new Plays on the Stage, but when driven to it by absolute Necessity' (*Miscellanies*, vol. I, 5), and it has been calculated that in the season of 1726–7 only 5 new mainpieces were presented at the repertory theatres, from a total of 115 plays.[11] It is in this context that the hapless Mr Wilson of *Joseph Andrews* lovingly crafts a five-act comedy which, though accepted at the theatre, is mothballed for the season and then returned to him too late to be placed elsewhere. (The managerial practice of accepting plays without intending to stage them, so cutting off the supply to rival playhouses, was a standard complaint, made, for example, by Fielding's friend Henry Carey in a play-text of 1736.)[12] Without the influence of Montagu, who attended two performances and no doubt also delivered her elite circle, *Love in Several Masques* might well have suffered this kind of fate.

Yet Fielding was right to remain confident, in words prefixed to his second comedy, *The Temple Beau* (January 1730), that 'this our Stage may be the Road to Fame' (*Plays*, vol. I, 111). By an accident of timing no less important to his career than the fortuitous *Pamela* sensation of 1740, *Love in Several Masques* came to performance just as two other new plays, Cibber's *The Provok'd Husband* and Gay's *The Beggar's Opera*, were demonstrating beyond question the potential of original drama to outperform the inherited repertoire. At Drury Lane, the record-breaking run of Cibber's comedy (based on an unfinished Vanbrugh script) was such that a key member of Fielding's cast was left disabled by a 'violent Fatigue'; at Lincoln's Inn Fields, Gay's intoxicating blend of innovative form and transgressive satire dominated the season and engrossed 'the whole Talk and Admiration of the Town' (*Plays*, vol. I, 20–1). The consequences for *Love in Several Masques* were severe. Not only eclipsed, the confident debut intended by Fielding suddenly looked staid and outmoded, an exercise geared to a repertory climate on the cusp of transformation. In the long term, however, fresh opportunities had now been created for the aspiring dramatist, especially one prepared to adopt the mould-breaking spirit of Gay's riotous ballad opera.

The odd thing is that Fielding was at first reluctant to embrace the generic lessons. It is an indication of his ambition to enter a hall of fame with Wycherley and Congreve that he continued to produce well-made five-act comedies for several more years, in the teeth of market conditions and with limited success. When he returned from studying at Leiden in 1729 with several new scripts in the traditional mode, the Drury Lane managers rejected *The Temple Beau* and discouraged him from working up an early version of *Don Quixote in England* (eventually completed and performed as a ballad opera in 1734); in the same period Lincoln's Inn Fields rejected *The Wedding-Day*, which languished in a bottom drawer until 1743. A new unlicensed theatre at Goodman's Fields in the city provided a fallback venue for *The Temple Beau*, where it ran for a worthwhile nine nights and enjoyed some later revivals, but this play was not to be performed in any major playhouse in Fielding's lifetime. Later five-act comedies were badly received or hung fire between composition and performance. Fielding's most successful exercise in the mode, *The Modern Husband* (February 1732), took more than a year after composition to reach the stage; so did his more pedestrian

*The Universal Gallant* (February 1735), which survived amidst boos and hisses for a mere three nights. *The Fathers; or, The Good-Natured Man* was rejected in 1735 and premiered only posthumously, in 1778. Even as he moved to more innovative, experimental and fragmented modes of drama in the 1730s, Fielding retained an equal and opposite commitment to neoclassical form, its deadening effects on his writing notwithstanding. Only in his final plays could he forthrightly mock the formulaic conventions involved in traditional comedy, as when the playwright Trapwit in *Pasquin* at last grasps the question when asked the 'Fable' or 'Design' of his latest play: 'Oh! you ask who is to be married! ... I hope you think I understand the Laws of Comedy, better than to write without marrying somebody.'[13]

Fielding's reluctant and halting break with conventional dramatic forms, beginning in the spring of 1730, was inaugurated in characteristically self-conscious style. Thwarted as 'Mr Fielding', the writer of genteel comedy for the patent theatres, he took refuge at the Little Haymarket in March 1730, producing over the following year a series of satirical plays in the teasing alternative guise of 'Scriblerus Secundus'. The pseudonym is central to Fielding's emerging project in the plays of this period, evoking as it does the cultural politics and ironic techniques of Scriblerian satire: the satire of Pope, Swift, Gay, and their circle, in which vulgarizations and debasements of literary form are burlesqued and derided, held up to exemplify the moral, aesthetic, and political corrosions of modern commercial society. Not content with a single persona, Fielding also creates, in the playwright Luckless of *The Author's Farce* (his first play in the Scriblerian persona, and almost as big a hit as *The Beggar's Opera*), an unmistakable avatar for his own condition as a writer torn between high aesthetic ideals and pressing financial need. As Scriblerus Secundus, he satirizes the commodification of literature and the dumbing-down of taste; as Luckless, he advances the process himself, abandoning his original principles of art in pursuit of commercial success. The paradox is that in turning from prestigious to popular modes of drama, Fielding also made his creative breakthrough, releasing his genius for theatrical havoc from the strictures of conventional form.

Central to the action of *The Author's Farce* are the competing pulls of serious comedy and irregular entertainment, and Fielding embodies the competition in his three-act structure, which finally displaces the standard patterns of Acts I and II with an exuberantly nonsensical mixture of balladeering, puppetry, and gratuitous theatrical pyrotechnics. 'A Farce brings more Company to a House than the best Play that ever was writ', announces the disillusioned Luckless: 'For this Age would allow *Tom Durfey* a better Poet than *Congreve* or *Wycherly*' (*Plays*, vol. I, 256; III.i). Here is the lesson of Luckless's experience as a would-be author in the opening acts, when he hawks his cherished comedy without success to a mercenary bookseller and a pair of philistine theatre managers, Marplay and Sparkish (thinly disguised proxies for Cibber and Wilks). The funniest and most telling scenes involve the publisher Bookweight, master of a literary sweatshop where penniless hacks and ignorant dunces translate Virgil from prior translations, thrash poems out of dictionaries of rhyme, and manufacture and prolong controversies simply to sell more print. But Marplay and Sparkish are no less significant than Bookweight as agents of cultural degeneration, and in keeping with Fielding's Scriblerian pretensions their attitude to plays as mere 'Merchandize' (*Plays*, vol. I, 243; II.i) suggests a more widespread corruption – this being an age when one no more hears sense in a playhouse than 'Honesty talked of at Court, Conscience at *Westminster*, Politeness at the University' (*Plays*, vol. I, 236; I.vi).

In its chaotic final act, a rehearsal of Luckless's catchpenny entertainment 'The Pleasures of the Town', Fielding's play lurches abruptly into burlesque mode. Unable to get his comedy accepted, Luckless offers his audience a hectic spoof of the dumbed-down fare it prefers to consume, in which puppets representing inane new fashions in cultural production – Haywood gets an outing as 'Mrs Novel'; Cibber is now recast as Sir Farcical Comick – sing, squabble, and flirt in Punch-and-Joan style. The farce is explained in advance by Fielding's satirical thesis in the previous acts, and dramatizes the aesthetic consequences of a marketplace in which the lowest common denominators of taste determine literary production. Yet it also draws energy and life from the lowbrow phenomena it mocks, repeating and exaggerating the established Scriblerian satire from *A Tale of a Tub* onwards to plunge into imaginative sympathy with its ostensible target. Consciously or otherwise – one suspects the former – Fielding's parody of popular styles of modern entertainment is also a gleeful immersion in their liberating absurdities, and an exploitation of their market appeal that swung between derisive mimicry and engaged participation. (The pattern persists to the end of Fielding's playwriting career, notably in *Tumble-down Dick* (April 1736), a riotous travesty of Rich's production style that mocked while also replicating the pleasures of pantomime extravaganza.)

In later performances as a freestanding afterpiece, 'The Pleasures of the Town' was literally cut loose from the larger explanatory context of *The Author's Farce*. But it escapes control in any case, taking off from its original parodic premise in a dazzling display of nonsense as self-conscious art. With its sudden representational shifts and jumbled mimetic levels (puppets representing humans are played by human actors, and at last interact directly with the cast of Acts I and II), 'The Pleasures of the Town' conjures from its unpromising sources a wayward, brilliant exercise in metatheatrical play.

Whatever his early ambitions to emulate or rival Wycherley and Congreve, Fielding was already achieving something more: he anticipates the modernism of Pirandello, or Ionesco and the theatre of the absurd.

The creative ambivalence of Fielding's satire in his pseudo-Scriblerian phase at the Little Haymarket is also attested by *Tom Thumb* (April 1730) and its elaboration in *The Tragedy of Tragedies* (March 1731), which similarly escape and transcend their founding satirical logic. A burlesque of heroic drama that misapplies the grandiloquent rhetoric of tragedy to a trivial chapbook world, *Tom Thumb* does for high literature what *The Author's Farce* does for low (and the plays regularly featured as a double bill, on thirty-four occasions in their opening season). While sending up tragic bombast and fustian, *Tom Thumb* also ridicules the squandering of attention in modern theatre on inconsequential matter – the minuscule size of the play's hero rendering the point more intense. There is little satirical severity in Fielding's tone, however, and a knockabout comedy of sheer incongruity prevails. Nonsense again takes on life of its own, and the play was regularly received or attacked as participating in the trends it mocked. William Shenstone was sympathetic, citing *Tom Thumb* to illustrate 'how large the number is of those that mistake burlesque for the very foolishness it exposes'. But others took a less charitable line, among them the pointedly named 'Scriblerus Tertius', probably Fielding's future friend Thomas Cooke. In *The Candidates for the Bays* (1730), Cooke depicts Fielding as a drunken, snuff-bedaubed plagiarist and bully who, far from defending traditional values and aesthetics, had banished all sense from the stage: '*Tom Thumb* and such Stuff alone tickle this Age'.[14]

No less perplexing than Fielding's stance towards popular entertainment was the political alignment of his play, in which glancing allusions to the public realm fail to indicate straightforward or consistent allegiance. 'A political stick for both sides', as Ronald Paulson puts it, *Tom Thumb* was denounced by one of Fielding's targets in *The Author's Farce*, the flamboyant preacher John Henley, as seditious antiministerial propaganda. But it also drew fire from the Opposition press as illustrating the debasement of culture in Walpole's England; one journalist noted with relish that the Prime Minister himself was a repeat attender during the opening run.[15]

Fielding's Scriblerian affectation is most fully substantiated in *The Tragedy of Tragedies*, a witty elaboration of *Tom Thumb* that ran for a respectable fifteen nights in its first season. It was to prove one of Fielding's most enduring plays, with intriguing later revivals: Frances Burney played Huncamunca in private theatricals of 1777, and there was a domestic production by the Austen family at Steventon in 1788; the eminent (and prodigiously tall) critic W. K. Wimsatt was the giantess Glumdalca at Yale

University in 1953.[16] But it is as a printed text that this work has its most interesting existence. In a distinction made by the philistine Bookweight in *The Author's Farce*, 'there are your Acting Plays, and your Reading Plays' (237; I.vi); *The Tragedy of Tragedies* is emphatically the latter, though not for the reasons given by Bookweight, for whom acting plays depend on 'Buffoonery and Gestures' in the performance, reading plays on 'Wit and Meaning' in the text. In *The Tragedy of Tragedies*, the most sustained buffoonery goes on at the foot of the page, in a fog of annotation thrown up around the text by Fielding's obtuse editorial persona. With its busy accumulation of bogus sources, irrelevant analogues, and other dim-witted misdirections (ten passages, five of them from Dryden, are cited to gloss the line 'I'm so transported, I have lost my self' (574; II.ix)), the pseudo-scholarly apparatus of *The Tragedy of Tragedies* employs a technique familiar from Pope's recent *Dunciad Variorum* (1729). As in Pope, risible annotation competes on the page with the primary text, at times almost squeezing it out. The superbly absurd premise of this pseudo-Scriblerian paratext, how-ever, is all Fielding's own. Far from being the work of 'Mr. P——' or 'Mr. F——', insists 'H. Scriblerus Secundus' at the outset, *Tom Thumb* is the corrupted text of an Elizabethan or even Shakespearian play, which Restoration and later tragedians have plagiarized. In one of the most famous examples, a sitting duck from James Thomson's *Sophonisba* (1730) – 'Oh! Sophonisba! Sophonisba! oh!' – is burlesqued as 'Oh! Huncamunca, Huncamunca, oh, / Thy pouting Breasts, like Kettle-Drums of Brass, / Beat everlasting loud Alarms of Joy'; a deadpan footnote then accuses Thomson of stealing 'this beautiful Line, which ought . . . to be written in Gold' (*Plays*, vol. I, 567–8; II.v). The *Sophonisba* example also indicates the efforts being made by Fielding to update his original focus on Restoration tragedy by targeting very recent plays. As Lockwood notes, the speech in question here moves on from Thomson to parody Benjamin Martyn's atrocious *Timoleon* (1730), in which 'heaving Breasts . . . beat Alarms to Joy' (*Plays*, vol. I, 601; Fielding's inspired substitution of 'pouting' for 'heaving' may also take a cue from Wycherley's *The Plain Dealer* ('those infallible proofs, her pouting swelling breasts' (v. ii)).

Thus Fielding not only parodies the diction of heroic tragedy and tips it into bathos; in a gesture of pure comic surplus, he also arraigns the plays he mocks for having plagiarized his send-up of them. More even than Dryden, Thomson, and the rest, the real butt of the laughter here is Scriblerus Secundus himself, with his fatuous and misdirected pedantry. He knows Restoration bombast well enough to associate 'O, *Tom Thumb! Tom Thumb!* Wherefore art thou *Tom Thumb?*' with a line from Otway's *Marius* (1680), but seems never to have read *Romeo and Juliet* (*Plays*, vol. I,

564; II.iii). He detects Dryden's *All for Love* (1678) behind 'Your *Huncamunca*. / *Tom Thumb's Huncamunca*, every Man's *Huncamunca*', but fails to spot the play on *Much Ado about Nothing*, which Fielding leaves hanging for the reader (*Plays*, vol. I, 575–6; II.x).

With fun at a premium over satirical rage, and topical allusion undirected by partisan drive, Fielding's theatrical output of 1730–1 makes clear the opportunist character of his pseudo-Scriblerian garb. Though happy to ride in the slipstream of Pope and Swift at their peak, and to borrow some of their themes and techniques, he never aligned himself wholeheartedly with the cultural or political project associated with the Scriblerus Club. In unpublished fragments of verse from the same early period, he distances himself unmistakably from the Toryism (and also the misanthropy) of Pope, and it has even been suggested that the surface affiliation of *The Tragedy of Tragedies* with Scriblerian writing masks genuine antipathy.[17] Whatever the case, Fielding's arrogation of the Scriblerus name seems not to have been resented by its original owners. Swift reportedly commended Fielding as a wit, declaring that he had laughed only twice in his life, the second instance being 'the Circumstance of *Tom Thumb*'s killing the Ghost' in the accelerated pile-up of corpses that closes the farce.[18] Pope may even have turned Fielding's invasion to advantage by helping himself in return, the expanded four-book *Dunciad* of 1743 suggesting memories of *The Author's Farce* in its adoption of specific targets from Act III and its exaggerated use of theatrical tropes as indices of a tawdry culture.

For Fielding himself, however, the value of the association was near its end. After two more outings as Scriblerus Secundus – *The Letter-Writers* (March 1731) and *The Welsh Opera* (April 1731), with its unperformed revision *The Grub-Street Opera* – he dropped the appellation after the season of 1730–1. A related factor was the uproar surrounding production at the Little Haymarket of *The Fall of Mortimer* (May 1731), probably by Eliza Haywood's lover William Hatchett, a historical drama with ostentatious application to the ministry of Walpole. The authorities responded by suppressing *The Fall of Mortimer* as 'a false, infamous, scandalous, seditious, and treasonable libel',[19] and the Little Haymarket was forced to close until the following year. As the rhetorical overkill suggests, topical application tragedies could arouse anxieties about public order that satire rarely involved, not least when the play ended by urging, as here, that in cases of ministerial corruption 'A Hempen Collar's always to be had'.[20] But *The Welsh Opera* had been an afterpiece to *The Fall of Mortimer* on several occasions, and sounded genial comic echoes of Hatchett's public themes: now Walpole becomes Robin the Butler, who steals the spoons. Fielding's satire is characteristically scattershot here, taking in Opposition leaders as well, but *The Welsh Opera* was still contextually implicated in the furore. Fielding seems to have felt the need to distance himself from antiministerial writing of every kind (even producing, for *The Modern Husband* in 1732, a dedication to Walpole that has frustrated several critical efforts to read it as ironic), and that included Scriblerian satire. Moreover, he needed a new venue, and Scriblerus Secundus was not the ideal persona in which to court the real-life targets of *The Author's Farce*. In the event, Cibber and Wilks played true to form as Marplay and Sparkish, struck more by the commodity value of Fielding's recent plays than by their content or meaning. For the remainder of their managerial tenure, Drury Lane was to provide him with a stable venue in probably the most lucrative phase of his playwriting career.

Fielding embraced the opportunity to reinvent his authorial self on returning to the prestige of a patent theatre. Erasing the pseudo-Scriblerian identity, and its association with theatrical havoc and disrupted form, he instead revived something like the persona of his Drury Lane debut. With its affectation of gentlemanly authorship and its emphasis on purity of structure, *The Modern Husband* boldly renews his early claims to seriousness of purpose in both moral and aesthetic terms. The comedy was the work of 'HENRY FIELDING, Esq.', and Fielding persisted with this suffix in the published texts of several later plays, to the derision of hostile journalists. Leading the charge was another set of self-appointed Scriblerians, the writers of the weekly *Grub-Street Journal*, who loftily ignored the plays of Scriblerus Secundus but virulently attacked Mr Fielding, the catalyst being his dedication to Walpole of *The Modern Husband*. 'I pay a deference to his birth, but cannot think it a title to wit, any more than it is to a fortune', wrote 'Prosaicus' in the *Grub-Street Journal*, neatly putting Fielding back in his box as a writer of hackney for bread.[21] Fielding also used his prologue to *The Modern Husband* – spoken by the egregious Wilks – to make explicit, almost in a spirit of recantation, that his youthful frolics with experimental drama were now at an end. No longer will he debase comedy to farce, he vows, or entertain the town with 'unshap'd Monsters of a wanton Brain'. He will write dignified moral drama in appropriate form, restoring the honour of the stage through exemplary practice: 'The Stage which was not for low Farce design'd, / But to *divert*, *instruct*, and *mend* Mankind.'

The play itself is a grim satire on cynicism and adultery in fashionable life, and lives up to its didactic billing (even anticipating aspects of *Amelia*) with sometimes unpleasant rigour. But Fielding also found less acerbic ways of restoring his credentials as an exponent of neoclassical form. By adapting two Molière comedies in the same period (*Le Médecin malgré lui* as *The Mock Doctor* in June 1732; *L'Avare* as *The Miser* in February 1733), he could present himself as reviving the essential proprieties of a theatrical golden age. The cue was obediently taken in an anonymous satire on contemporary taste that hails Fielding as '*England's Moliere*', the solitary upholder of 'Virtue and Wit' in a period when theatre is otherwise nothing but 'Gaiety and Air'.[22]

Yet the public image crafted by Fielding masked, as so often, a more mixed position. For all its noisy pretensions to unified form, *The Modern Husband* also slips in several gratuitous scenes, sacrificing coherence of dramatic structure for the sake of topical appeal. The play was in fact a 'motly composition', alleged the *Grub-Street Journal* with some justice, singling out the irrelevant but crowd-pleasing episode of Lord Richly's levee (which alludes, though without more than token hostility, to Walpole's well-known rituals for distributing patronage and favour).[23] Other Drury Lane plays of 1732–3 are less discontinuous with their pseudo-Scriblerian predecessors than it would seem from the professions of Mr Fielding (or, as he becomes in *The Old Debauchees* of June 1732, 'the Author of the MODERN HUSBAND'). *The Covent-Garden Tragedy* (June 1732) resurrects the burlesque techniques and targets of *Tom Thumb*, though without the revelry of the earlier play, and its setting is a pointed violation of theatrical decorum: the scene is a brothel, the characters prostitutes and hoodlums. Earlier in the same year, *The Lottery* recycles some of its material from *The Grub-Street Opera*. Both this play and *The Old Debauchees* are rowdy generic hybrids, making brisk satirical capital of the talk of the town: respectively, the notorious profiteering of stockjobbers in the state lottery held the previous autumn, and a recent sex-and-religion scandal featuring Jesuit priests. Potentially the most interesting work of the period, a lost afterpiece to *The Miser* entitled *Deborah* (April 1733), was probably an obscene burlesque of Handelian oratorio, perhaps with the superaddition of political hints.

Some of these plays were failures, but Fielding was reported by a reliable insider to have made 'little less than a thousand pounds' from *The Lottery* and *The Modern Husband*: the income of the gentleman he insisted he was, and five times the sum he was to regard as handsome payment for *Joseph Andrews* a decade later.[24] In terms of popularity and remuneration, Fielding had found a perfect middle way, harmonizing his ambition for serious comedy with his aptitude for irregular farce, and deftly appealing to the multiple tastes of his London audience by blending (or at least juxtaposing) disparate theatrical modes, from lofty didacticism to low burlesque. The strategy moves close to the surface in the dramatized introduction to *Don Quixote in England* (April 1734), where another of the many internal dramatists in Fielding's plays (known this time simply as 'Author') casts doubt on the value of prologues: 'But of what Use is a Bill of Fare to any Entertainment, where the Guests are not left to their Choice what Part they will pick at, but are oblig'd to swallow the Whole indifferently?' ('Introduction'). Fielding's surrogate author is pessimistic here, as though the heterogeneity of his play is more an encumbrance than an opportunity, offering no one satisfaction. Yet these words also contain the germ of Fielding's celebrated opening chapter to *Tom Jones* ('The Introduction ... or Bill of Fare to the Feast'), which makes a virtue of the novel's capacity to cater simultaneously, with its 'prodigious Variety' of subject matter, to multiple audience tastes.[25] If the plays do indeed anticipate the novels, it is not least in their awareness that the public for literature is unpredictably diverse, and in their strategy of maximizing audience appeal by diversifying content and style.

The appeal of individual plays could also be freshened, and another marked characteristic of Fielding's career as a dramatist is his treatment of play-scripts as provisional and malleable works, always open to revision or redirection in the context of ongoing events. *Tom Thumb* and *The Welsh Opera* had both been enlarged and updated as distinct new plays, and even *The Lottery* (topical as it stood) was revised a month after its first performance with a new scene satirizing the drawing ceremony, the effect being to double its run. The most interesting cases date from the period when Fielding's flourishing career at Drury Lane was derailed by external factors. At first he survived the sudden disintegration in September 1732 of the long-lived managerial triumvirate, but the following spring the theatre was thrown into chaos, and eventually closed, by an actor rebellion against the new management led by Cibber's abrasive son, Theophilus Cibber. Creatively, the power struggles between rival claimants to authority at Drury Lane played out to Fielding's advantage, lodging in his head the pervasive satirical analogies between theatrical and state politics that energize his last plays, and stimulating first of all a clever revival and revision of *The Author's Farce* (January 1734). Among more localized topical adjustments, Sparkish disappears (Wilks having died) to be replaced by Marplay junior, who outdoes even his father as a dead hand on dramatic production. His own most recent humourless effort, as Marplay junior proudly declares with reference to Fielding's familiar touchstones, is not 'cram'd with a pack of Wit-traps, like *Congreve*, and *Wycherly*, where every one knows when the Joke was coming. I defy the sharpest Critick of 'em all to have known when any Jokes of mine were coming' (*Plays*, vol. 1, 315; I.vi).

In strictly practical terms, however, the revised *Author's Farce* was an ill-judged work, trumpeting Fielding's allegiance to what proved within days to be the losing side at Drury Lane. Deprived of his former security, he zealously courted audiences over the year that followed by highlighting elements of topical appeal while also ensuring that no important constituency within his audience would sense an alienating bias. His early script of *Don Quixote in England*, rehearsed by 'the distrest [i.e. loyalist] Actors in *Drury-Lane*' ('Preface') but displaced to the Little Haymarket when Theophilus Cibber and the rebels returned, was enlivened by farcical new hustings scenes, written with reference to the impending general election of 1734. However, these scenes were contrived to avoid offending any spectator on partisan grounds, the laugh falling on both political sides. There is evidence that Fielding even self-censored plays in performance through fear of audience hostility or boycott. In a somewhat aggrieved note to the cast-list of *An Old Man Taught Wisdom* (January 1735), he informs 'the Spectator of this Farce' that only readers of the published text have access to the play as he wrote it: 'whereas the Audience at its first Performance seemed ... to express a Dislike to one particular Character, to comply with their Opinion, that Character hath been since entirely omitted'. The grammar is evasive, and perhaps the cut was made by Marplay junior (now supervising productions at Drury Lane, to which Fielding had returned from the Little Haymarket in a disempowered position). But the character in question also vanishes from later published editions, which suggests Fielding's own hand, or at least his acquiescence. Either way, the episode offers an intriguing clue to the gender politics of theatre in the 1730s, the character being a student, Bookish, almost all of whose speeches are misogynist slurs.

Yet none of these gambits could prevent Fielding's income as a playwright from collapsing. While writing with his usual enthusiasm about cash transactions (Quixote's encounter with 'the Knight of the *Long-Purse*' (*Don Quixote in England*, 22), a venal Tory candidate, is an inspired case), he was making little himself from a remuneration system that rewarded playwrights with the profits from every third mainpiece performance in an opening run. Hume notes that Fielding gained just two benefit nights in 1733–4, earning a total annual income from the theatre of perhaps £100, 'and in 1734–5 it may have been significantly less'.[26] In a pained headnote to the unpopular *Universal Gallant*, Fielding meditates publicly on the competing motives behind authorship, as though preparing himself to abandon a pose of gentlemanly authorship that looked increasingly at odds with his hack condition. 'Every Man who produces a Play on the Stage, must propose to himself some Acquisition either of Pleasure, Reputation, or Profit', he writes in categorical style ('Advertisement'). But indulging 'the Itch of Scribling' is a juvenile and transient pleasure, and the amateur pursuit of reputation that animates Fielding's early plays no longer presses hard. Implicitly, but forcefully so, he now identifies himself as a professional more than a genteel author, casting his detractors instead as the leisured 'Gentlemen', and reworking Blotpage's 'Hackney for Bread' song from *The Author's Farce*

(*Plays*, vol. I, 226; II.iii) in a melancholy key. If an author 'be so unfortunate to depend on the success of his Labours for his Bread, he [the gentlemanly detractor] must be an inhuman Creature indeed, who would out of sport and wantonness ... make a jest of starving him and his Family'.

A year later it was '*Henry Fielding*, Esq.' who claimed authorship on the title page of *Pasquin*, but this was the last play in which Fielding so designated himself, and he was now developing a far more assertive, and emphatically commercial, persona. Nothing could be further from the caution that dulls the plays of 1734–5 than the imaginative recklessness of his last two seasons as a professional playwright, as though there was now nothing to lose, and indeed everything to gain, by switching from compliance to provocation. The shift is marked in practice by relentless explosion of the mimetic illusion. Cast in the self-reflexive form of the rehearsal play, *Pasquin* resumes the metatheatrical games of *The Author's Farce* more fully than in any interim work, and makes the locus classicus of the rehearsal form – a satire on Dryden, by the Duke of Buckingham and others, entitled simply the *Rehearsal* (1671) – look dramaturgically conservative by comparison. Two plays within the play are rehearsed before their authors and a critic, and the satirical implications of both (Trapwit's comedy of corrupted elections, Fustian's allegorical tragedy of the murder of Queen Common Sense) are at once exposed and complicated by the erratic commentaries – largely foolish, occasionally cogent – of the observing authors.

The debased condition of contemporary theatre returns to prominence as a topic here, and Fielding's recognition that he had no sustainable future within the established playhouses remains apparent in the satirical abandon of subsequent plays. *Tumble-down Dick* cleverly parodies the lowbrow pantomimes that Rich was now producing at his new playhouse in Covent Garden; in *The Historical Register*, the theatre world is one of 'lying, flattering, dissembling, promising, deceiving, and undermining' (16; I.97–8). Though *Eurydice* was performed at Drury Lane for its one and only night in February 1737 (brilliantly, Fielding followed this disaster with an afterpiece entitled *Eurydice Hiss'd*), the commercial and creative freedom to be found elsewhere more than compensated for the lack of elaborate machinery and expensive costumes. From the premiere of *Pasquin* on 5 March 1736 to the defiant last night of *The Historical Register* and *Eurydice Hiss'd* on 23 May 1737, Fielding remained at the Little Haymarket, acting in effect as manager of his own scratch company (which he may have intended to make permanent in a theatre of his own). As well as satirizing the established patent-theatre managers within these farces, Fielding presented and performed his operations at the Little Haymarket as a living, running parody of their management style. For the remainder of his career as a playwright, Scriblerus Secundus and Mr Fielding gave way to 'the Great Mogul', a designation with inescapable resonance at a time when theatre managers were regularly compared to types of impulsive autocracy, especially oriental potentates. (Furious at his high-handed treatment by Charles Fleetwood, patentee of Drury Lane from 1734, Henry Carey railed against 'the bad Taste and monstrous Partiality of the Great *Mogul* of the Hundreds of *Drury*'.)[27] The earliest announcement of Fielding's new persona seems to have come in an advertisement of 24 February 1736 for *Pasquin* '*By the* Great Mogul's *Company of* English Comedians',[28] and thereafter it marked his exuberant public performance of the impresario role.

With its allusion to dictatorial rule, Fielding's pose as the 'Great Mogul' also connected the satire on theatrical degeneration in his plays of 1736–7 with their other most prominent and controversial concern, political corruption and abuse of power. *Pasquin* was criticized by the *Grub-Street Journal* for interspersing its antiministerial barbs with allegations of Opposition hypocrisy, so displaying Fielding's familiar pragmatic detachment, and *Tumble-down Dick* leaves largely latent its analogy between Rich and Walpole as purveyors of shoddy illusion for personal profit. Performances of the latter play may have been more explicit than the published text, however, perhaps by borrowing meanings encoded in topical application tragedies and other Opposition dramas: Tiffany Stern notes the spaces left open for extemporization in Fielding's script, and some of these spaces, as when '*the* Tragedy King *repeats a Speech out of a Play*; *the Manager and he quarrel about an Emphasis*', offer unmistakable potential for political innuendo.[29] In the following season, *The Historical Register* and *Eurydice Hiss'd* commit themselves unequivocally to the antiministerial campaign, most strikingly when developing the analogies between politics and theatre that Fielding had been toying with since *The Author's Farce*. Power is abused, virtue corrupted, and standards debased in both arenas, and Fielding reiterates the point by conflating or superimposing dual satirical targets (prime minister, theatre manager) within single figures on stage. Expanding on his case for 'a strict resemblance between the states political and theatrical', the playwright Medley compares the mercenary new 'Prime Minister theatrical' at Drury Lane (Theophilus Cibber) with the established master of political theatre at Westminster: 'And though the public damn both, yet while they both receive their pay, they laugh at the public behind the scenes' ('*Historical Register*' and '*Eurydice Hissed*', 36; II.290–8). In *Eurydice Hiss'd*, the figure of Pillage connotes theatrical plagiarism and political peculation alike, while Sourwit moralizes that ''Tis all a cheat, / Some men play little farces and some great' (54; lines 48–9) – thus glancing back to the most notorious moment of *The Historical Register*, when Medley likens 'politics ... to a farce' (16; 1.16).

The disrupted forms and unstable meanings of these plays complicate their status as partisan interventions, and ideological rigour may not be the only explanation for their character at a time when Opposition satire, as the campaign against Walpole gained momentum, was a commodity in strong demand. But Fielding raised the political stakes in the severe 'Dedication to the Public' affixed to the published version of *The Historical Register*, which anticipates the voice of incorruptible Opposition that he was to cultivate in the *Champion* three years later. As manager of a company, he added to the offence by staging other Oppositional plays such as the anonymous lost drama *A Rehearsal of Kings* (March 1737), and compounded it further by advertising what would have been the first production of *Polly*, Gay's scandalous follow-up to *The Beggar's Opera*, which had been banned on political grounds in 1729. He was even rumoured to have written *The Golden Rump*, a scurrilous and seditious farce that Walpole used to ease the passage of the Licensing Act (and may have commissioned from a hired pen for just this purpose).

Fielding was not alone in precipitating the Licensing Act, and recent accounts stress the prevalence and increasing stridency of Opposition drama in every playhouse except Covent Garden during the 1737 season. An extreme example is William Havard's application tragedy *King Charles the First* at Lincoln's Inn Fields, which rewrites history in the topical language of ministerial corruption and misgovernment. To Fielding's enemies at the time, moreover, his new extremism had more to do with the profit motive than with political awakening, and as well as feeding the tastes of the season he may even have been courting hush money. Lockwood takes seriously Eliza Haywood's suggestion that he wrote 'in the hope of having some post given him by those whom he had abused, in order to silence his dramatic talent', and suggests that after the passage of the Act 'Fielding's own wordless disappearance from the midst of the affair' may reflect one among several other possible occasions on which he took money from Walpole to suppress existing writing or refrain from producing more.[30] Whatever the case, Fielding's career as a playwright was decisively halted, not so much by the requirement that new plays be submitted for censorship as by the stifling of competition entailed by the reinforcement of the old monopoly system. The Little Haymarket and venues like it had no viable future following the Licensing Act, and the patent theatres relapsed into torpor, leaving little room for the innovative, experimental drama that had been Fielding's greatest achievement. As Colley Cibber gloated in 1740 with mock-heroic reference to Herostratus, the fame-seeking arsonist of classical myth, Fielding had perpetrated a grand act of creative self-immolation in his last few plays, and in effect 'he set Fire to his Stage, by writing up to an Act of Parliament to demolish it'.[31] The conflagration and demolition cleared a space from which, in the years that followed, the novels could arise. But they also curtailed a meteoric career in the theatre that was potentially no less important, and no less rich in its capacity, had circumstances been different, to energize and transform a whole genre.

## NOTES

1. James Harris, 'An Essay on the Life and Genius of Henry Fielding Esqr.', in Clive T. Probyn, *The Sociable Humanist: The Life and Works of James Harris, 1709–1780* (Oxford: Clarendon Press, 1991), 307, 306. The word 'merely' was deleted in Harris's manuscript (see above, p. 10).
2. J. Paul Hunter, *Occasional Form: Henry Fielding and the Chains of Circumstance* (Baltimore: Johns Hopkins University Press, 1975), 69; see also Arthur Murphy, 'An Essay on the Life and Genius of Henry Fielding', in *The Works of Henry Fielding, Esq.*, ed. Arthur Murphy, 4 vols. (London, 1762), vol. I, 9, 25–6.
3. *General Advertiser*, 30 March 1748, quoted by Martin C. Battestin, 'Fielding and "Master Punch" in Panton Street', *Philological Quarterly* 45 (1966), 193; see also, on the first performances of *Miss Lucy in Town* (1742) and *The Wedding-Day* (1743), Martin C. Battestin with Ruthe R. Battestin, *Henry Fielding: A Life* (London: Routledge, 1989), 359–65.
4. Henry Fielding, *Plays*, vol. I, *1728–1731*, ed. Thomas Lockwood (Oxford: Clarendon Press, 2004), xvii. In the present chapter, all Fielding plays of this period (*Love in Several Masques, The Temple Beau, The Author's Farce, Tom Thumb, The Coffee-House Politician, The Tragedy of Tragedies, The Letter-Writers*) are cited from Lockwood's definitive edition. Unless stated otherwise, later plays are cited from first editions.
5. Robert D. Hume, *Henry Fielding and the London Theatre, 1728–1737* (Oxford: Clarendon Press, 1987), ix. For the theatre calendar of 27–9 April 1736, see Battestins, *Henry Fielding: A Life*, 232.
6. Henry Fielding, *'The Historical Register for the Year 1736' and 'Eurydice Hissed'*, ed. William W. Appleton (Lincoln: University of Nebraska Press, 1967), 64 (lines 261–3); subsequent references appear parenthetically in the text. Murphy, 'Essay', 27.
7. George Bernard Shaw, Preface to *Plays Unpleasant* (1898), in *Henry Fielding: A Critical Anthology*, ed. Claude Rawson (Harmondsworth: Penguin, 1973), 319.
8. Henry Fielding, *Joseph Andrews*, ed. Martin C. Battestin (Oxford: Clarendon Press, 1967), 89; II.i.
9. Henry Fielding, *Miscellanies*, vol. I, ed. Henry Knight Miller (Oxford: Clarendon Press, 1972), 155. Subsequent references will be given parenthetically in the text.
10. Mary Wortley Montagu, *Complete Letters of Lady Mary Wortley Montagu*, ed. Robert Halsband, 3 vols. (Oxford: Clarendon Press, 1965–7), vol. III, 66 (23 July 1754).
11. Hume, *Henry Fielding and the London Theatre*, 15.
12. See *Joseph Andrews*, 215–17; III.iii; Henry Carey, Preface to *The Honest Yorkshire-Man, A Ballad Farce, Refus'd to be Acted at Drury-Lane Playhouse* (London, 1736).

13. Fielding, *Pasquin: A Dramatick Satire on the Times* (London, 1736), 12; I.i.
14. William Shenstone, letter of 17 or 18 May 1742, in *Henry Fielding: The Critical Heritage*, ed. Ronald Paulson and Thomas Lockwood (London: Routledge, 1969), 120; 'Scriblerus Tertius', *The Candidates for the Bays* (London, 1730), 2.
15. Ronald Paulson, *The Life of Henry Fielding* (Oxford: Blackwell, 2000), 55 and 339 n., citing Henley's *Hyp Doctor* for 10 June 1740 and *Fog's Weekly Journal* for 1 August 1730.
16. See Thomas Lockwood's introduction to *The Tragedy of Tragedies* in *Plays*, vol. I, *1728–1731*, 518–19; also, for the Austen production (which may have been of the original version, *Tom Thumb*), Paula Byrne, *Jane Austen and the Theatre* (London and New York: Hambledon Press, 2002), 12.
17. Isobel Grundy, 'New Verse by Henry Fielding', *PMLA* 87 (1972), 213–45; Howard Weinbrot, 'Fielding's *Tragedy of Tragedies*: Papal Infallibility and Scriblerian Satire', *Harvard Library Bulletin* 7 (1996), 20–39.
18. Laetitia Pilkington, *Memoirs of Laetitia Pilkington*, ed. A. C. Elias Jr, 2 vols. (Athens: University of Georgia Press, 1997), vol. II, 312. Either Swift or Pilkington misremembers here, Tom's being the ghost that gets killed.
19. Vincent J. Liesenfeld, *The Licensing Act of 1737* (Madison: University of Wisconsin Press, 1984), 18, citing the presentment of the Middlesex Grand Jury, 7 July 1731.
20. *The Fall of Mortimer* (1731), 64.
21. *Grub-Street Journal*, 24 August 1732, in *Henry Fielding: The Critical Heritage*, ed. Paulson and Lockwood, 67; see also, on Fielding's feud with this journal, Bertrand A. Goldgar, *Walpole and the Wits* (Lincoln: University of Nebraska Press, 1976), 94–8, 113–14.
22. *The Connoisseur* (London, 1735), 20–1.
23. *Grub-Street Journal*, 30 March 1732, in *Henry Fielding: The Critical Heritage*, ed. Paulson and Lockwood, 33.
24. Aaron Hill, *See and Seem Blind* (1732), 7–8, quoted by Hume, *Henry Fielding and the London Theatre*, 125; on Fielding's contract with Andrew Millar for *Joseph Andrews*, see Fielding, *Joseph Andrews*, ed. Battestin, xxviii–xxx.
25. Henry Fielding, *The History of Tom Jones: A Foundling*, ed. Martin C. Battestin and Fredson Bowers (Oxford: Clarendon Press, 1974), 32; I.i.
26. Hume, *Henry Fielding and the London Theatre*, 191; see also 185.
27. Carey, *Honest Yorkshire-Man*, A2.
28. Quoted from the *London Daily-Post* by Battestins, *Henry Fielding: A Life*, 192.
29. Tiffany Stern, *Rehearsal from Shakespeare to Sheridan* (Oxford: Oxford University Press, 2000), 238; Fielding, *Tumble-down Dick* (1736), 17.
30. Thomas Lockwood, 'Fielding and the Licensing Act', *Huntington Library Quarterly* 50 (1987), 388 (quoting Haywood, *Betsy Thoughtless* (1751), vol. I, 76–7); 380.
31. Colley Cibber, *An Apology for the Life of Colley Cibber*, ed. B. R. S. Fone (Ann Arbor: University of Michigan Press, 1968), 156.

# 3

THOMAS LOCKWOOD

# *Shamela*

*Shamela* was the first and most famous parody of Richardson's *Pamela*, but Fielding never acknowledged having written it. Nor did those who studied and wrote of Fielding for the next century and a half show any more inclination to claim it for him, despite the signs of his authorship which lay here and there in plain sight, and only within the past sixty years has it really been shown to be his.[1] Yet there is nothing dubiously recent about this attribution, which is not so much the invention of a latter day as the willing forgetfulness of a former. It was Fielding himself who first studied to forget his title to this work, for though it was cheerful and brilliant, it was very low. *Joseph Andrews* and *Tom Jones* had that mark upon them too, but only from the low scenes or characters they descended to treat: or in other words only because they were stooping to truth. To that meritorious form of the low Fielding would gladly claim the title, mocking the bigotry of critics and taunting them with their own cant word itself of 'low'.[2] But *Shamela* was another matter. There it is not the vulgar story but the vulgar tone – Shamela's tone – that engrosses the work and puts it beyond respectable ownership. Whatever Shamela talks of she cheapens, with an effortless spirit and charm uncalculated by her but on Fielding's part very carefully calculated to please and to frustrate disapproval. She is indulged so freely and so sympathetically by her creator that no pretence of condemnation, no post-scripted report of her having been caught in bed with Williams and turned out of her house, can make it seem that she is not also beloved of her creator, or that all this comic indecency from her does not simply amount to indecent comedy from him. Fielding understandably would have had no good reason to own such a work – and he may also not have known that the book he was blackening had been written by the friend and neighbour of his four sisters – but even so it is ironic to consider how determinedly unconscious he appeared to remain of the very existence of a work that so obviously gave him a whole new consciousness of what he might create on a page. *Shamela* is the purest parody Fielding ever wrote, and for that matter one of the purest parodies to be found anywhere on the shelf of the period literature: this painstakingly imitative send-up of a literary original being an art of more flourishing growth in the next century. But if *Shamela* is in that way a work of specialized parody, rather than what might be called burlesque, it is a work which does not achieve its main strength through parody, if indeed (as I would argue) its real genius does not lie in another quarter altogether. Of course the parody is there, and very energetic, as in the dedicatory address, copying Conyers Middleton's style of obsequious self-importance, the pretence of authorship by Colley Cibber, or those puffed-up letters commendatory fronting *Pamela*, for the mockery of which Fielding had to do little more than transcribe them as they stood. As for the work itself, the episodes and dialogue of the story follow their counterpart originals with a grinning funhouse-mirror fidelity, and that imitative satirical relation between *Shamela* and *Pamela* has been thoroughly charted already.[3] I believe however that the work deserves closer consideration for the vital if not fully legible record it gives of what seems to me a crucial turn in Fielding's creative history, when he had left off writing plays but had not yet quite begun to write novels.

For the story of *Shamela* Fielding single-mindedly battens upon *Pamela*; but for the whole of the *Shamela* pamphlet with framing preliminaries, as his commentators have long observed, Fielding embraces not only Richardson but also Middleton and Cibber in the scheme of his parody, copying or otherwise recalling somehow the memorably ridiculous in all three authors. From this diversity of objects it has been argued that Fielding had in mind a general theme of corporate ridiculousness, an abstract something, such as corruption in church, state, and literature, which might be held to be the satirical principle governing the whole.[4] Possibly so; although it seems to me that the integrity of the work, such as it is, is a unity of tone rather than theme. However the link between framework and story is rationalized for the purposes of criticism, Fielding does not really succeed in making them seem parts of any unified creative whole – nor for that matter does he seem to try. For real mastery of total form Fielding's great success to this time was probably *The Tragedy of Tragedies*, compared to which *Shamela* will rightly seem a work more of two forms than one.

Not that it really matters, because *Shamela* lives by its story, not its editorial paraphernalia. It is not Parson Oliver's opinions on *Pamela* we remember, but Shamela's opinions on life: 'It would be hard indeed that a Woman who marries a Man only for his Money should be debarred from spending it'.[5] Fielding has his heart or at least his head in the opinions of *Pamela* we hear from Oliver, but they are merely Fielding's meditated critical views, projected self-consciously and unimaginatively through that stand-in. 'Many more Objections might, if I had Time or Inclination, be made to this

Book' (343), he says, although the five he has entered and numbered on
Fielding's behalf seem already somewhat too many, because so feebly and
irrelevantly challenging the book on moral grounds. The true lesson of
*Pamela* was not moral, after all, but artistic – showing not that such a
story might be virtuous but that it might seem true. The critical and editorial
view Fielding takes through Parson Oliver seems to miss some vital creative
question, oddly enough in the same way that Richardson's conscious editorial grasp of his own work can seem so narrowly didactic or beside the point.
If we trust the Richardsonian tale over the teller, it is likewise to Shamela, not
Shamela's author, that we should look for an estimate of what Richardson's
book meant to Fielding creatively. *Pamela* roused Fielding's critical dislike
of course but more significantly roused a creative desire to bring his own
character to life. And while much of the result is copied or caricatured
from the Richardson original, Shamela herself is not. Fielding puts her into
the scenes of *Pamela* and replays them in her lovably low-toned key, but, as
I have argued elsewhere, Shamela as an imaginative construction comes from
Fielding's theatrical past, the latest and most transgressive scripting of a
character represented by the smart-talking *soubrettes* and other heroines of
self-seeking in the plays he wrote for his great musical comedienne Catherine
Clive.[6] In what follows here I will try to indicate more precisely how he
realizes this character within the narrative, particularly as a narrating character herself, and what the result may signify.

The book of *Shamela* is made up of many parts and letters not belonging to
Shamela herself, who can be heard directly in only eight of the twenty-three
different letters of the book, and is only one of ten persons writing letters at
one time or another. Her letters are some of the longest, but even so her share
of the whole text (frame material included) amounts only to a little more than
half. She is nevertheless the star of the show, without whom this work would
be nothing. Even those who share the stage now and then to memorable
effect, like Booby, do so as it were only on her sufferance, as characters
brought to life in her own words and letters. Between Shamela herself and the
considerable remainder of the book that bears her name there is some
obvious difference of imaginative force. What is it?

Whatever it is, this difference does not appear right away. Nor is the
Shamela we meet at the beginning quite like the Shamela we know later
on. Her first letter is intended to establish her circumstances and 'true'
character but, apart from her outburst of longing for the balcony of the
Old House, is merely informational, with nothing of herself present. Fielding
makes her misspell words ('Ludgin' for lodging, 'wil' for while) to show
the vulgar servant-girl behind the mask of Pamela, as he does also with
Jonathan Wild in his love-letter to Laetitia,[7] but then drops the device

thereafter. The effect of the bad spelling is to remind the reader not so much of an ignorant letter-writer as of a knowing author copying ignorant spelling (an effect more dramatically obvious in the Wild letter), and Fielding undoubtedly sensed that any more of the same would be a distraction. With Letter II he finds the form in which his character can breathe and talk without such editorial over-management – the form of the letters in *Pamela* – and his abbreviated version of that epistolary monologue, with its narrative immediacy and personal presence, turns out to be perfect for Shamela, who rolls happily away in that vehicle as if it belonged to her.

Where Fielding copies scenes or circumstances from *Pamela* into *Shamela*, the result is not so much caricature as contemptuous abbreviation. The brevity of the retelling or reformulation makes part of the joke, and Shamela's personality expresses itself by the brutally summarizing form she gives her accounts of what happens. It is almost as if she herself has read *Pamela*, impatiently, and in retelling bits of that story to show what really counts or matters will drive to the point – her point, anyway – at high speed. In the shoulder-slapping episode with Mrs Jewkes, for example (Letter IX), it isn't simply the comic reversal of violent Shamela for victimized Pamela that produces the entertainment, but also the quick work Shamela makes both of Mrs Jewkes and of the storytelling itself: 'How now, Mynx, says she; Mynx! No more Mynx than yourself, says I; with that she hit me a Slap on the Shoulder, and I flew at her and scratched her Face, i'cod, 'till she went crying out of the Room; so no more at Present, from ...' (324). This little narrative goes back to the original episode for that word 'Mynx', the slap on the shoulder, and our memory of the Pamela helpless to respond. But it is not really a 'reading' of that episode, even parodically, or an unmasking of Pamela, because Shamela so thoroughly acts her own non-helpless character both in striking instantly back and recording the result in those rapid few words of uninflected, slightly bored-sounding summary. On the other hand, where Fielding is making a distinct effort to strip away the supposedly false covering of the original to show what 'really' happened, as in his copy of the scene of Pamela's presumed drowning in the pond (Letter X), he leaves a slight taint of editorial determination over Shamela's account of the event, because she must explain his intended meaning, with correspondingly less freedom to tell the story simply as herself. The result is a two-paragraph narrative which, while accomplishing its external purpose of showing Pamela's unintended suicide scare to have been a planned contrivance, and her thoughts of drowning herself merely a 'Fib', is somewhat characterless and not very funny. 'So much for this Matter', she says at the end, however, sounding more like herself again.

Shamela's second letter shows only light editorial traces, like the parenthetical 'for so I am called here' following the Squire's address to her as Pamela, or her notations that she 'pretended to be shy' and 'pretended to be Angry', necessary to the exposure of the Richardson original but also slightly interrupting the flow of words otherwise springing purely from the world and outlook of Shamela herself: as 'the young Squire hath been here, and as sure as a Gun he hath taken a Fancy to me', or 'then he kissed me again, and breathed very short, and looked very silly' (315). This is also the first of her narrative letters, setting what is to be her usual tone of brisk summary by way of implied contrast with the dilated circumstantiality of *Pamela*. Her next letter (IV) is part of the mother-daughter exchange about Shamela's 'slip' with Parson Williams and puts her back into less entertaining duty as an informant, through whom we learn more of the 'truth' behind the *Pamela* story and are reminded, somewhat clumsily, of the corrupt influences at work here: like mother like daughter.

But in Letter VI she makes a vivid showing, and this is where Fielding really begins to find his best vein. Shamela's first appearance as a narrator had come in Letter II with the brief account she gives of that first little passage of rude kissing from her master, but here she takes over the book in fully characteristic form, telescoping her slanging match with Booby into a comically concentrated rush of dialogue:

> – No, forsooth, says I, as pertly as I could; why how now Saucy Chops, Boldface, says he – Mighty pretty Words, says I, pert again. – Yes (says he) you are a d–d, impudent, stinking, cursed, confounded Jade, and I have a great Mind to kick your A–. You, kiss – says I. A-gad, says he, and so I will … (317)

The reader of *Pamela* would recognize the original of Squire B's own slightly ludicrous backstairs language like Saucy Chops and Boldface in the mockingly speeded-up redaction here, improved upon with language not recognizable from the original except as it were by poetic licence or extension of the character and his speech from the slightly to the utterly ludicrous ('impudent', yes, but not 'stinking', and obviously never with any threats of arse-kicking). The reminders of *Pamela* here, and the Booby makeover of Squire B, are part of the satirical fun, but it is Shamela herself who intensifies the fun and sets it off by the slightly deadpan manner of her narration, including the tick-tock speech attributives or 'inquits' in her vulgar historical present ('says I … says he') that mark and vivify her style:

> And so I flung from him in a mighty Rage, and pretended as how I would go out at the Door; but when I came to the End of the Room, I stood still, and my Master cryed out, Hussy, Slut, Saucebox, Boldface, come hither – Yes to be

sure, says I; why don't you come, says he; what should I come for, says I; if you don't come to me, I'll come to you, says he; I shan't come to you I assure you, says I. (317)[8]

The dramatic and comic high point of this part of her story comes in her bogus fainting fit, eyes open in a fixed stare, while Booby sits pale and trembling in the moonlight until she pretends to come to after half an hour. In all the parts of this letter, from the opening episode with Booby to her conversation with Mrs Jervis and the bedroom scene, and then the morning-after threat of her being turned off along with Mrs Jervis, the narrative and its tone belong wholly to Shamela, in that Fielding has withdrawn from the proceedings as to any authorial pointing or management and left his heroine to tell the story in her own fashion and with her own editorial notations: 'After having made a pretty free Use of my Fingers, without any great Regard to the Parts I attack'd, I counterfeit a Swoon' (318).

Shamela's narrative manner is not so strongly marked as her character itself, though it is certainly characteristic even so, mostly in its rather businesslike tone and subtle but definite impression of impatience for getting on with the story, as also of course in the abiding contempt for her master that saturates her speech. Letter VII, from Mrs Jervis to Shamela's mother, relates the episode of the humbly dressed Shamela's being mistaken by her master for a tenant's daughter, and the more strictly informational manner of that narration can be contrasted with Shamela's own idiom. When Mrs Jervis describes the Squire's discovery of the mistake, and the ensuing back and forth between them, it is impossible not to imagine how differently the same scene would have run – especially the part of it Mrs Jervis covers by saying 'and Miss defended herself with great Strength and Spirit' (320) – had Shamela herself been reporting.

With Letter IX and the remaining three letters Shamela comes completely into her own as a character representing herself by her narrative. Her signature tone of arch determination can be heard in small but resonantly typical comments: as in reference to Mrs Jewkes, who 'now designs I see, to sell me to my Master; thank her for that; she will find two Words go to that Bargain' (322). There are moments in these letters when the pressure of some editorial purpose leaves a slight dent in a text otherwise mostly belonging to Shamela. In her description of Parson Williams's sermon on the text of 'Be not righteous over-much' (Letter IX), Fielding requires Shamela to exhibit what she remembers of Williams's teachings in a naïve summary crafted by sophisticated authorial purpose to expose a self-serving doctrine of religious observance over moral action – 'That to go to Church, and to pray, and to sing Psalms, and to honour the Clergy, and to repent, is true Religion' – and the impression of puppeteering inevitably compromises the result there, as to the free representation of Shamela herself.

Letter X is a little masterpiece of narration tuned wholly to the voice and outlook of its narrating character, including Shamela's tryst in the garden with Parson Williams, the arrival of Squire Booby with yet another slanging match in the parlour, the after-dinner occasion where Mrs Jewkes drinks the 'dear *Monysyllable*' (328), followed then by the bedroom scene of Booby's attempt to ravish Shamela ('Mrs *Jewkes* crying why don't you do it?'), so memorably defeated by that 'genital hammerlock'[9] prepared by the heroine, with the morning-after sequel of the settlement proposals. This letter gets its verve partly from the rapid theatrical timing of all these little episodes of action, the reader being assumed to be (like Shamela herself) a lover of quick changes and getting to the point. But though the episodes themselves are extravagant and funny, they would fall flat without the narrative voice producing them, and the key there is Shamela's peculiarly rushed, slightly forward-leaning discourse, particularly in the scenes with her master, where her words practically tread upon his: 'Hussy, says he, don't provoke me, don't provoke me, I say' (327).[10] Or she will mix direct quotation within her own narrative to similarly jumbled effect, as in '*Pamela*, says he, the Moment I came in, you see I cannot stay long from you' (327), where 'the Moment I came in' seems at first to be words of her master. And sometimes the break between her words of self-quotation and of narrative likewise may be missably faint: 'Sir, says I, I shall be always glad to do what is in my power, and so I pretended not to know what he meant' (328). At their characteristic best her renditions of the story depend on a fuzzy mix of quotation and narrative, direct and indirect discourse, with minimal routinized markers of speech, often displaced somewhat so that 'says he' and 'says I' will bookend a pair of speeches not otherwise shown as belonging to two different speakers. The result is a blended flow of words and references at first a little disorientingly unclear as to speaker or reference but always bracingly clear as to Shamela's own tone and outlook:

> Well, *Pamela*, said he, what Answer do you make me to this. Sir, said I, I value my Vartue more than all the World, and I had rather be the poorest Man's Wife, than the richest Man's Whore. You are a Simpleton, said he; That may be, and yet I may have as much Wit as some Folks, cry'd I; meaning me, I suppose, said he; every Man knows himself best, says I. (329)

The singsong dialogue is also typical of many such scenes, perhaps suggesting the impertinence or back-talking gift that Shamela burnishes so brightly. And the speech markers supply a kind of musical accompaniment to the back and forth, in this case also enhancing the audible presence of the dialogue slightly by the shift from past to present. Fielding's ear for the tone of head-tossing maidservantly comment ('every Man knows himself best') is pitch perfect. More broadly speaking, Shamela as a narrator bathes everything and everybody she describes in her own strangely innocent if also predatory light. In her letters even Squire Booby calls it 'Vartue' ('Doth the Resistance you make to my Attempts proceed from Vartue only … ?', 331, Letter XII).

There are moments in Letter X too when Fielding fuses his own critical outlook on *Pamela* almost seamlessly with his evocation of Shamela's character: 'Mrs *Jewkes* remembered the Smart of my Nails too well to go farther, and so we sat down and talked about my Vartue till Dinner-time', or 'And so we talked of honourable Designs till Supper-time' (328). Fielding, not Shamela, is the one who is looking to expose the emptiness of talk about virtue. Nor can we really imagine the talk that ran here till dinner-time, or how it could possibly have sounded in character, since Shamela does not talk at length anyway, let alone about virtue. But she is reporting her own speech here so distantly and indirectly that the textual result presents no question of credibility in that way, while the dismissive manner of her *not* reporting the talk except as a matter of indifference, or time-filler not worth recording, is very much in character, one of those narrative occasions when she seems almost to be scanning the pages of *Pamela* on Fielding's behalf and editing out the unnecessary bits.

Letter XII, where the Squire tells Shamela he is thinking of marrying her, until her professions of disbelief set off his comically short fuse yet again, is notable among other things for her speech to Mrs Jewkes pretending to welcome her dismissal, another beautifully tuned rendition of the self-dramatizing maidservant on her high horse, this time with Shamela quoting herself not directly but indirectly:

> So, truly, I resolved to brazen it out, and with all the Spirit I could muster up, I told Mrs *Jewkes* I was vastly pleased with the News she brought me; that no one ever went more readily than I should, from a Place where my Vartue had been in continual Danger. That as for my Master, he might easily get those who were fit for his Purpose; but, for my Part, I preferred my Vartue to all Rakes whatever – And for his Promises, and his Offers to me, I don't value them of a Fig – Not of a Fig, Mrs *Jewkes*; and then I snapt my Fingers. (331–2)

'Vastly pleased' suggests another punctuating toss of the head, and 'Vartue' if anything is even funnier in this form of free indirect self-quotation.

The unnumbered thirteenth and last letter of the series, accounting for her post-marital mastery of her husband, is also Shamela's longest. The mix of narrative and dialogue is somewhat altered in favour of a greater share of narrative, with the exchanges of speech seeming somewhat more closely embedded within Shamela's recitation of events, as if reflecting her now more authoritative control of those events. In the long paragraph describing the morning of her request for the third supply of one hundred guineas in as many days, we are given yet another row between Shamela and Booby, where the tone however is slightly amended now, politer and more restrained than their earlier blow-ups, with Booby far more tractably husband-like and herself playing the injured wife: 'For if you begin to use me in this manner already, I reckon you will beat me before a Month's at an End. I am sure if you did, it would injure me less than this barbarous Treatment' (336). With an expression like 'barbarous Treatment' Shamela has made a convincing transition from the archly vulgar tone of her servant's rhetoric to the much better-bred language (and tears) of a lady of fashion, as she now identifies herself. She talks more, and in more sophisticated form, than she had before, though in her managing art and irrepressible spirit of self-seeking she is as recognizable as ever.

In the remainder of the letter Shamela perfects her character of put-upon wife, as well as perfecting her construction of Booby's own character of abusive or irrationally suspicious husband, as when he looks black at the sight of Williams poaching his hare and she 'begins with him first', as she puts it: 'La, Sir, says I; what makes you look so Angry and Grim? Doth the Sight of Mr *Williams* give you all this Uneasiness? I am sure, I would never have married a Woman of whom I had so bad an Opinion, that I must be uneasy at every Fellow she looks at'. And then she completes her preemptive strike:

> No, no, I am the Hare, for whom poor Parson *Williams* is persecuted; and Jealousy is the Motive. If you had married one of your Quality Ladies, she would have had Lovers by dozens, she would so; but because you have taken a Servant-Maid, forsooth! You are jealous if she but looks (and then I began to Water) at a poor P–a–a–rson in his Pu–u–u–lpit, and then out burst a Flood of Tears.
>
> (337)

This is Shamela in top form: from a mastery of her talent for impertinence, a quality necessarily belonging to the class she has left behind, she has graduated here to a whole new level of theatricalized brass or 'impudence', as Fielding liked to call it. Toward the end of this letter Fielding reaches an editorial hand into the text again, when he sends Shamela to the room where Williams is drinking with the mayor and aldermen so she can report her husband's angry reflections on them and their 'Pollitricks'. But on the whole the letter represents Shamela in fully and freely realized form, well in control of the respectable world she has commandeered, and sounding rather respectable herself, though still never far away either from one of those spontaneous moments of innocent vulgarity that make her shine, in her way, as when she is admiring Williams in the tobacco-clouded room drinking with the worthies of the borough: 'he hath pure round cherry Cheeks, and his Face look'd all the World to nothing like the Sun in a Fog. If the Sun had a Pipe in his Mouth, there would be no Difference' (340).

Richardson said that *Pamela* taught Fielding 'how to write to please',[11] which as to *Shamela* is true enough, in that the epistolary narrative method he copied from Richardson made it possible for him to write himself into his character with a totalizing power he had never experienced with play-scripts or journal essays. That was new, and while Fielding wrote in letter form only this once, the lesson it taught him was that a narrative might be controlled completely, and given all its life and excitement, by the presence and outlook of its narrator. In a manner of speaking, what he gave to Shamela he ended up wanting for himself. At any rate, Fielding certainly does not ever again let one of his characters tell the story, except in the limited space of an interpolated narrative – all of which, like Mr Wilson's story in *Joseph Andrews* or that of the Man of the Hill in *Tom Jones*, stand out as level patches of uninflected, characterless narration within a landscape of otherwise vividly potent and characterful storytelling.

Only Shamela, among his other part-time fictional narrators, has anything like Fielding's own freedom to create or realize a character for herself within the narrative. The type played on the stage to such perfection by Catherine Clive, from Isabel in *The Old Debauchees* to Lappet in *The Miser* and Lucy in *The Virgin Unmask'd*, was a character much gifted in an art of self-interested managing and supervision. Shamela also inherits that gift, extending it in a sense to a part of her world to which Isabel and Lappet have only the most limited access, namely the representational control of the persons and events she manages. That of course is Fielding's own art, or would shortly become so, and Shamela – thanks to Richardson's provision of the epistolary method – turned out to be a try-out partner for Fielding in something like the personally inflected narrative manner he made his own in the novels. He identifies with Shamela as to the form of her discourse, projecting himself into her narrating self, and that is one link or affinity between Fielding and Shamela otherwise forbidden by the rules of his own game in ridiculing *Pamela*. But the affinity goes beyond form. However coarse or conniving Shamela must be for the sake of the satire on Richardson, however unacceptably low and wicked, it seems to me obvious that Fielding nevertheless identifies devotedly with his character in spirit, for the reckless freedom from hypocritical respectability she represents. And as *Shamela* itself and the other work of this period shows, from the later plays through *Joseph Andrews* and *Jonathan Wild*, it was the love of such freedom, or longing for it, that could set his comic and artistic imagination ablaze like nothing else.

## NOTES

1. See particularly Charles B. Woods, 'Fielding and the Authorship of *Shamela*', *Philological Quarterly* 25 (1946), 248–72.
2. As e.g. *Tom Jones*, 326; VII.i: 'And all the young Critics of the Age, the Clerks, Apprentices, &c. called it Low, and fell a Groaning'.
3. See Henry Fielding, *An Apology for the Life of Mrs. Shamela Andrews*, ed. Sheridan W. Baker, Jr (Berkeley: University of California Press, 1953), xi–xxxvi; Ian Watt's introduction to *Shamela*, Augustan Reprint Society, no. 57 (Los Angeles: William Andrews Clark Memorial Library, University of California, 1956), 9–11; Bernard Kreissman, *Pamela-Shamela* (Lincoln: University of Nebraska Press, 1960), 10–22; Ulrich Broich, 'Fieldings *Shamela* und *Pamela or, the Fair Imposter*: zwei Parodien von Richardsons *Pamela*', *Anglia* 82 (1964), 172–90; Ronald Paulson, *Satire and the Novel in Eighteenth-Century England* (New Haven and London: Yale University Press, 1967), 110–13. Fielding's parody of the preliminary matter Richardson included with the second edition of *Pamela* is well surveyed in *The Pamela Controversy*, ed. Thomas Keymer and Peter Sabor, 6 vols. (London: Pickering and Chatto, 2001), vol. I, l–liii. For an excellent general analysis of *Shamela*, suggestively arguing for a view of it as in part less attack upon than 'grateful comic development' of *Pamela*, see Thomas Keymer's introduction to *'Joseph Andrews' and 'Shamela'*, ed. Douglas Brooks-Davies (Oxford: Oxford University Press, 1999), ix–xxiv (quotation p. xvii).
4. See Baker, ed., *Shamela*, xv–xxvii; Eric Rothstein's powerful argument in 'The Framework of *Shamela*', *ELH* 35 (1968), 381–402; and Hugh Amory, '*Shamela* as Aesopic Satire', *ELH* 38 (1971), 239–53.
5. Unnumbered Letter XIII, in the revised Oxford World's Classics edition, ed. Douglas Brooks-Davies and rev. by Thomas Keymer (Oxford: Oxford University Press, 1999), 336. In the absence of the forthcoming Wesleyan Edition volume containing *Shamela*, quotations are from this edition, identified within the text by letter number or other reference to its place in the original, with page number in this edition following the quotation.
6. Thomas Lockwood, 'Theatrical Fielding', *Studies in the Literary Imagination* 32 (1999), 107–10, and 'Fielding from Stage to Page', in *Henry Fielding, Novelist, Playwright, Journalist, Magistrate (1707-1754)*, ed. Claude Rawson (forthcoming 2007).
7. Beginning 'Most Deivine and adwhorable Creture' (*Jonathan Wild*, in *Miscellanies*, vol. III, ed. Hugh Amory, intro. and commentary Bertrand A. Goldgar (Oxford: Clarendon Press, 1997), 108; III.vi).
8. The classic analysis of this whole exchange for its characteristic vitality and 'metallic exuberance' is Claude Rawson, *Order from Confusion Sprung* (London: Allen and Unwin, 1985), pp. 261–5, 274. My own approach to *Shamela* is indebted to the lead taken by Rawson, almost alone among critics, in

concentrating closely on the representational form and significance of its dialogue rather than its content as a parody of Richardson.

9. Carl Wood, '*Shamela*'s Subtle Satire: Fielding's Characterization of Mrs. Jewkes and Mrs. Jervis', *ELN* 13 (1976), 267.
10. Cf. also 'Will you promise to forgive me: I forgive you! D – n you (says I) and d – n you says he, if you come to that' (319, Letter VI).
11. Letter to Dorothy Bradshaigh, in Samuel Richardson, *Selected Letters*, ed. John Carroll (Oxford: Clarendon Press, 1965), 134.

# 4

PAUL BAINES

# *Joseph Andrews*

A key moment in Fielding's first novel finds Parson Adams holed up (as often) in an inn, reading his beloved manuscript of Æschylus. Suddenly he notices Fanny Goodwill, the virtuous dairymaid under his protection, swoon: '*Adams* jumped up, flung his *Æschylus* into the Fire, and fell a roaring to the People of the House for Help'.[1] At once Joseph Andrews, on his way home to see Fanny and providentially located in the next room, appears, and the lovers are for the time being reunited. But the manuscript, 'his dear Friend, which was the Work of his own Hands, and had been his inseparable Companion for upwards of thirty Years' (155), is gone for ever.

We might think about this moment in relation to Henry James's point, in the classic essay 'The Art of Fiction', written in 1884, that there is no essential distinction between novels of incident and novels of character. True, an early reader of the novel, Thomas Gray, finds himself led to separate the aspects in a letter to Richard West of 8 April 1742: 'the incidents are ill laid ... but the characters have a great deal of nature, which always pleases even in her lowest shapes. Parson Adams is perfectly well; so is Mrs Slipslop'. It is also true that the understanding of 'character' here does not have a subtle, extended, Jamesian depth, but is derived from the principle Fielding learned in comic drama, that selfhood has to be quickly recognizable and not subject to much change or development. The crabstick-wielding Adams, with his finger-snapping, forgetfulness, indomitable energy ('brisk as a Bee'), sexual innocence (despite his prodigious brood of children), fearless generosity of spirit, and mildly culpable pride in learning, was always the 'character' that readers were tempted to extract from the book. Once initially identified, character is all but absolute, even slightly Bunyanesque: Beau Didapper, for example, does not appear until Book IV, but is summed up in an essay-like sketch (IV.ix). Fielding tells us that his prudent and calculating lawyer is 'not only alive but hath been so these 4000 Years' (189; III.i). Nonetheless, character is always shown in interaction with circumstance: Adams is often ludicrously at odds with his milieu, but in practice he is never completely separable from it, and one of the points of the book is to find appropriate locations for particular characteristics.

As an incident, the loss of the Æschylus is memorable, with a number of significant ramifications. As an expression of character, it bears much freight. Adams's jump is one of many gestures in the novel reminding us of the moral importance of brisk physical action over contained reflection. Adams does not begin to calculate for possible complications in his response, and discards a prized possession in a moment of someone else's need. It is a small demonstration of that active, practical virtue which Fielding promoted over mere private faith as the essence of Christianity. Adams has already rescued Fanny from rape, and unhesitatingly uses fist and crabstick in the defence of virtue throughout.

But the Æschylus has more to tell us. The loss is comic, despite the tragic content of the manuscript's pages, typifying Adams's careless tendency to become detached from material things such as money and horses. It is, too, an over-reaction, for Fanny has only fainted; dropping the book would have sufficed. It is a great personal loss to Adams, whose classicism is a clear signal of his class and intelligence. It is not that the classical mindset itself is diminished: Adams solaces himself with a phrase from Theocritus at the end of this episode and is never without the resources of his thorough Greek and Latin knowledge. His unimpeachable learning is contrasted with the malapropisms of Mrs Slipslop, daughter of a curate and perennially over-doing her attempts to show class and standing by the use of 'hard Words' (26; I.iii). As with many of Fielding's women, the failed aspiration to a high language betrays an essential limitation of mind. Adams laments that his wife does not read Greek, though Wilson seems more in tune with the novel's line in being content that his wife's understanding is limited to 'the Care of her Family' (227; III.iv); Joseph's masculine quality, meanwhile, is signalled by Adams's judgement that he should be taught Latin. The loss of the manu-script does however constitute a motif: the classical inheritance under threat.

It is especially intriguing in a novel which persistently alludes to classical texts in order to mark itself off as properly literate, in contrast to the new breed of anti-classical, uneducated novels by Defoe and Richardson, and which includes a number of mock-heroic pastiches for the 'Entertainment' of 'the Classical Reader' (4; Preface). Fielding's Preface, one of the key docu-ments in the early theory of the novel, is at once keen to identify his book as a 'kind of Writing, which I do not remember to have seen hitherto attempted in our Language' (3) and to characterize its newness in relation to detailed classical precedent. In explaining that a comedy based on a satiric appre-hension of the disparity between aspiration and reality in human affairs can have a wider social scope and a higher moral efficacy than a worthy but dull 'serious Romance', and in differentiating the novel's mode from that of the simply burlesque caricature, the Preface offers itself to the reader as a kind of Aristotelian supplement, a set of definitions by which to understand the new hybrid genre of 'comic Epic-Poem in Prose' (4; Preface). Classical values are infused into the modish form of the novel and brought up to date; or, perhaps, modern values are made to look comic when held in literary tension with classical forms which hold a ruefully intermittent sway.

By the time Adams throws it into the fire, the Æschylus manuscript has already featured as a sign of the world's crassness when it is treated with suspicion by the ignorant and corrupt crowd who accuse Adams and Fanny of theft; the local parson who surmises that Adams must have stolen it declares it is a religious work (II.xi). Moreover, the Æschylus is actually one of many missing, disputed, or rewritten books in the novel. Indeed, during Adams's impassioned extempore dissertation on Homer (passing through Sophocles, Aristotle, Euripides, and Seneca on the way), delivered partly in Greek to the somewhat less well-equipped Wilson, attention is drawn to a profound gap in the textual history of that great fount of Western literature:

> [Homer] was the Father of the Drama, as well as the Epic: Not of Tragedy only, but of Comedy also; for his *Margites*, which is deplorably lost, bore, says *Aristotle*, the same Analogy to Comedy as his *Odyssey* and *Iliad* to Tragedy.
>
> (197–8; III.ii)

This is an important 'ideal' text to bear in mind, partly because Fielding has already mentioned it in the Preface and partly because the novel deliberately invokes a Sophoclean tragic model: during the crisis of identity at the end of the book, when the family histories of Joseph and Fanny remain to be sorted out to determine whether their proposed marriage is incestuous or not, the lovers 'felt perhaps little less Anxiety in this interval than *Oedipus* himself, whilst his Fate was revealing' (336; IV.xv). In bringing together the ancient motif of the fostered child, the birthmark, and the low-class witness (in this case, the pedlar), Fielding brings his denouement close to a familiarly tragic ending, but opts instead to toss tragedy into the fire and produce a latterday *Margites*.

These careful negotiations around images of classical texts have a sort of counterpart in Adams's official productions as a clergyman: the sermons. Adams's journey to London is undertaken in the naïvely optimistic belief that he can sell his manuscript sermons (variously enumerated as three and nine volumes) for publication. This is deeply unlikely in commercial terms, as the bookseller (a descendant of Fielding's own Bookweight from *The Author's Farce*, 1730) informs him (I.xvii). While plays may sell (much to Adams's disgust), only controversial sermons of 'enthusiastic' turn, such as those of George Whitefield (54–5), are worth the printing. Adams's attempt to use a volume of sermons ('as well worth a hundred Pound as a Shilling was worth twelve Pence', 73; I.xvi) as a pledge for the unpaid bill at Tow-wouse's inn meets with a similar rebuff. But, comically, it transpires that Adams has not even brought the sermons with him, his practical wife having substituted some useful shirts for them (II.ii). Again, this illustrates character at a moment of loss, with extended significance for the progress of the narrative. Later, Adams tries to deliver a sermon on vanity which – in his vanity – he reckons his 'Master-piece'; this too is absent (214; III.iii). Adams is deceived by the illusory promise of an old Greek manuscript into giving a sermon as part of what turns out to be yet another humiliating experience, the trick which results in a soaking in III.vii: another apparent defeat for Adams's sermons (and his classicism). Books are not doing well. Adams's argument, expressed both to Joseph and to an innkeeper, that 'Knowledge of Men is only to be learnt from Knowledge of Books', Plato and Seneca in particular, and that the mental travel of armchair study provides him with all the knowledge of men that he needs, looks progressively more Quixotic as he fails time and again to judge the characters of those he meets (176, 181–2; II.xvi and xvii; Fielding's own essay 'On the Knowledge of the Characters of Men', from the first volume of his *Miscellanies* of 1743, strengthens the point). It is not the least irony of the book that the character proposed as 'not to be found in any Book now extant' (10; Preface) is the one most steeped in literature.

His literary ancestry is, on the other hand, impeccably ancient, for the bedrock of his identity is the Bible: Abraham Adams is named after a patriarch and the first human being. Part of the comedy of the book depends on the disparity between these august names and his generally dishevelled appearance; yet something emblematic remains, drawing a not wholly comic energy from the biblical forbears. In the same way, Lady Booby's sexual advances to Joseph are explicitly aligned with the biblical Joseph's rejection of Potiphar's wife, though the abuse of power is comically softened through Joseph's naïvely puzzled response; the brutal robbery that leaves him naked and half-dead, to be rescued (reluctantly, and for prudential rather than charitable reasons) by travellers who take him to an inn, is a caustic modernization of the parable of the Good Samaritan. But Adams must undergo a process whereby the secular and modern texts with which he protects himself are stripped away, like his money and his horse, leaving him to sermonize extempore, from the heart, as he does repeatedly in discussion with characters through the book: not only in theological discussions about faith, works, chastity, and charity with antagonistic fellow clergymen such as

Barnabas and Trulliber, but more generally: with the keepers of alehouses, with Wilson, and with Andrews, his protégé. He must also give the greater sermon that is his life and character, without knowing it. We are less interested in the texts he knows he has written than in the text that he makes unconsciously in the novel that produces him.

Even when absent, missing or lost texts function as a continual reminder of the processes of literary production. *Joseph Andrews* is the most overtly literary of the novels associated with the 'rise of the novel'. True, it has a realistic sense of detail, especially in areas of description: the open road, inns, stables, kitchens, pigs. But it wears its text on its sleeve as Swift's fictions do, foregrounding literary processes at every turn. Not many novels have the title character quoting what they overheard 'Squire *Pope*, the great Poet' say at table of the charitable works of men that educated readers would at once recognize as the Man of Ross and Ralph Allen (235; III.vi). Drama, the most obviously professional form of writing, which Fielding had by now been effectively forced to abandon, also features very distinctly. The poet and the player who assist in the abduction of Fanny (III.x) comically dispute where the success of drama lies: their failures and vanities are expertly captured in the upstart genre of the novel. It is part of Wilson's 'rake's progress' to have written, in economic desperation, a play which was not acted. He gives Adams an insider's view of the literary marketplace to which Adams has been refused entry, and tells how as an 'excellent Penman' he commenced 'Hackney-writer to the Lawyers', a final inglorious reduction of the economics of writing (217; III.iii). (Even his lost lottery ticket might be considered as another cancelled writing, and Wilson has, like the brothers in Swift's *Tale of a Tub*, controverted the text of his father's will.) Drama might be another form for the novel to demote, since Adams denounces plays as vehemently as any Jeremy Collier (with the exception of Addison's classically minded *Cato* and Steele's *Conscious Lovers*, a supposed comedy which Adams thinks 'has some things almost solemn enough for a Sermon', 267; III.xi). Given that Aeschylus and Sophocles were dramatists, however, there is some irony here. Moreover, Joseph is able to understand some of Lady Booby's conduct partly because he has seen drama (I.vi) while in London. It is at once a breach of innocence and a handy forewarning. He also quotes Shakespeare, apparently a closed book to Adams, to solace himself in a moment of loss (267), and drama retains a residual force throughout.

These alternate cancellations and invocations of prior texts and surrounding genres come together when we consider the relation of Fielding's novel to the emergent genre as a whole, as represented by Richardson's smash-hit *Pamela* (1740) and, to a much lesser extent, the earlier fictions of Defoe. *Joseph Andrews*, published on 22 February 1742, a few weeks after

Richardson's own sequel to *Pamela*, is an attempt to refound the novel on recognizably traditional lines: not only Homer, but the prose fiction as represented by the European tradition of Cervantes, explicitly acknowledged on the title page as the source of narrative 'manner'. Literary experience is foregrounded in ways which are quite foreign to the vivid impersonations of Defoe, the master of the first-person narrative of the self-made hero/ine, and Richardson, who presents a subjectivity supposedly emerging immediately from the event in letters which we are privileged to spy on. Adams's hand-copied Æschylus is a precious writing, a labour of love, but not in the way that Pamela's letters are: her texts present (supposedly) the authentic pressure of experience and individual virtue, while Æschylus presents a timeless and universal tragic vision.

There is no illusion of the *Pamela* type in Fielding: we are always definitely reading a book, as the narrator, with his direct addresses to and constructions of readers high, low, female, male, moralistic, or bored, keeps reminding us. This is not a private experience, a visionary sympathy with the sufferings of a single figure, but a public engagement by a multiplicity of variant readers with an overtly material book. We have a four-book structure, a classical epic division used for example by Virgil in the *Georgics* and Milton in *Paradise Regained* – and, for satiric purposes, in Swift's *Gulliver's Travels*. We have chapters, eschewed by Defoe's stream of telling and rendered otiose by Richardson's moment-by-moment structure. We have headings, prefaces, essays on biography, a table of contents: a full textual grid to view the narrative through and to protect us from the seductions of an individual subjectivity. The last line of the novel indicates in a final intertextual hit the kind of text we have, and have not, been reading: Joseph 'declares he will imitate [his parents] in their Retirement; nor will be prevailed on by any Booksellers, or their Authors, to make his Appearance in *High-Life*' (344; IV.xvi) – unlike Pamela, whose very privacy, blazoned endlessly (as in John Kelly's unauthorized continuation, *Pamela's Conduct in High Life*, 1741), is always regarded by Fielding as a form of calculated display.

Criticism of the relationship between *Joseph Andrews* and *Pamela* has sometimes argued that Richardson's novel is merely a minor irritant, or stimulant, to Fielding; or that, having begun a further *Shamela*-like parody, the novel somehow got out of hand and Fielding found himself accidentally writing a 'proper' novel. Given the geometric planning of the novel, it is more convincing to see *Pamela* as a pervasive presence in it, partly as a source of parody and partly as a foil against which to test new solutions for problems (sexual, social, literary) raised by that fiction. Fielding has Joseph write to Pamela, guiltily, about the sexual approaches of his employer (I.vi and I.x), cheekily appropriating the very ground of her literary self-presentation; at the end of the book she actually appears, married to Squire B (pointedly, as in *Shamela*, renamed Booby). Familiar as the device is to an age of post-modern rewritings and intertextual games, the transplantation of Richardson's character ('with a lewd and ungenerous engraftment', as Richardson complained in a letter to Lady Bradshaigh)[2] into his own novel was a bold experiment for Fielding, in some ways bolder than the more purely parodic *Shamela*. *Joseph Andrews* tries something more difficult and complex: an overwriting, a kind of viral infection of the prior text which reads Pamela's character in a more negative light but also tries to produce a valid fictional combination of new issues with classic form.

Pamela's opposite number is of course to begin with her supposed brother, Joseph, the chaste servant who emphatically does not seek cross-class marriage but pursues his original, given, pure affection for a dairymaid. Fanny, who turns out to be Pamela's actual sibling, is also a carefully targeted example of real, unselfconscious, uncalculating female virtue. Mrs Slipslop takes the role of Mrs Jewkes and turns it into a miniature comic epic of sexual and social frustration. Adams stands as a robust, if Quixotic, response to Richardson's ineffectual Parson Williams, though the other clergy figures in the novel remind us of the range of theological positioning available. More or less every aspect of Richardson's story finds some reversed mirror-image in Fielding's.

Richardson's novel works by claustrophobic concentration on a single sexual-political encounter from which there is no escape: the problems caused by cross-class desire and ambition are resolved internally by internal reform, love, marriage, and consummation. Only at that point does the outside world return to deal with the now established couple/unit, who have to a large extent been sealed off. To some readers, *Pamela*'s fascination with sexual chastity has always seemed covertly pornographic, and in *Joseph Andrews* we have a much more open and straightforward eroticism, where eroticism has a purposeful place: Fanny is described lusciously for the reader early on (II.xii) and once again later, slightly undressed, for Joseph's more particular benefit (IV.vii), so that there is no possible ambiguity about her sexual status. Moreover, we have a much broader dynamic of interaction and interference: Joseph is also depicted in sexually alluring terms by way of explanation for his perennial subjection to female desire, the great motor of the plot (I.viii).

Joseph is pursued sexually not only by Lady Booby, but also by Mrs Slipslop, whose sense of status and sexual lack renders her relationship with her mistress very unstable; and by casual Pamela-level women like Betty, the amiable servant who tends Joseph's wounds. Fanny herself is

throughout the book the subject of repeated sexual harassment and preda-
tion, a fact which places her squarely under the correct protection of her male
keepers, Adams and Joseph, since – in a violent world where men hold all the
real power, physical and legal – Pamela-like reliance on virtue and chastity,
however covertly effective for that heroine, is not likely to help much. The
novel construes Fanny's desire for Joseph as healthy and legitimate in comparison with Pamela's autoerotic sham-modesty. After a series of increasingly warm physical encounters, Joseph and Fanny retire to enjoy a sexual
union which is quite explicitly superior to considerations of rank: their
'Rewards' are 'so great and sweet, that I apprehend *Joseph* neither envied
the noblest Duke, nor *Fanny* the finest Duchess that night' (343; IV.xvi).

To be sure, much of the sexual action is comic and indeed farcical: the
adventures of the night in which Parson Adams manages in all innocence to
end up in bed with both Slipslop and Fanny, constitute a benign version of
the folk-tale motif of the bedswap, as used by Chaucer and Shakespeare. But
the episode is also a recognition of a wider world of sexual misunderstanding, mishap, and frustration. Slipslop's pursuit of any man within range
is comically placed by, among other techniques, an elaborate comparison
between her and a female tiger (33–4; I.vi); but perhaps, in the end, the
humour is not without some feeling. It is a mark of Fielding's moral understanding and latitude that Lady Booby, wicked stepmother though she is,
breaker of all the rules of rank, age, and gender, seems a stronger and more
interesting character than Fanny. Fielding is suspicious of private emotion,
and the central trio all express strong feeling in public, in conventional
rhetorical language, guarding against the private, spontaneous, inward commission to paper to which we are granted voyeuristic access in *Pamela*. Much
of what might be termed the internal psychological processing of the novel is
concentrated in Lady Booby's tormented self-deceptions and internal vacil-
lations, on which Fielding expends considerable energy, bordering on a kind
of sympathy. Furthermore, Fielding is careful not to punish her indiscretions
with more than internal pain, even granting her a kind of consolation prize
at the end, in the shape of 'a young Captain of Dragoons' (344; IV.xvi).
Fielding will get noticeably tougher on the sexual indiscretions of women
in later novels: Lady Bellaston (in *Tom Jones*) and Miss Matthews (*Amelia*)
have much less to redeem them than Lady Booby.

Fielding does not want to concentrate on the success of one single
Cinderella narrative, and that is one reason for the insertion of so many
narratives of courtship and marriage from what look like other universes, a
feature which has troubled some readers. The parallel narratives can seem
to be pasted in from other genres, as if a colour film had suddenly changed
to monochrome, or the characters had started talking in Italian. The story

of Leonora and Horatio, with its romance names, Frenchified villain, and near-tragic defeat, is in one sense loosely attached (it is told by an unnamed lady in a coach as the travellers happen to pass Leonora's house); but Adams is one of the hearers – occasionally intervening to correct female pronunciation of Latin – and the story of grown-up misunderstanding and romantic failure is integrated into the greater narrative of heterosexual coupling as a window on to a different kind of experience and a different literary tradition: it is one of the more obvious evidences of the manner of Cervantes.

Similarly, Wilson's first-person confessional narrative of his misadventures as an amorous and ambitious young man, from which he is rescued by an ideal wife figure, is a short story in itself (and sometimes considered to be a kind of covert apology for Fielding's own failings); but it is integrated into the novel by the presence of Adams as auditor and interlocutor. Moreover, Wilson's narrative sets up the very model of a domestic future for Joseph and Fanny, an ideally detached and self-sustaining rural system, declared by Adams to represent 'the Manner in which the People had lived in the Golden Age' (229; III.iv). The system is completed and closed, but only because the narrative has a sense of wider scope to close off from. The story of Leonard and Paul (IV.x) which Adams's son Dicky reads aloud also functions in this sidelong manner: in its tragic-comic demonstration of a friendship unravelling under the new priorities of marriage, it reminds us of other possible modes of literary discourse on the subject, and affords us some glimpse of married life beyond the conventional closure produced by the marriage and imminent parenthood of Joseph and Fanny on their ready-made miniature estate, conveniently funded by Squire Booby and stocked by Wilson.

That sense of destination might remind us of another way in which Fielding's fiction contrasts itself with that of his precursors. Defoe's heroes zoom hyperkinetically all over the world as part of their self-creation, but Richardson's Pamela is effectively immured in one place, driving reflection inward. Her escape exists only in the pure expressiveness of her letters, smuggled out through the wall. But as with desire, so with place: Fielding's fiction wants to look more broadly at social interactions and situations, and it does so partly through geographical means. Between the official residences in which the action begins (Lady Booby's house in London) and ends (her place in the country) lies an oddly uncharted hinterland of England, dotted with dangerous woods, obscure hamlets, the occasional country house, and a vast number of variously graded inns and alehouses, places of casual encounter and interchange. Inns here replace Odyssean sites of hospitality in which feasting is supplemented with tale-telling: they are like miniature states, forming a lesson in economy and placing in themselves, the innkeepers poised between demand and subservience as the class and economic substance of each visitor is determined.

The landscape of England is here actually an almost undifferentiated moral geography of selfishness: servant, lawyer, steward, clergyman, Squire, and Lady are all devoted to their own interests and desires above everything. Fielding's experiment is to set his characters walking through this rough world, a traditional (and Cervantesque) metaphor for self-discovery. To begin with, this is a novel of displacement: everyone has left a fixed point. Joseph is kicked out, his 'character' traduced, his uniform removed; physically he is robbed, stripped, abandoned. Fanny abandons a half-milked cow and sets off on foot; she is sexually attacked and robbed. Parson Adams leaves his curacy for London, but never gets there, undergoing a series of humiliating defeats and, like the others, getting robbed. Where Defoe's heroes accumulate goods and money, Fielding's relinquish them. Joseph actually has less to keep him going than the shipwrecked Crusoe, who at least manages to salvage a useful toolkit – and, indeed, some money. Fielding's novel strips its characters of the signs that key them into the hierarchy of rank, so that Adams, his clergyman's costume awry and caked in mud, is mistaken for a pig-dealer and identified as a criminal. The ever-diminishing shilling finally leaves the three of them cast back upon the most basic human resources: honesty, fellow-feeling, courage. Having demonstrated high-value moral essence, the characters are then prepared for a reasoned shift in social status: Adams is promoted out of his poverty, and Joseph and Fanny take up their rightful roles within the minor gentry.

But actually it is a kind of return: the characters pass the test and prove to be what they always 'really' were – the last thing to be stripped away is the world's false estimation of them. The strawberry birthmark on Joseph's body, through which his true identity as the lost son of Wilson is recognized, is at once a cavalier throwback to the oral culture of fairy tales and lost children, and a contemptuous dismissal of socially mobile self-making as practised and promoted by the supposedly naturalistic techniques of Defoe and Richardson. Joseph begins as a sort of cleaned-up version of the 'low' and dispossessed heroes of Defoe's fiction, but has nothing of their ability and desire to remake themselves through exertion, transgression, and imagination. He is quite happy being a footman, and this relocation simply befits his internal moral qualities and indeed his upbringing: he is an already-reformed and educated version of his father. It has little to do with effort or ambition or sentimental education: this is who, and what, Joseph has always been. The strawberry birthmark itself ('as fine a Strawberry as ever grew in a Garden', 338; IV.xv) might be read symbolically for its suggestion of a beautiful and fruitful rural England into which he is now planted.

The rejigging of family relationships through these losses and discoveries is also the final twist of the relationship with the earlier novel. Joseph innocently adores Pamela, but the reader sees her as vain, snobbish, and conceited; perhaps as an acknowledgement (soon rescinded) of Richardson's literary quality, his heroine is Joseph's blind spot. How can Joseph and Pamela be related? By substituting Fanny for Joseph as Pamela's sibling Fielding gives himself another opportunity to demonstrate Pamela's sniffiness about rank. But Fanny also blanks the self-indulgence and hypocrisy of the scribbling Pamela's self-representation (and the emergent literary genre she represents) by her complete insulation from the world of written discourse: she cannot read or write, a purer woman even than Wilson's domesticated wife. Joseph, it transpires, is actually the offspring of a classically educated, fallen but rediscovered patriarch who now emerges from hiding to claim the future of the novel.

One of the few things that Fielding shares with the earlier novelists is the familiar satiric point that rank on its own has no visible connection with moral quality. Indeed, in many ways Fielding, a distant cousin of more than one aristocrat, has a more authoritative contempt for social rank than Richardson, the self-made printer-novelist. Joseph is refused entry to a coach (for the second time) on the grounds of his 'lowness' of rank, precipitating an argument over who is higher than whom in the pecking order but demonstrating quite clearly the lack of charity evident in those who consider themselves 'high'. As often in Fielding, snobbery is the giveaway sign of an essentially 'low' nature. Another sign is the abuse of power, for everyone in the novel who has worldly power is corrupted by it (perhaps a small reminder to us of the timing of the novel, just as the great master of political 'management', Sir Robert Walpole, was toppling).

Not only does Lady Booby misapply her domestic authority in attempting to seduce Joseph and turning him out after a sort of mock trial; she uses the tricks of the lawyer Scout to obstruct the marriage of Fanny and Joseph, arranges for Beau Didapper to assault Fanny's virtue, and tries to browbeat Adams into neglecting to read the banns. Adams's principled refusal here, like his open rebuke to Squire Booby and Pamela for laughing in church, constitutes one of his claims to higher authority (342; IV.xvi). Peter Pounce, Lady Booby's embezzling steward, rescues Fanny from yet another rape attempt, but corrupts the rescue by desiring Fanny himself (III.xii). Squire Booby himself exerts a certain amount of helpful authority, rescuing Joseph and Fanny from a magistrate he happens to know. But he is no Allworthy: his views are essentially limited to private comfort, which features here as coercive. Joseph, as brother-in-law to the squire, now counts as socially superior to Fanny and the Squire refuses to countenance their marriage – a clear sign of hypocrisy, given his own marriage. (The problem is repeated in another guise when Joseph turns out to be Wilson's son and thus actually superior to Fanny; but the morally superior Wilson accepts that in the light of her virtue, 'the Disadvantages of Birth and Fortune might be compensated', 340; IV.xvi).

The squire who wantonly shoots Wilson's daughter's pet dog is just one of the mean-spirited and self-interested authority figures who populate the book (III.iv). We quickly learn to expect nothing from the regulatory power of the law, which always operates in defence of power, interest, and ignorance. Adams only escapes from the rigged proceedings against him through the intervention of a 'gentleman' who happens to be present and able to vouch for him; once his rank is established, the magistrate is as arbitrarily for him as he had been against him. Courts are merely the locus of fraud and oppression (to the extent that Fielding almost seems to be identifying a future project to clean up the legal act). Meanwhile a genuine thief escapes by bribing the officer guarding him (I.xvi). The lawyer in the coach advises the rescue of Joseph on legal and prudential grounds alone, but the postillion who fulfils the biblical command to hand over his cloak in rough but pure charity is first censured for swearing and 'since transported for robbing a Hen-roost' – (53; I.xii). Virtue is found among the low: the ex-army pedlar whose common-law wife supplies the vital piece of information leading to the discovery of Joseph's parentage has already established his claim by bailing out the penniless travellers when his social superiors fail to do so; he is rewarded with a low but stable position in the Excise office, one of the novel's few slight gestures towards possible reform of the apparatus of power.

Adams is once more at the centre of these problems of rank and authority, partly because, despite his worldly innocence and moral energy, he is not an unimpeachable figure. As a clergyman, his rank is that of a gentleman; as a curate he is all but penniless, and thus always an object of uncharitable suspicion to those around him. He is repeatedly subject to the great slapstick tradition of English comedy, tripping over in the mud, falling down hills, getting soaked, ragged, and filthy. Ending up in bed with the wrong women is the last humiliating test of his uxorious but domestically inept character. Yet there are questions to be asked of Adams as an authority figure. His confidence in the muscular interpretation of Christianity is complete and probably in line with Fielding's views; but his confidence in his abilities as a schoolmaster is gently mocked (III.iv). His early history, discreetly concentrated in a single chapter (II.viii), recounts his troubled accommodations with political and clergy hierarchies. He appears to align himself with the high-church supporters of the alarmist Henry Sacheverell, and his superstitious foibles about witches and apparitions post a further satirical marker. Adams is nearly as much under the thumb of his wife as Mr Tow-wouse, and his daughter is unpleasantly close to Pamela rather than to Fanny in character.

The crucial exchange comes when a neighbour sees Adams's favourite son Dicky fall in a river and, instead of doing something useful like pull the boy out, comes instead to report his certain death, a typical instance of veiled low-level malignity. Adams has been here before: he has lost five of his eleven children, and advises Wilson, expressing grief for the loss of his son, to 'submit to Providence' (224; III.iii). (Wilson's comment, setting up the eventual recovery of Joseph, is that he could have accepted his son's death as the will of God, but not his abduction.) When the report of his own favourite son's death comes, Adams has been lecturing Joseph (who at this stage believes he cannot marry Fanny because she is his sister) on absolute submission to the will of God. But the modern Abraham proves to be a patriarch who is not willing to sacrifice his child, and he raves inconsolably, to Joseph's understandable puzzlement, until the alarm proves false (IV.viii). When Samuel Johnson came to incorporate and rewrite this episode in *Rasselas*, in the case of the stoic philosopher who reacts to the news of his daughter's death by complete emotional collapse, the child remains dead, the philosopher discredited, the enquirer more firmly disillusioned. Joseph does not go quite this far, but his challenge to Adams is interrupted rather than resolved.

Indeed, Joseph is not simply the passive projection of his mentor's teaching, and in some ways supplies some of the gaps and failings that Adams demonstrates. In the Æschylus incident with which this discussion opened, Joseph is singing a song of a surprisingly bawdy character, which Fanny hears and Adams does not. He confesses that during Lady Booby's spirited seduction attempt, he nearly forgot all his mentor's discourses of chastity. His understanding of worldly and sexual urges actually has its uses out on the road: Joseph is quick, and right, to suspect the validity of the huge promises made by yet another flawed gentleman, while Adams is completely fooled (II.xvi). His momentary anger on finding Adams (innocently) in bed with Fanny is a necessary rite of separation from his mentor as he reaches full manhood. He has been out in the world, and learned enough to survive and protect himself; Adams's reliance on books and on his own authority is never quite sufficient.

The only authority figure who might be thought beyond criticism is the narrator, for *Joseph Andrews* was the first book in which Fielding developed the voice of programmatic control that distinguishes the narration of *Tom Jones*. Cajoling, witty, firmly in command, reminding us always of where we are in the chapter, and telling us whether or not we are likely to like the next one, the voice is every inch the gentleman, outside the events it providentially arranges, aware of and sympathizing with the emotional states of the characters but by no means subjected to them. The reader is welcome to partake, or not: 'Then *Joseph* made a Speech on Charity, which the Reader, if he is so disposed, may see in the next Chapter; for we scorn to betray him into any such Reading, without first giving him Warning' (233; III.v). Yet here too, in the very marrow of the fiction that he opposes to the apparently authorless, self-generating works of Defoe and Richardson, there is a concern to distinguish authority from tyranny. Conservative as the literary style is, it condescends with gusto, making itself flamboyantly dependent on low comedy, to the distress or scorn of many of the novel's first readers, and plugging its classicism into quotidian detail:

> Now the Rake *Hesperus* had called for his Breeches and, having well rubbed his drowsy Eyes, prepared to dress himself for all Night; by whose Example his Brother Rakes on Earth likewise leave those Beds, in which they had slept away the Day. Now *Thetis* the good Housewife began to put on the Pot in order to regale the good Man *Phœbus* after his daily Labours were over. In vulgar Language, it was in the Evening ... (37–8; I.viii)

The extended mock-heroic description of Joseph beating with his ancestral cudgel the hounds that are pursuing a fleeing Adams, with its invocations of literary muses, modern geniuses (Swift, Mallet), and classical authorities (Virgil, Horace, Cicero), functions at once to question Adams's authority, hand the cudgel of righteous violence to Joseph, announce a super-educated narrator, and give a comic edge to the narrative mastery (III.vi). The Patrician narrator, indeed, likes to play at insufficiency, in a proto-Sternean manner: 'As we cannot therefore at present get Mr *Joseph* out of the Inn, we shall leave him in it, and carry our Reader on after Parson *Adams*' (95; II.ii). Even the principle of 'extradiegetic' narration, performed by a narrator not involved in the action and thus in a position of authority, is comically limited by moments which reset the frame: 'Indeed, I have often been assured by [Joseph and Fanny], that they spent these Hours in a most delightful Conversation; but as I never could prevail on either to relate it, so I cannot communicate it to the Reader' (168; II.xv). In its public restraint and wink to the reader, the gesture communicates more than the supposed private conversation would. Fielding's intervention in the history of the novel appears to hijack Richardson's heroine and repackage her subjectivity, her style, and her social mobility in an authoritative novel of classic literary breadth and direction. But the unnamed narrator, our guide throughout, reminds us that power, even narrative power, is at its best when it allows itself to include, or artfully highlight, complication, imperfection, and self-mockery.

# 5

JENNY DAVIDSON

# *Jonathan Wild*

Approach Fielding's *The History of the Life of the Late Mr Jonathan Wild the Great* (1743) with an eye to the realistic depiction of character and human psychology and you will bump up against the literary equivalent of a brick wall. This is not to say that Fielding's not interested in psychology – far from it – but that *Jonathan Wild* frames psychology rather as an instrument of ethics than as an aid to portrait-painting. Near the beginning, the narrator claims that reading the lives of great men may be instructive as well as entertaining: besides helping readers to attain 'a consummate Knowledge of human Nature in general; its secret Springs, various Windings, and perplexed Mazes', he asserts, 'we have here before our Eyes, lively Examples of whatever is amiable or detestable, worthy of Admiration or Abhorrence, and are consequently taught, in a Manner infinitely more effectual than by Precept, what we are eagerly to imitate or carefully to avoid.'[1] This description is partly tongue-in-cheek – Fielding's narrative is sharper and more satirical than the emphasis on exemplary morality would suggest – but the book is undoubtedly far less realistic in its depiction of people in their day-to-day lives than Daniel Defoe's *True and Genuine Account of the Life and Actions of the Late Jonathan Wild* (1725), a contemporary chronicle of the rise and fall of the real-life thief-taker Jonathan Wild in 1720s London. (Though the difficulty of matching up the prolific Defoe with his anonymous publications has led a number of scholars to question his authorship of this life of Wild, Defoe's recent biographer persuasively points to the 'obvious signs of Defoe's unique style' and calls him 'certainly responsible for it'.)[2]

As the name suggests, the thief-taker's job involved capturing everyone from housebreakers to highwaymen and testifying against them in court; a zeal for returning goods to their owners often proved compatible, however (it was certainly so in the case of Wild, the century's most notorious thief-taker), with fencing stolen goods, organizing gangs of criminals, and turning over one's own close associates to the law, no matter that they were likely to be hanged for their offences. Defoe is interested not just in the economics of crime and its policing but in the interior life of the thief-taker himself, and he excels in his treatment of Wild's moral complexity; despite his daily dealings with thieves, Wild 'acquired a strange, and indeed unusual, reputation for a mighty honest man, till his success hardened him to put on a face of public service in it, and for that purpose to profess an open and bare correspondence among the gangs of thieves, by which his house became an office of intelligence for inquiries of that kind, as if all stolen goods had been deposited with him in order to be restored.'[3] Defoe's *Account* was one of a host of similar narratives, and Jonathan Wild attained almost mythic status in his own lifetime (first as enforcer of the law, then as its abuser, and at last as its victim), a reputation consolidated after his death when his story became a pretext for lampooning the corruption of the highly unpopular politician Sir Robert Walpole, Britain's first Prime Minister at a time when the name was not an official title but rather a nasty epithet.

In contrast to Defoe's Jonathan Wild, the protagonist of Fielding's novel is less a historical than an allegorical figure, the novelist even choosing to bestow on Wild (although his historical counterpart was baptized in May 1683, most probably as a baby) a birth-date of 'the very Day when the Plague first broke out in 1665', with obvious implications.[4] Indeed, in the Preface to the three-volume *Miscellanies* (of which *Jonathan Wild* made up the final volume), Fielding disclaims any design of competing with the chroniclers of the real historical Wild: 'To confess the Truth', he continues, 'my Narrative is rather of such Actions which he might have performed, or would, or should have performed, than what he really did; and may, in Reality, as well suit any other such great Man, as the Person himself whose Name it bears.'[5]

Despite the term 'Life' in the work's title, then – equivalent to our term 'biography', which had not yet come into general use as a synonym for a life story – Fielding's 'Narrative' is not straightforward biography but prose fiction or satire. Bursting with rhetorical energy and literary allusions, *Jonathan Wild* reveals its author's tactical pillaging of history, epic, biography, the novel, and the picaresque tradition, as well as of more specific sources such as proverbs and jestbooks, mock-genealogy, and the work of individual writers from the Greeks and Romans to Erasmus and Cervantes.[6] The debt to epic is particularly apparent, not surprising in a period whose greatest literary accomplishments included those ambivalent responses to epic called mock-epics (Pope's *Dunciad* (1728, 1729, 1743) and *Rape of the Lock* (1712–14) among them), poems written against the background of a thoroughgoing humanist critique of the warlike values of traditional epic. Claude Rawson has observed that 'Jonathan Wild's schoolboy celebration of the gangster-virtues of Homeric and Virgilian heroes is a version of an old connection, made especially familiar in our time in several formulations by Auden and Isherwood, between the ethics of heroes, gangsters and schoolboy toughs.'[7]

In his influential 1957 book *The Rise of the Novel*, the literary critic Ian Watt coined the phrase 'formal realism' to describe the 'narrative embodiment' of the premise or convention 'that the novel is a full and authentic report of human experience, and is therefore under an obligation to satisfy its reader with such details of the story as the individuality of the actors concerned, the particulars of the times and places of their actions, details which are presented through a more largely referential use of language than is common in other literary forms.'[8] As distinct from the 'uncompromising' realism of Defoe and Richardson, Watt suggests, Fielding's style – heavily rhetorical, highly literary – tends 'to interfere with his technique as a novelist, because a patent selectiveness of vision destroys our belief in the reality of report, or at least diverts our attention from the content of the report to the skill of the reporter'.[9] For reasons both temperamental and artistic, Fielding seems to have enjoyed going head-to-head with contemporaries striving to define what prose fiction could and should do. The literary innovation he would achieve in *Joseph Andrews* (1742) and perfect in *Tom Jones* (1749) originated in *Shamela* (1741), Fielding's hilarious and rhetorically powerful parody of Richardson's immensely popular epistolary novel *Pamela, or Virtue Rewarded* (1740). Similarly, Fielding's choice of Jonathan Wild as a subject lets us juxtapose Fielding to Defoe as a practitioner of criminal biography. (While the editors of the best scholarly text of *Jonathan Wild* argue that Fielding composed it after *Joseph Andrews*, most scholars share 'a broad consensus that the bulk of the book already existed in draft before *Joseph Andrews* appeared in February 1742', and this essay will treat *Jonathan Wild* as Fielding's first major prose fiction.)[10]

Where Defoe's language works to paint a picture of Jonathan Wild amidst a dense web of real circumstances, that is to say recognizable places and people and practices, Fielding instead depicts the Great Man at a relatively high level of abstraction. Like the novelist, Wild reveals himself to be a theorist of human motivation and human society; he is also a master of manipulation. Adopting a manner quite different from Defoe's sociological reportage, Fielding uses Wild to expose the general tendencies of human nature rather than to detail the particulars of the actual thief-taker's method and practices. The following passage, for instance, sums up Wild's treatment of his 'prigs', thieves he sets to impeach and bear witness against each other, often with fatal consequences:

> With such infinite Address, did this truly GREAT MAN know to play with the Passions of Men, and to set them at Variance with each other, and to work his own Purposes out of those Jealousies and Apprehensions, which he was

wonderfully ready at creating, by Means of those great Arts, which the Vulgar call Treachery, Dissembling, Promising, Lying, Falshood, &c. but which are by GREAT MEN summed up in the collective Name of Policy, or Politicks, or rather *Pollitricks*; an Art of which, as it is the highest Excellence of Human Nature, so perhaps, was our GREAT MAN the most eminent Master. (67; II.v)

The narrator here sounds rather like one of Jonathan Swift's mad projectors, exposing (by celebrating qualities generally found odious) a genuinely sinister aspect of greatness and its philosophical underpinnings.

Disingenuous thinkers may 'confound the Ideas of Greatness and Goodness', the narrator states early on, but in fact 'no two Things can possibly be more distinct from each other':

> For Greatness consists in bringing all Manner of Mischief on Mankind, and Goodness in removing it from them. Now, tho' the Writer, if he will confine himself to Truth, is obliged to draw a perfect Picture of the former in all the Actions which he records of his Hero, yet to reconcile his Work with those absurd Doctrines above-mentioned, he is ever guilty of interspersing Reflections in Reality to the Disadvantage of that great Perfection, Uniformity of Character; for Instance, in the Histories of *Alexander* and *Cæsar*, we are frequently reminded of their Benevolence and Generosity. When the former had with Fire and Sword overrun a whole Empire, and destroyed the Lives of Millions of innocent People, we are told as an Example of his Benevolence, that he did not cut the Throat of an old Woman, and ravish her Daughters whom he had before undone[.] (9; I.i)

Fielding's initial satirical choice here involves the redefinition of greatness as something more culpable than admirable. He makes a subsidiary joke about the literary convention of uniformity or consistency of character, the point being that the details instanced in support of the benevolence of so-called heroes like Alexander or Julius Caesar are ludicrously trivial in proportion to the havoc such men wreak. Throughout the narrative, Fielding wittily plays on the parallels between greatness in high life and greatness in the lower orders. 'But without considering *Newgate* as no other than Human Nature with its Mask off, which some very shameless Writers have done, a Thought which no Price should purchase me to entertain', he writes in the Preface (the last phrase a savage and somewhat Swiftian aside), 'I think we may be excused for suspecting, that the splendid Palaces of the Great are often no other than *Newgate* with the Mask on. Nor do I know any thing which can raise an honest Man's Indignation higher than that the same Morals should be in one Place attended with all imaginable Misery and Infamy, and in the other, with the highest Luxury and Honour.'[11]

This critique of the hypocrisy that lets a society execute a thief for house-breaking while rewarding men in high office for pillaging the national treasury runs as a thread throughout the work, and the book is motivated in part by the desire to attack Sir Robert Walpole, the government minister who served as target for much of the satirical animus of the plays Fielding wrote in the 1730s. *Jonathan Wild* was not published until after Walpole left office, though, and in a later edition Fielding seems to have made the political references less specific (topical material is often the quickest thing to become out-of-date in satirical writing). There has been considerable speculation as to the extent of the book's immediate political motivation as well as about the dates of its composition.[12] But Wild is undoubtedly far more than simply a stand-in for Walpole, and the speeches Fielding gives his protagonist display interesting rhetorical instabilities. Sometimes Wild voices a thoughtful critique of social values; at other times he becomes the mouthpiece for a self-aggrandizing and rather obtuse philosophy of personal promotion. Dividing great men into four main categories, for instance, Wild asserts that '*Conquerors, absolute Princes, Prime Ministers*, and *Prigs* ... differ from each other in GREATNESS only, as they employ *more* or *fewer* Hands. And *Alexander* the Great was only *greater* than a Captain of one of the *Tartarian* or *Arabian Hords*, as he was at the Head of a larger Number' (48; I.xiv). 'In what then is a single *Prig* inferior to any other GREAT Man', the thief-taker goes on to ask, 'but because he employs his own Hands only; for he is not on that Account to be levelled with the Base and Vulgar, because he employs his Hands for his own Use only. Now, suppose a *Prig* had as many Tools as any Prime Minister ever had, would he not be as GREAT as any Prime Minister whatsoever? Undoubtedly he would. What then have I to do in the Pursuit of GREATNESS, but to procure a Gang, and to make the Use of this Gang center in myself?'

This passage works in a number of different ways. On the one hand, it is an absurd philosophy, an idiotic misapprehension of greatness in history. On the other, though, it cuts Alexander and the Prime Minister down to size, showing each to be little more than an ordinary thug or schoolyard bully (and Wild meanwhile picks up a little lustre himself by his association with one of the best-known heroes of the ancient world). Like many of his contemporaries, Fielding systematically demolishes the values associated with epic, adopting mock-heroic tropes and language to attack violence in its incarnation as political power. The mode of mock-epic attracted many of the greatest writers of the late seventeenth and early eighteenth centuries; sick of war and warlike values, their writings nonetheless remain steeped in the sometimes bloodthirsty language and ethos of poems such as the *Iliad* and the *Aeneid*. When the narrator calls Wild's friend and colleague Fireblood 'the *Achates* of our *Æneas*, or rather the *Hæphestion* of our *Alexander*' (101; III.iv), the effect is 'to arrest the flowering of the strictly epic fiction by means of a reminder of distasteful *historical fact*', in Rawson's words: but despite Fielding's evident desire to limit his critique of the hero to classical history rather than to the great epic poems, the narrative also displays what Rawson describes as 'an uneasy consciousness of the fact that the great heroic poems do celebrate exploits of war and plunder not always manifestly different from the actions of bad men like Alexander and Caesar'.[13]

Fielding explicitly likened his own practice as a novelist to the work of the epic poets when (in the Preface to *Joseph Andrews*) he introduced the phrase 'comic Epic-Poem in Prose' to describe his comic romance.[14] Though *Tom Jones* is commonly considered Fielding's masterpiece in the comic epic vein, *Jonathan Wild* includes several lovely burstings-forth of the epic simile, usually delivered with considerable self-consciousness on the part of the narrator. 'And now, Reader, if thou pleasest, as we are in no great Haste', he says at one point, 'we will stop and make a Simile':

> As when their Lap is finished, the cautious Huntsman to their Kennel gathers the nimble-footed Hounds, they with lank Ears and Tails slouch sullenly on, whilst he with his Whippers-in, follows close at their Heels, regardless of their dogged Humour, till having seen them safe within the Door, he turns the Key, and then retires to whatever Business or Pleasure calls him thence: So with louring Countenance, and reluctant Steps mounted the Count and *Bagshot* to their Chamber, or rather Kennel[.]     (45; I.xiv)

This is partly Fielding showing off the delightful effortlessness with which he can transpose a Homeric simile to his own time and place, here adopting the distinctly English-countryside conceit of the hunt with its whippers-in to describe a con-artist and a highwayman retiring to their cell (the 'nimble-footed Hounds' surely come off considerably better than the two men, who are degraded by the repetition of the word 'Kennel' at the end of the passage). An even funnier epic simile (Fielding introduces such similes sparingly here, in contrast to their frequency in a 'straight' epic like the *Iliad* or *Paradise Lost* (1667), England's last great epic poem in the heroic vein) crops up at the moment when Wild catches Fireblood 'in the Arms of his lovely *Lætitia*', the phrase introducing a comic incongruity (it would be more conventional to describe finding one's wife in the arms of another man than the other way round, and there is something mildly homoerotic in the verbal implication that Wild is more upset by seeing Fireblood with his wife than his wife with Fireblood). First Wild is compared to a bull bellowing at the incursion of a male competitor into a herd of cows he considers 'all his own Property':

> Not with less Noise, nor less dreadful Menaces did the Fury of *Wild* burst forth, and terrify the whole *Gate*. Long time did Rage render his Voice inarticulate to the Hearer; as when, at a visiting Day, fifteen or sixteen, or perhaps twice as many Females of delicate but shrill Pipes, ejaculate all at once on different Subjects, all is Sound only, the Harmony entirely melodious indeed, but conveys no Idea to our Ears; but at length, when Reason began to get the Better of his Passion, which latter being deserted by his Breath, began a little to retreat, the following Accents leapt over the Hedge of his Teeth, or rather the Ditch of his Gums, whence those Hedge-stakes had by a Pattin been displaced in Battle with an *Amazon* of *Drury*.                                             (170; IV.xi)

Playful and knowing, this simile supplants the initial image of a bull lowing at his sexual rival with an outrageous comparison of Wild's cries to the sound of a crowd of ladies having a not very melodious drawing-room visit: the uncertainty over the number ('fifteen or sixteen, or perhaps twice as many') is an amusing rhetorical gesture, and the diction deliberately inflated. The last part of the passage compounds the absurdity by introducing another metaphor. First Wild's teeth are likened to a hedge, then the image is corrected to reflect the fact that his gums are toothless because of the encounter with a patten (a wooden sole attached to shoes to raise them out of the filthy water that flowed through the streets and gutters of Georgian London) wielded by 'an *Amazon* of *Drury*'. Drury Lane had become synonymous with prostitution, and the last phrase simply means 'whore', while the Amazonian woman was a favourite trope of Fielding's;[15] the double effect of this passage is to make Wild ridiculous and to display Fielding's linguistic virtuosity.

Critics have generally agreed that the least successful aspect of *Jonathan Wild* concerns Fielding's depiction of Heartfree and his virtues. Rather like Milton's Satan, who is famously more engaging than the poem's other male principals (Adam, God, the Son), Fielding's Jonathan Wild (who at one point bathetically echoes Satan when he says that he 'had rather stand on the Summit of a Dunghil, than at the bottom of a Hill in Paradise' (20; I.v)) is far more lively than the story's moral exemplars. The ironic language in which Fielding celebrates greatness works more to erode than to shore up the real virtue of goodness. Here is an example of the instabilities of tone that characterize such passages in *Jonathan Wild*, the narrator moralizing here on Heartfree's readiness to trust the thief-taker:

> I am sensible that the Reader, if he hath but the least Notion of GREATNESS, must have such a Contempt for the extreme Folly of this Fellow, that he will

be very little concerned at any Misfortunes which befal him in the Sequel; for, to have no Suspicion that an old School-fellow, with whom he had, in his tenderest Years, contracted a Friendship, and who, on the accidental renewing their Acquaintance, had professed the most passionate Regard for him, should be very ready to impose on him; in short, to conceive that a Friend should, of his own Accord, without any View to his own Interest, endeavour to do him a Service; must argue such Weakness of Mind, such Ignorance of the World, and such an artless, simple, undesigning Heart, as must render the Person possessed of it the lowest Creature, and the properest Object of Contempt imaginable, in the Eyes of every Man of Understanding and Discernment. (55; II.ii)

Yet a little contempt for Heartfree *does* infect the reader who learns of this extreme gullibility and naïveté. Even Heartfree's name, with its too-obvious allegorical freight, suggests that he is neither historically nor psychologically persuasive as a character, in a clear breach of the new patterns of naming that were coming to be associated with the realist novel. Ian Watt writes of 'the way that the novelist typically indicates his intention of presenting a character as a particular individual by naming him in exactly the same way as particular individuals are named in ordinary life',[16] and Heartfree fails to come across as an individual partly because of the name Fielding has chosen for him. The narrator's affected contempt for Heartfree also lessens our own affection for him, in other words, so that when the sight of his children in prison after their mother has left 'brought a Flood of Tears into the Eyes of this weak, silly Man, who had not GREATNESS sufficient to conquer these low Efforts of Tenderness and Humanity' (94; III.i), we feel that while it may be right and proper to cry on such an occasion, it *is* also slightly weak and silly, at least when the narrator lingers on the details in this manner. Most readers agree that *Jonathan Wild* fails in its representation of goodness.[17]

In contrast to Heartfree's soppiness, Jonathan Wild is portrayed with a refreshing combination of energy and humour. He is allowed to voice the hero-as-thug critique, for one thing, albeit at some cost to the consistency of his character (see especially II.iv); he also shows an appealing rough courage. Fielding gives Wild a wonderful monologue after he has been cast out to sea in a small boat with few provisions and little chance of surviving. Wild first blasphemes God, then accuses lust as 'the unhappy Occasion of his present Sufferings' (it is his attempt to force himself on Mrs Heartfree that has prompted the French captain to throw him off the ship):

At length, finding himself descending too much into the Language of Meanness and Complaint, he stopp'd short, and soon after broke forth as follows. 'D–n it, a Man can die but once, what signifies it! Every Man must die, and when it is over it is over. I never was afraid of any thing yet, nor I won't begin now; no, d–n me, won't I. What signifies Fear? I shall die whether I am afraid or no: Who's afraid then, d–n me?' At which Words he looked extremely fierce, but recollecting that no one was present to see him, he abated the Terror of his Countenance, and pausing a little, repeated the Word, *D–n*! 'Suppose I should be d–ned at last, when I never thought a Syllable of the Matter! I have often laughed and made a Jest about it, and yet it may be so, for any Thing which I know to the contrary. If there should be another World it will go hard with me, that is certain. I shall never escape for what I have done to *Heartfree* ... D–n me, I will think no longer about it. – Let a Pack of cowardly Rascals be afraid of Death, I dare look him in the Face. But shall I stay and be starved! – No, I will eat up the Biscuits the *French* Son of a Whore bestowed on me, and then leap into the Sea for Drink, since the unconscionable Dog hath not allowed me a single Dram.' Having thus said, he proceeded immediately to put his Purpose in Execution, and as his Resolution never failed him, he had no sooner dispatched the small Quantity of Provision, which his Enemy had with no vast Liberality presented him, than he cast himself headlong into the sea.                                    (82; II.xi)

Wild's attempt at fierceness, his rather endearing lapse into self-examination, his honesty about his own crimes, his brisk dismissal of remorse after a brief interval of considering possible penalties in the afterlife, the combination of greed and common sense that makes him eat his biscuit before taking the plunge: all these culminate in the almost attractive bravado of the last gesture. Comically, though, Wild has second thoughts and climbs back into the boat, illustrating the truth of the proverb that the man who is born to be hanged will never be drowned.

Fielding's depiction of Wild includes echoes of some of Shakespeare's most engaging villains. Wild's nightmares in prison, haunted by the idea of Heartfree being under sentence of death as a consequence of Wild's own actions, are reminiscent of the nightmares of Richard III the night before his final battle;[18] emerging from these dreams, we learn, Wild 'no sooner recovered his waking Senses than he cry'd out: "I may yet prevent this Catastrophe. It is not too late to discover the whole." He then paused a Moment: But GREATNESS instantly returning to his Assistance, checked the base Thought, as it first offered itself to his Mind' (148; IV.iv). Wild's first words here call to mind the moment near the end of *King Lear* when the bastard Edmund, dying after his combat with Edgar, recants some part of his villainy: 'I pant for life. Some good I mean to do, / Despite of mine own nature' (V.iii.244–5). Though Edmund sends a servant to stop the writs of death for Lear and his daughter, his gesture comes too late to save Cordelia; Wild, of course, does not lapse nearly so far into goodness.

Fielding made his name as a playwright before the Licensing Act of 1737 (a measure pushed through by Walpole to prevent Fielding and others from using the stage as a medium for political satire, the act required all new plays to be approved and licensed by the lord chamberlain) led him to turn to prose fiction, and *Jonathan Wild* is often self-consciously theatrical in its metaphors. When Wild decides to accuse Heartfree of having sent away his wife and property to defraud creditors, the narrator introduces a telling comparison between the world and the theatre:

> What remained to consider was only the *Quomodo*, and the Person or Tool to be employed; for the Stage of the World differs from that in *Drury-Lane* principally in this; that whereas on the latter, the Hero, or chief Figure, is almost continually before your Eyes, whilst the Under-actors are not seen above once in an Evening; now, on the former, the Hero, or GREAT MAN, is always behind the Curtain, and seldom or never appears, or doth any thing in his own Person. He doth indeed, in this *grand Drama*, rather perform the Part of the *Prompter*, and instructs the well-drest Figures, who are strutting in public on the Stage, what to say and do. To say the Truth, a Puppet-show will illustrate our Meaning better, where it is the Master of the Show (the GREAT MAN) who dances and moves every thing; whether it be the King of *Muscovy*, or whatever other Potentate, *alias* Puppet, which we behold on the Stage; but he himself wisely keeps out of Sight; for should he once appear, the whole Motion would be at an End. (124; III.xi)

As a great man, Wild may work behind the scenes to pull off his elaborate machinations; as a figure in Fielding's narrative, however, he is 'continually before your Eyes' just like his dramatic counterparts.

Towards the end of the narrative, Fielding's language becomes even more self-conscious, as when the narrator is careful to label Heartfree's reprieve 'at least as natural as delightful' so that it should not 'seem to resemble [the unexpected reprieve] in the *Beggar's Opera*' (152; IV.vi). Here Fielding invokes the popular and innovative musical play by John Gay that casts a long shadow over *Jonathan Wild*, in its low-life material and satirical parallels between high and low as well as in its self-aware theatricality. Gay frames his play with a pair of metatheatrical characters who exist outside the play's main story, the Player and the Beggar. Near the play's denouement – the protagonist Macheath is on the verge of being hanged – these two characters return to the stage to decide the highwayman's fate. The Player expresses his dismay at the Beggar's intention to do 'strict poetical Justice' – Macheath is to be hanged, and the audience to suppose 'the other Personages of the Drama ... all either hang'd or transported' – and argues for a different outcome on the grounds that an opera, unlike 'a down-right deep Tragedy', 'must end happily'.[19] The Beggar grants a reprieve, the Player admitting in response that such choices are made 'to comply with the Taste of the Town'. The Beggar answers him with the play's credo, one to which Fielding might also have subscribed:

> Through the whole Piece you may observe such a similitude of Manners in high and low Life, that it is difficult to determine whether (in the fashionable Vices) the fine Gentlemen imitate the Gentlemen of the Road, or the Gentlemen of the Road the fine Gentlemen. – Had the Play remain'd, as I at first intended, it would have carried a most excellent Moral. 'Twould have shown that the lower Sort of People have their Vices in a degree as well as the Rich: And that they are punish'd for them.

Wild's closest analogue in *The Beggar's Opera*, though, is not the charismatic womanizer Macheath whose dramatic reprieve ends the play but rather Peachum, the cynical and calculating thief-taker who responds to the news that his daughter has married the engaging highwayman by trying to have Macheath hanged (for the reward, of course, not out of malice towards him personally).

The execution of the real historical Jonathan Wild in May 1725 (less than twenty years earlier) would have been still strongly present to Fielding and his readers. Ample documentation shows that the thief-taker (unlike either the debonair Macheath or Fielding's darker but still courageous representation of Wild) spent his final days at Newgate in a state amounting to abject terror; he questioned the prison clergyman about the theological consequences of suicide, tried to kill himself by drinking laudanum, and had only partly recovered by the time he was taken to be hanged at Tyburn.[20] In a sense, then, Fielding gives back to Wild what Defoe – and what life in its ending – took away from him, letting Wild retain the boldness and somewhat ludicrous energy that have characterized him throughout the narrative. Even as he is on the verge of being hanged, the narrator observes, Wild's character remains consistent: 'We must not however omit one Circumstance, as it serves to shew the most admirable Conservation of Character in our Hero to his last Moment, which was, that whilst the Ordinary was busy in his Ejaculations, *Wild*, in the midst of the Shower of Stones, *&c.* which played upon him, applied his Hands to the Parson's Pocket, and emptied it of his Bottle-Screw, which he carried out of the World in his Hand' (188; IV.xv). At once ridiculous and touching, this detail offers a comic instantiation of Fielding's theory of fictional character.[21]

The intense humanity of Fielding's fiction is not always borne out by his other writings. Despite the sympathy with which he treats some of the inmates of Newgate in *Jonathan Wild*, in his later career as a magistrate (and as the pioneer of a central intelligence office that fulfilled many of the same functions as the real-life Jonathan Wild's once-thriving Office for the Recovery of Lost and Stolen Property), Fielding would go on to publish *An Enquiry into the Causes of the Late Increase of Robbers* (1751), a work whose social conservatism and general lack of tolerance for the poor and criminal classes have horrified many of Fielding's most passionate admirers. Fielding sounds here as if he had never written *Jonathan Wild* at all, with its moral contempt for the plots of great men, its sparks of sympathy for the unjustly imprisoned, and its condemnation of the betrayals and politicking associated with the practice of thief-taking. 'I will venture to say, that if to do Good to Society be laudable, so is the Office of a Thief-catcher', states the *Enquiry* with no hint of levity; 'and if to do this Good at the extreme Hazard of your Life be honourable, then is this Office honourable. True, it may be said; but he doth this with a View to a Reward. And doth not the Soldier and the Sailor venture his Life with the same View? For who, as a Great Man lately said, serves the Public for nothing?'[22] There is a touch of the old mock-heroic technique here, subordinated now to the serious end of defending the thief-taker (to Fielding's contemporaries, thief-taking was tainted by a squalid history in which the government's well-intentioned decision to provide a monetary incentive for capturing criminals led individuals like Jonathan Wild to manipulate the justice system for their own profit, often at the cost of the lives of men and women who had been their own immediate colleagues and partners in crime). 'What was the great *Pompey* in the Piratic War? What were *Hercules, Theseus*, and other the Heroes of old[?]' Fielding asks in conclusion, sounding rather like his old protagonist Jonathan Wild at his most grandiose and self-rationalizing. 'Were they not the most eminent of Thief-catchers?'[23]

In his Foucault-inflected reading of power and surveillance in eighteenth-century literature and culture, John Bender points out that the first publication of *Jonathan Wild* 'predates the formal inauguration of Fielding's magistracy by more than five years' but that Fielding's fictionalization of Wild's history 'as a struggle to master narrative resources entirely complements his actual experimentation, as a justice of the peace, with methods to increase the number of viable indictments by improving the interception of evidence and suspects'.[24] Unlike policing, however, fiction 'can realize the fantasy of omniscient authority', and Bender suggests that by adopting methods akin to those of the real historical thief-taker Jonathan Wild, Fielding was able in his fiction (if not always in his administration of justice) to internalize control over the fates of good- and evil-doers.[25] Rather as Fielding's contempt for the loathsome ethics of thief-taking proved surprisingly compatible with his adoption of the thief-taker's most effective practices, *Jonathan Wild* also reveals the novelist's deep ambivalence towards hypocrisy. The 'Character' or trait on which the fictional Wild most prides himself and which he values most in others is hypocrisy (IV.xvi). Fielding hates hypocrisy, and yet something in him is also drawn to it, especially to its brazen outrageousness: no voice in Fielding's fiction is more distinctive and engaging than Shamela's, although the character was invented mostly to expose what Fielding saw as the hypocrisy of the title character of Richardson's best-selling *Pamela*.[26] Alexander Welsh offers a psychologically convincing account of why novelists sometimes identify with the hypocrite in a story, the remarkable rhetorical force with which Dickens endows Uriah Heep being an obvious case in point. Since the hypocrite displays two faces (virtue and vice, self-sacrifice and self-aggrandizement), anyone who identifies with both sides at once risks a 'moral objection to falsity or insincerity', yet Welsh suggests that as soon as that objection is done away with, 'as in unconscious or conscious play, . . . it becomes possible to be attracted to hypocrisy on its own grounds, for the powers of concealment and manipulation that two-sidedness confers'.[27] Just so does the role of prompter or puppet-master fill the novelist with a combination of admiration and abhorrence, and the mix of the two qualities makes *Jonathan Wild* genuinely unsettling.

## NOTES

1. Henry Fielding, *The History of the Life of the Late Mr Jonathan Wild the Great*, in *Miscellanies by Henry Fielding, Esq.*, vol. III, intro. Bertrand A. Goldgar, text ed. Hugh Amory (Oxford: Clarendon Press, 1997), 7; I.i. All references are to this edition and will be given parenthetically in the text by book and chapter number. Thanks to Adela Ramos for help with library research; I am also grateful to the Guggenheim Foundation and the Visiting Scholars Program at the American Academy of Arts and Sciences for their generous financial support.
2. Maximillian E. Novak, *Daniel Defoe, Master of Fictions: His Life and Ideas* (Oxford and New York: Oxford University Press, 2001), 641.
3. [Daniel Defoe], *The True and Genuine Account of the Life and Actions of the Late Jonathan Wild* (1725), in *Defoe on Sheppard and Wild*, ed. Richard Holmes (London: Harper Perennial, 2004), 89.
4. Fielding, *Jonathan Wild*, 14; I.iii. The authoritative modern biography of Wild is Gerald Howson, *Thief-Taker General: The Rise and Fall of Jonathan Wild* (London: Hutchinson, 1970). See also Lucy Moore's joint biography of Wild and Jack Sheppard, *The Thieves' Opera* (New York: Harcourt Brace, 1997); and, on Fielding's use of historical sources, William Robert Irwin, *The Making of Jonathan Wild: A Study in the Literary Method of Henry Fielding* (1941; rpt. Hamden, CT: Archon Books, 1966).
5. Fielding, *Miscellanies by Henry Fielding, Esq.*, vol. I, ed. Henry Knight Miller (Oxford: Clarendon Press, 1972), 9.
6. See especially the relevant chapters in Claude Rawson, *Henry Fielding and the Augustan Ideal under Stress* (London: Routledge and Kegan Paul, 1972; corrected edn, Atlantic Highlands, NJ, and London: Humanities Press International,

1991); and Rawson's introduction to the Oxford World's Classics edition of the novel, *The Life of Mr Jonathan Wild the Great*, ed. Hugh Amory (text), notes by Linda Bree (1999; Oxford and New York: Oxford University Press, 2003), ix–xxxii.

7. Claude Rawson, 'Pope's *Waste Land*: Reflections on Mock-Heroic', in *Order from Confusion Sprung: Studies in Eighteenth-Century Literature from Swift to Cowper* (London: Allen and Unwin, 1985), 201–21; the quotation is on 215.

8. Ian Watt, *The Rise of the Novel: Studies in Defoe, Richardson and Fielding* (London: Chatto and Windus, 1957), 32.

9. Watt, *Rise of the Novel*, 30.

10. For a summary of the relevant historical and textual issues, see Claude Rawson's review of Amory and Goldgar's edition, 'Walpole and the Highwaymen', *TLS* (27 Feb. 1998).

11. Fielding, *Miscellanies*, vol. I, 10.

12. See especially Martin C. Battestin with Ruthe R. Battestin, *Henry Fielding: A Life* (London and New York: Routledge, 1989), 280–2; and Ronald Paulson, *The Life of Henry Fielding: A Critical Biography* (Oxford: Blackwell, 2000), 100, 121–2, 131–2, 316. Hugh Amory provides the most detailed account of the differences between the first and second editions and the subsequent fate of each of these texts; see 'Appendix I: Textual Introduction', in *Miscellanies*, vol. III, 197–224.

13. Rawson, *Henry Fielding and the Augustan Ideal under Stress*, 154, 156.

14. Henry Fielding, 'Preface', *Joseph Andrews*, ed. Martin C. Battestin (Oxford: Clarendon Press, 1967), 4.

15. See Nina Prytula, '"Great-Breasted and Fierce": Fielding's Amazonian Heroines', *Eighteenth-Century Studies* 35:2 (2002), 173–93.

16. Watt, *Rise of the Novel*, 18.

17. On this quality of silliness, see Rawson, *Henry Fielding and the Augustan Ideal under Stress*, 228–59.

18. Shakespeare, *Richard III*, V.iii.177–206; both this reference and the quotation from *King Lear* given later in the paragraph are from *The Riverside Shakespeare*, ed. G. Blakemore Evans, 2nd edn (Boston and New York: Houghton Mifflin, 1997).

19. These lines and the ones quoted below can be found in John Gay, *The Beggar's Opera*, in Gay, *Dramatic Works*, 2 vols., ed. John Fuller (Oxford: Clarendon, 1983), vol. II; III.xvi.

20. On the pathos of the historical Wild's final days, see *The Ordinary of Newgate his Account, Of the Behaviour, Confession, and dying Words of the Malefactors, who were Executed on Monday the 24th of this Instant May, at Tyburn* (London, 1725); and *True and Genuine Account*, 114.

21. On the effects of the corkscrew, see also Rawson, *Henry Fielding and the Augustan Ideal under Stress*, 185–6, 207.

22. Henry Fielding, *An Enquiry into the Causes of the Late Increase of Robbers and Related Writings*, ed. Malvin R. Zirker (Oxford: Clarendon Press, and Middletown, CT: Wesleyan University Press, 1988), 153.

23. Fielding, *Enquiry*, 154.

24. John Bender, *Imagining the Penitentiary: Fiction and the Architecture of Mind in Eighteenth-Century England* (Chicago: University of Chicago Press, 1987), 165.

25. Bender, *Imagining the Penitentiary*, 165–6.
26. See also the discussion of Fielding's relationship to hypocrisy in Jenny Davidson, *Hypocrisy and the Politics of Politeness: Manners and Morals from Locke to Austen* (Cambridge: Cambridge University Press, 2004), 138–41.
27. Alexander Welsh, *From Copyright to Copperfield: The Identity of Dickens* (Cambridge, MA: Harvard University Press, 1987), 25.

# 6

NICHOLAS HUDSON

# *Tom Jones*

*Tom Jones*, observes David Richter, 'is in danger of being thought an easy read'.[1] This danger has lurked through readings of the novel since its first publication. Samuel Johnson famously accused Fielding of presenting only the clock-face of human nature, in contrast to his great rival Richardson, who exposed humanity's hidden springs and wheels.[2] In the twentieth century, F. R. Leavis was only echoing prevailing orthodoxies when he dismissed 'Fielding's attitudes, and his concern for human nature' as 'simple', and therefore unworthy of the English novel's 'Great Tradition'.[3] This alleged simplicity was redeemed to some extent by formalist criticism of the 1950s and 1960s, which valued the classical symmetry of the novel's stylistic architecture, the neat order of its eighteen-book division, its balancing of episodes at the beginning and the end. But in the wake of post-structuralism and post-modernism, with their fetish for dissonance and disharmony, *Tom Jones* has again seemed as outmoded as a Palladian façade or manicured lawn. The beneficiary of this assessment has remained Richardson. If *Clarissa* delves into the dark paradoxes of sexuality and textuality, it is claimed, *Tom Jones* exhibits only the rough *bonhomie* of old-fashioned masculinity; if Richardson heralds a modern age of democracy and feminism, Fielding holds fast to the patriarchal privileges and property rights of a feudal age that was passing even as he wrote.

This judgement has not gone entirely unchallenged. William Empson, while conceding that it seems 'particularly absurd' to 'leap to ambiguity' in order to explain *Tom Jones*, nonetheless theorizes on Fielding's 'double irony'[4] – his technique of holding opposed judgements on moral matters in ironic suspension. Empson's famous assessment looked forward to Richter's more recent argument that Fielding is unattractive to post-modernism precisely because he undermines and dissolves the binary oppositions that this school of criticism favours in its quest for logical indeterminacy. The old view of Fielding as a rigid conservative has also been challenged by scholars who have noted an unexpected complexity in his social and political thought.[5] As I will contend in the following chapter, this defence of Fielding's ultimate subtlety and deftness makes particular sense if we view his master-piece in its social, political, and philosophical context. For *Tom Jones* appeared at a moment of social and political transition in English society – a transition reflected in a novel characterized by, as John Richetti has put it, intense ideological 'contestation and negotiation'.[6] Old values and stand-ards were being questioned without being merely exploded; an older political and social order was being challenged while also being enfolded within the evolving mentality of the modern age. There is every reason to believe that Fielding lived personally right at the nexus of these transitions, and that his values and authorial choices were shaped by the myriad pressures and deliberations that surrounded him.

In order to understand properly this ideological change in Fielding's era, one must set aside the simplistic paradigm that a rising 'middle class', dominated by capitalists, overthrew an old feudal regime, replacing the peculiar attitudes of this old order with values of its own. It is true that the hereditary elite was widely resented: the aristocracy had become decadent and frivolous, it was said, its males effeminate and useless, its females idle, affected, and sexually wayward. On the other hand, the vulgar Cit, coarse and money-grubbing, also became the widespread target of moralistic and satiric literature of the time. Significantly, a major complaint was that a newly moneyed class was appropriating the symbols and privileges of the traditional ruling class. The title 'gentleman' (and its associated signifiers 'Mr' and 'Esq.') had become so pervasive as to be rendered virtually mean-ingless, as any merchant, trader, or even journeyman able to afford a sword and laced coat could bow and ogle indistinguishably alongside his 'betters'. With regard to young women empowered by the new wealth to dress and behave like 'ladies', the potential for social disruption was even greater. Legal measures such as the 1753 Marriage Act set out to control the sup-posed pandemic of social miscegenation, the squandering of fortunes on charming but worthless gallants, that accompanied the erosion of bound-aries that had previously separated the classes.[7]

In short, the salient phenomenon of the time cannot be well characterized as 'class conflict' between distinct and easily identified social blocks, the old and the new. Rather, the anxieties of the mid-eighteenth century derived from the sense that the markers and physical boundaries that previously delineated the social hierarchy had become unmanageably fluid and con-fused. The era's obsession with masquerade, both as reality and as metaphor, reflects the dismayed perception that the stable verities of title and privilege had become a simulacrum of shifting surfaces. Beneath these surfaces lay that expansive category of eighteenth-century discourse, 'human nature'.

Differences that had at one time seemed 'natural' increasingly appeared to be arbitrary, inscribed over a multifarious but essentially consistent humanness whose inherent nature absorbed the century's philosophical debates. That these differences belonged to the realm of culture not 'nature' did not, however, make them less important. Indeed, the strenuous effort of the century's moral, philosophical, and political dialogue, including its novels, focused on the need to establish standards of education, manners, taste, and political responsibility conducive to a stable and beneficial social order of a new kind.

No novelist of the eighteenth century reflected so seriously and intelligently on these problems as did Fielding. Biographically, Fielding was peculiarly well positioned to range over the complex and changing society of his day. The conventional view of Fielding as temperamentally 'patrician', locked into the embattled ideology of the *ancien régime*, is surely exaggerated. While he was linked to the nobility on his father's side – albeit an Irish branch of the nobility – Fielding's mother's family came from landed gentry, legal professionals, and merchants. There is good evidence that Fielding felt a strong attachment to this distinctly bourgeois half of his family, even in preference to the rather shoddy nobility of his wayward father. As a mature author, his novels and social pamphlets were filled with contemptuous descriptions of the '*Beau Monde*' as essentially '*Frivolous*' (*Tom Jones*, 744; XIV.i); the minor character who most recalls Fielding's aristocratic heritage, the Irish lord who appears in *Tom Jones* as Mrs Fitzpatrick's 'protector', is seedy and sinister. With regard to the lower orders, Fielding was notorious among his contemporaries for his 'promiscuous intercourse with persons of *all* ranks',[8] including the inhabitants of gambling halls and brothels. This is a flexibility that Fielding even paraded as a virtue. In *Tom Jones* he writes that the 'Historian', as opposed the mere writer of 'Romances', had learned from conversation 'with all Ranks and Degrees of Men' (494; VII.i).

All these groups had value for Fielding because the scope of *Tom Jones* embraces the entire social order. From the opening chapter of this novel, Fielding proclaims that he will exhibit not just one class, with its corresponding literary forms and moral priorities, but rather that preoccupying category of eighteenth-century philosophy, 'HUMAN NATURE' (32; I.i). This was a 'Provision', Fielding writes, that varied like a dish of meat in its 'dressing . . . up' rather than its substance (33). Much in *Tom Jones* indicates that the 'Ranks and Degrees of Men' represented only such a 'dressing up', exterior and essentially artificial differences superimposed over the deeper uniformity of human nature. For differences of social rank in the novel, particularly within that contested zone of the 'gentleman', are as blurred and changeable as the confused social hierarchy of Fielding's England.

While the novel's pre-eminent muddle of class identity is the genteel foundling Tom, it is also worth considering his adopted 'father', Allworthy. Early in the novel, Fielding presents Allworthy presiding benevolently over a sweeping landscape like the 'Sun', even the Sun King: 'in the full Blaze of his Majesty, up rose the Sun; than which one Object alone in this lower Creation could be more glorious, and that Mr *Allworthy* himself presented; a human being replete with Benevolence, meditating in what manner he might render himself most acceptable to his Creator, by doing most good to his Creatures' (43; I.iv). As so often in the novel, Fielding draws on the symbols and values of a declining social order. Oddly for an author who vociferously defended the Hanoverian reign against the Jacobite Rebellion, an event that serves as the historical backdrop of the novel, Fielding conjures images that recall the *jure divino* power of a monarch like Louis XIV. Allworthy's power over his little realm, which is little less than absolute, seems sanctioned by the Creator Himself. His dependants submit implicitly to his word as law, at least outwardly. Nor does Fielding entirely subvert the benefits of this power. When Allworthy benignly restrains the hand of Thwackum from whipping Tom, or when he finally banishes Blifil and reinstates Tom to favour, we surely feel that Allworthy's power has the effect of sustaining a benevolent order.

Characteristically, however, Fielding evokes the imagery and values of the *ancien régime* only to hedge them round with ironies and doubts. Even the comparison of Allworthy with the sun seems ponderously inflated, as Claude Rawson points out.[9] And we soon learn that Allworthy is in fact a half-blind Sun King whose authority is constantly circumvented by a household of modern sneaks and social aspirants. Unlike the Sun King, moreover, Allworthy's power truly derives from neither God nor nature, nor from the beneficence that Fielding's narrator claims as the source of his authority over his 'new Province of Writing' (77; II.i). Regardless of the imagery derived from antiquated modes of social authority, Allworthy is no feudal lord. Fielding offers only tantalizing hints concerning his exact origins. At one point, for example, Western claims to have known Allworthy at university, where 'many a Wench we two had together', but this story is immediately contradicted by Parson Supple, who had thought that 'he had never been at the University' (190; IV.x). In Fielding's life, Allworthy's closest counterpart is a man who shared the first syllable of his name, Ralph Allen.[10] And so far from being a representative of the traditional ruling class, Allen was a self-made entrepreneur effusively praised in *Tom Jones* as the very model of the upwardly mobile businessman (402; VIII.i). This is the model that best fits the owner of Paradise Hall. The untitled Allworthy wields authority not from divine right, much less from his goodness, but from the mundane fact that, for reasons left conspicuously unclear, he owns a great deal of land. His moral goodness retains importance because, in contrast to his potential heir Blifil, he appears morally qualified to stand as equal alongside a hereditary ruling class recalled by imagery indebted to the *ancien régime*. In this very respect, however, Allworthy's status reflects the precepts of eighteenth-century writers attempting to hammer the shapeless mass of an evolving social hierarchy into a new political and ideological symmetry. While imagined though the lens of traditional symbolism, Allworthy exemplifies contemporary attempts to define a new ruling class.

The interlarding of traditional imagery and new social realities also typifies the presentation of the novel's hero, Tom. An educated literary sensibility quickly identifies all that is traditional and conventional about Tom. Tom is the knight errant who rescues and beds threatened maidens; he strangely conforms with Jacobinical motifs of dispossessed and exiled princes. It is nonetheless a measure of Fielding's ambivalent relationship with the old regime that his hero actually enlists in the army that marches against the Jacobites. More generally, *Tom Jones* repeatedly raises the following question: can Tom legitimately claim the title of 'gentleman', and the social authority that title entails? As in the case of Allworthy, the reader's answer to this question is hindered by the obscurity of Tom's origins. Even when this obscurity is cleared, and Tom is revealed to be the son of a clergyman trained only by means of Allworthy's charity to be a 'gentleman', he remains illegitimate, and in no way authorized by birth to enter the ruling class. While not exactly a *parvenu*, therefore, Tom relies on the very modern qualifications of the property he will inherit from Allworthy, and on the respectability of his conduct and morals.

From almost his first appearance, Tom is a class anomaly, a grey-zone that stirs meditation about the whole structure of authority and deference around him. As a young man in Paradise Hall, he plays the double role of the local lad who beds Molly, who calls him 'my Gentleman' (185; IV.ix), and the reputed 'son' of Allworthy, educated with the Latin and polished manners of his adoptive class. Having been expelled from Paradise Hall, Tom becomes the repeated subject of speculation concerning his status as either a 'gentleman' or, as the landlady on the road to Bristol deems, 'an arrant Scrub' (412; VIII.iii). When Tom volunteers as a regular soldier in the regiment marching north to meet the Jacobites, the Lieutenant puzzles over the status of a young man 'very well dressed, and . . . naturally genteel' (370; VII.xi). But rumours of his 'low' birth instigated by Lawyer Dowling lead Mrs Whitefield in Bristol to conclude that he is 'a sorry Scoundrel' (434; VIII.viii), though she is presented as fair-minded and benevolent. The debate concerning Tom's gentility continues at the inn at Upton, and in conversations between Lady

Bellaston and Sophia in London (see 737; XIII.xii). As for Sophia, she repeatedly rises ardently to the defence of Tom's status as a 'gentleman' on the grounds of his benevolent nature (see 200; IV.xiv, 903; XVII.viii). But even she will not take Tom as a husband, much less a lover, until he has been given the sanction of social convention, no matter how unreasonable or arbitrary. As in the case of Allworthy, princely imagery drawn from an older, more stable hierarchy in fact sets up problems concerning the more nebulous parameters of social order in the present day. And these problems of liminality extend to virtually all the characters of the novel. The landlord on the road to Bristol 'had been bred, as they call it, a Gentleman' (428; VIII.vii), and lounges about his house with the genteel affliction of the gout. Squire Western has the land and authority of a country gentleman, but is ultimately deemed unworthy of a duel when he insults Lord Fellamar. Even the undeniably upper-rank characters in the novel, Fellamar and Lady Bellaston, are portrayed with the jaundiced disdain typical of middle-rank polemics against the failures of the old elite.

Significantly, the tension between traditional forms of representation and modern social realities characterizes even the portraits of the serving class. At many points, Fielding does seem to resort to the mocking treatment of the lower-orders typical of literary convention before the eighteenth century. The mock-epic depiction of the battle of the mob in the churchyard in Book IV, Chapter viii, would seem, superficially, to be such a place. Yet it is easy, here and throughout the novel, to underestimate the unruliness of Fielding's irony: the battle itself is prompted by Molly's disruption of social order by wearing a handsome dress supplied by Tom, proving that 'the great are deceived if they imagine they have appropriated Ambition and Vanity to themselves' (177). Typical of Fielding's form of mock-epic, the battle implies as much about the violence and vulgarity of the original classical heroes as about the lowness of the plebeian combatants. Similarly, Partridge conforms in important respects to the foolish and tiresomely loquacious servant conventional in romance. Yet conventional servants do not quote Latin, however bad, and Partridge refuses to allow himself to be deemed Tom's servant: Partridge's smatter of learning, one ingredient of gentility, complicates the conventional portrait and his relationship with Tom. 'None of your Magisters', he insists, 'I am no Man's Servant, I assure you' (515; IX.vi). Comparably, Jenny Jones technically occupies the very lowest possible rank, servant in the penurious household of Partridge and his wife. On the other hand, she speaks better Latin than her erstwhile master and ends up as 'Mrs Waters' with passable credentials as a corrupted gentlewoman, her apparent status at the inn at Upton. Black George presents even more subtle problems of social identity. While a kind of servant to Allworthy and later

Western, Black George enjoys a privilege shared by both gentlemen and gamekeepers – the right to hunt on private land. He is not in every respect a mere subject of ruling-class power, for he legally exercises the responsibility of enforcing the state's gaming laws, including the notorious Black Act of 1722. Not untypically of gamekeepers in the eighteenth century, moreover, Black George is curiously upwardly mobile, finally attempting to invest the £500 he retained (but did not exactly 'steal') from Tom in land rather than taverns and brothels.[11]

On the one hand, therefore, Fielding draws on imagery and literary conventions typical of an age and its literature that distinguished unproblematically between the gentry and the serving class. But this traditional form contrasts in ironic ways with confusions and complications typical of the author's own social milieu. As professedly an author in a commercial marketplace, indeed, the narrator's own status in the social order is as liminal as that of Allworthy or Tom. For all his display of genteel learning, Fielding admits that those who 'take upon themselves the bad Trade of Writing' seldom have the advantages of 'Birth or Fortune' (742; XVI. 742). Writers usually provide only an absurd parody of upper-rank manners for the reason that they 'know nothing of it' (741). How *this* particular author has both adopted the modern trade of writing and also gained entry into the upper ranks stands as one more of the novel's mysteries of origin and status. It points to Fielding's personally confused and controversial relationship with the changing social hierarchy of his day. This nebulous status informs the author's 'carnivalesque' swings between 'high' and 'low'. His learned allusions and patrician tone again constitute an outward and provisional scaffolding, an old-fashioned 'dress', and these generate ironic tensions with the crude humour, the coarse fist-fights, the low women, and the squalid inns that dominate the action and settings of the novel. At points, we might sense a patrician dignity in the narrator's tone, as he describes, with throat-clearing circumlocution, the 'low' behaviour of his characters: '"Ho! Are you come back to your Politics," cries the Squire, "as for those I despise them as much as I do a F_t." Which last Word he accompanied and graced with the very Action, which, of all others, was most proper to it' (337; VII.iii). On the other hand, it would be wrong to confuse Fielding's narrator with a Basil Fawlty: in this passage, as in so many others, we also detect that a 'low' side of Fielding enjoys Western's fart, particularly as we imagine the wincing reaction of his ridiculously pompous sister.[12]

These difficulties of social definition, moreover, are inseparable from the problems of moral judgement that fill the novel. What many readers have regarded as the confidence and simplicity of Fielding's moral vision have been frequently contrasted with the supposed subtlety and uncertainty of

Richardson's novels. Yet it is doubtful that even the most apparently serious moral pronouncements in *Tom Jones* can be accurately read without a sensitivity to his ironic qualifications.

It is indeed a repeated error of Fielding's characters that they attempt to judge the world around them according to simple and universal rules or systems. These overly 'serious' characters – Allworthy, Square, Thwackum, even Tom at moments (as in his pious lectures on chastity to Nightingale) – never evade the narrator's irony. But the dangers of seriousness have also sometimes undermined Fielding's scholarly readers. To cite a notable example, scholarship on *Tom Jones* over the last forty years has frequently been absorbed by the question of whether 'prudence' is 'the dominant ethical theme of the novel'.[13] At one point Fielding seems to say as much:

> It is not enough that your Designs, nay that your Actions are intrinsically good, you must take care that they shall appear so. If your Inside be never so beautiful, you must preserve a fair Outside also. This must be constantly looked to, or Malice and Envy will take Care to blacken it so, that the Sagacity and Goodness of an *Allworthy* will not be able to see through it, and to discern the Beauties within. Let this, my young Readers, be your constant Maxim, That no Man can be good enough to enable him to neglect the Rules of Prudence. (141; III.vii)

It should be noted first that prudence, with its attention to commendable exteriors, represents a knowledge of the world's shifting surfaces, the modes of 'dressing up', that constitute the realm of social custom as opposed to 'human nature'. Every time Tom oversteps the novel's physical and moral thresholds – as first when he 'poaches' on Western's property, and later when he steps over the boundaries of Mrs Waters's and Lady Bellaston's bedrooms – he ends up *seeming* different than his natural impulses intended. Yet can even the above, most patently 'serious' statement in Fielding's novel be taken without major ironic qualification? It has been pointed out that the novel's most 'prudent' characters are its most dislikable, as epitomized by the 'prudent' Blifil. Significantly, Blifil has no 'Maxim' of prudence. He is villainous, but never absurd, because he has no constant rule whatsoever except engrossing the world's property for himself, an aim that requires that he adjust his behaviour in the myriad ways required by a particular moment and situation. Moreover, a steady attention to 'prudence' would effectively choke off most of the good that Tom does in the novel. A 'prudent' Tom would not have hastened to the rescue of Mrs Waters when she is attacked by Ensign Northerton; he would not have forgiven and relieved the highwayman who accosts him on the road to London. Tom's very goodness, in brief, is demonstrated by his willingness to rush beyond what the world deems decorous or wise when his good-hearted nature directs him. Similarly, while some critics have elevated Sophia into the exemplar of *sophia* or worldly wisdom, she shows a decided lack of prudence when she escapes her father's estate, for all appearances in pursuit of Tom. Her final act, facilitating the novel's happy closure, is forgiving and accepting Tom before he has been given 'Time' to prove the sincerity of his repentance, surely a highly 'imprudent' decision.[14]

Given that the novel's most admired characters, Tom and Sophia, frequently act in defiance of the 'world's' standards and morals, some scholars have concluded that these rules are therefore without real moral value. According to Martin Price, for example, Fielding values solely 'the flow' of 'active energy of virtuous feeling', an excess opposed to 'the structures' of 'those forms that are the frozen travesty of authentic order'.[15] Except when approving the benignity of a personage's inner character and motives, judgement of another's conduct is always suspect, and must always be tempered by a willingness to forgive.[16] In the face of this reading, Blifil presumably stands the glaring exception, for as his motives are purely selfish, he must be condemned by the same criteria that relieve the purely unselfish Tom of any moral guilt. But Tom, Sophia, and Blifil strike an important contrast with all the other characters of the novel. In keeping with his uncertain status in the social hierarchy, for instance, Fielding dramatizes Black George's mind as a courtroom of conflicting generous and selfish motives (319; VI.xiii). Notwithstanding the prevailing love of money that leads him to keep Tom's £500, Fielding tells us that 'he was of a compassionate Disposition' (917; XVIII.ii). Led to make a judgement not based on any clear rule that the novel has taught us, we are left to ponder how closely Tom's ultimate desire to forgive him truly 'borders on Injustice' (969; XVIII.xi). A similar blend of ungenerous and benign intentions form the personalities of Partridge, Jenny Jones, Western, Molly, and Honour and a cast of characters who, together, confound the notion that the mass of humanity can be judged easily in terms of purity of intention. Allworthy raises problems of a different sort. Critics have been quick to condemn his fallible exercise of his role as local magistrate. Yet if we are to judge only on the basis of goodness of motivation, then surely Allworthy must be exonerated, for his inherent generosity, if directed towards the welfare of society as a whole, seems comparable to Tom's towards individuals.

Even in the case of Tom, moreover, should we conclude that 'prudence' is a negligible form of wisdom in all cases? If prudence concerns an attention to how the world judges us in accordance with its abiding concern for reputation and appearance, then Tom does confine his natural energies within the bounds of convention in at least one important case – his love for Sophia. When Sophia and Tom meet early in the novel, notably when she tumbles from her horse into his arms, Fielding evokes the tremulous pressure of instinct pressing against but never surpassing a limit that must be, and is, respected throughout the novel. Tom and Sophia restrain themselves 'prudently' according to standards that enforce the virginity of unmarried women of a certain social rank and dictate a respect for property and authority, even that of the irrational and overbearing Western. As the philosopher Bernard Harrison has well observed, these standards do not represent 'goodness' or even true 'virtue'.[17] Showing a sophistication not often associated with him, Fielding distinguishes between artificial and changeable conventions of virtue and the true goodness of a selfless and morally courageous heart. Nevertheless, *Tom Jones* portrays a world in which happiness depends far more on obedience to external rules, a respect for appearance, and the appropriate 'dress' of social decorum, than on our desire to do good to others. It is precisely this consideration that withholds Tom from the sexual seduction of Sophia that he is repeatedly given the opportunity to undertake. Similarly, while engaging in drunken fisticuffs with his tutor, or revealing his love for a gentleman's daughter to an itinerant barber, does not undermine our sense of Tom's basic decency, these and other largely unreflective misdemeanors contravene a code of genteel conduct that the novel finally affirms to be necessary to his social rehabilitation. There can be no doubt that Tom's final ascendance to the title of landed 'gentleman', with the power that this role bestows, could not be achieved without the final clearing of his moral reputation, or without the land that he is destined to inherit from his patron. To a significant degree, that is, *Tom Jones* is concerned with how authority is adjusted and assessed in a world where the static order and codes of the old regime no longer offer consistent guidance.

Reviewing these various conflicts between spontaneous goodness and prudence in the novel, we in fact approach conclusions that might satisfy even post-structuralists, with the value they place on paradox and *aporia*. On the one hand, Tom's very heroism is exemplified by his willingness to defy worldly standards of respectable or 'wise' behaviour; on the other hand, Tom does respect these limits in certain cases, particularly that of Sophia, and he becomes a legitimate member of the novel's ruling class only by virtue of his deepened respect for the world's judgements. Prudence would seem, in the final analysis, neither the 'constant Maxim' proclaimed in Book II, Chapter vii, nor an attribute that can be rejected as a mere 'travesty'. Contrary to Price's appeal to an 'absolute order', Fielding makes clear that the world is *not* ideal. Nevertheless, Fielding rejects a nihilism that would logically paralyse all moral action or judgement. Act and judge we must, even if every decision cannot appeal to any overarching rule for absolute guidance, and must instead weigh the contingencies of each endlessly different situation. This demand is extended as well to the reader of *Tom Jones*. Despite the novel's scaffolding of literary convention and moral logic, it consistently focuses the reader on the evanescent circumstances of the present episode, the immediate moment. Nothing in the novel gives us exact direction about whether Tom should defend Sophia's honour against the insulting Northerton, as the benevolent lieutenant (to whom Tom defers) urges; nothing assures us whether Tom's charity to the highwayman, no matter how high-minded, will have either good or tragic consequences.

For this reason, the most sensitive reading of *Tom Jones* can never eschew an abiding sense of irony and an essentially comic disposition towards the novel and life itself. Such an ironic disposition is appropriate in a novel where our judgement of any episode may well turn out to be mistaken or insufficient – and the winking narrator in fact ensures that the first-time reader *will* be wrong about central facts such as Bridget Blifil's maternity of Tom. The irony of the novel is embodied by the narrator's coy reluctance, at innumerable points, to lay down authoritative judgements, his frequent deferral to imagined readers:

> There are two Sorts of People, who I am afraid, have already conceived some Contempt for my Heroe, on Account of his Behaviour to *Sophia*. The former of these will blame his Prudence in neglecting an Opportunity to possess himself of Mr *Western*'s Fortune; and the latter will no less despise him for his Backwardness to so fine a Girl, who seemed ready to fly into his Arms, if he would open them to receive her. (171; IV.vi)

Precedents in the novel subtly induce us to read this passage armed with an attention to irony. Fielding has shown himself contemptuous of both greediness for fortune and, rather less clearly at this point, a careless appetite for young women's bodies, though this is not the case with Tom's loving desire for Sophia. But against exactly *what* precept should this irony be measured? The narrator only exacerbates our uncertainty by assuring us that 'I shall not perhaps be able absolutely to acquit him of either of these Charges', and that 'Want of Prudence admits of no Excuse' (171) – the latter statement bearing a strong element of apparent truth if only in *this* case. The one appropriate response available to us is laughter. For only comic wisdom confronts a self-deluding seriousness that believes in our capacity to reduce the world and the novel to a comprehensive system. As Fielding observes in one of the novel's most fully 'serious' moments, 'I am not writing a System, but a History, and I am not obliged to reconcile every Matter to the received Notions concerning Truth and Nature' (651; XVII.vii).

Far more than his rival Richardson, in fact, Fielding gives us an atmosphere where social and moral demarcations are subtle and uncertain in ways that reflect the amorphous state of his changing world. In illustration of this deeply ironic and eclectic vision, let us consider a literal 'vision' in the novel, the description near the beginning of *Tom Jones* of Mr Allworthy surveying not only his own estate, but evidently all of southern England, from the fantastically high promontory of Paradise Hall.[18] Particularly notable about this landscape is its lack of all boundaries except the utmost limits of vision. In one direction, Allworthy's gaze wanders over 'an amazing Variety of Meadows and Woods' until it terminates at 'the Sea'. In another direction, he looks over 'several Villages', ending with an 'old ruined Abbey'. A third and final vista is limited only by 'the Clouds' (43; I.iv). The physical expansion of the scene corresponds with the limitless moral generosity of Allworthy, who at a climactic moment seems to shine benignly like the sun itself over the whole world. But from this height Allworthy must 'descend' (deflatingly, to take breakfast with his sister Bridget) to a world where vision is decidedly limited, particularly his own, and where the natural panorama is in fact crisscrossed with the property lines and various constraints imposed by its human inhabitants.

Acting as almost a symbolic prelude to the novel, this scene literalizes the contrast between the limitless and untrammeled beauty of 'nature' and the provisional, changeable, yet ultimately unavoidable lines of human conventions – the realm of irony. The problems of the novel are set. As soon as Tom appears in Book III, Chapter ii, we witness the conflict between nature and property, boundless spontaneity and social restraint, that will be the predominant theme of the whole novel. The young Tom and the gamekeeper, later revealed to be Black George, chase a covey of partridges which crosses the property line of a local 'Keeper of Game' (146; III.x) – later revealed to be Squire Western – pursued by Tom with all his wonted eagerness and importunity. (The partridges, vainly 'kept' within certain boundaries, form part of a menagerie of animals – foxes, hares, bucks, dogs – conjured in both the narrative and imagery of the novel, and evoking the boundless freedom of the natural landscape.) This transgression prefigures all of Tom's later breaches of social and moral convention, and the dilemmas they provoke. At many points, Tom's choices involve again the literal crossing of thresholds and boundaries. The novel is filled with doorways and property lines. Tom will go on to 'poach' again on Western's property, though his game will be more serious – no less than the squire's daughter Sophia, vehemently claimed by Western as a piece of property. Western, still thinking that Tom is pursuing Sophia's maid Honour, turns characteristically to the poaching metaphor, admonishing him to 'beat abroad, and not poach up the Game in his Warren' (225; v.iv). Later episodes dramatize Tom's crossing through the doorways of Mrs Waters's bedroom at the inn at Upton and of the house that Lady

Bellaston has prepared for his reception in Hanover Square. And each threshold represents a problem or test which, while sharing something in common with the others, is subtly differentiated. These tests all show Tom propelled across borders by spontaneous instincts of good nature and sexual appetite, which in his case are closely conjoined. But his affair with the seedy Lady Bellaston bears a different aspect from his one-night stand with Mrs Waters, in part because he is deluded by the world of fashionable London, and is motivated to bed the noble lady for strategic rather than purely altruistic or amorous reasons.

Only a reader prepared for the subtleties of Fielding's irony can properly distinguish between these and all the other situations in the novel. Given the essentially artificial nature of all the moral and social boundaries met in the novel, as well as the complexities of intention that motivate all but the major characters (and indeed even the major characters, though in more subtle ways), any reading that reduces *Tom Jones* to simple messages of any kind has not done the novel justice. The wider context of this irony and this comedy is, as I have insisted, an England in the midst of social transition and the upheaval of received values. The certainties of the old social order were being eroded without being simply overthrown or replaced. Lines of property were being redrawn in patterns that remained uncertain and unpredictable. Codes of morals and manners were undergoing a reformulation that by no means rejected ideas of virtue and politeness typical of the *ancien régime* while adjusting to the influx of new claimants to power and influence. Humour and irony seemed to Fielding the only responses that possessed the subtlety to bridge the old and the new, and to straddle the threshold of the serious and non-serious in the face of these changes. If we are still able to join with Fielding's laughter in *Tom Jones*, it is because the transformations and ambiguities of this emergent modern world have never ceased to unfold.

## NOTES

1. David H. Richter, 'The Closing of Masterpiece Theatre: Henry Fielding and the Valorization of Incoherence', in *Ideology and Form in Eighteenth-Century Literature*, ed. David H. Richter (Lubbock: Texas Tech University Press, 1999), 3.
2. See James Boswell, *Life of Johnson*, ed. G. B. Hill, rev. L. F. Powell, 6 vols. (Oxford: Clarendon Press, 1934–50), vol. II, 49.
3. F. R. Leavis, *The Great Tradition* (Harmondsworth: Pelican, 1962), 12.
4. William Empson. '*Tom Jones*', *Kenyon Review* 20 (1958), 218–19.
5. See Kay Weeks, 'Fielding Looks Down: *Tom Jones* and the Lower Orders', *Eighteenth-Century Novel* 3 (2003), 97–127; John Allen Stevenson, *The Real History of Tom Jones* (New York and Basingstoke: Palgrave, 2005), 17–46. On 'the many oscillations of emphasis, which run through Fielding's attitudes on questions of rank, social grace, and the like', see also Claude Rawson's *Henry*

*Fielding and the Augustan Ideal under Stress* (London and Boston: Routledge and Kegan Paul, 1972), 9.

6. John Richetti, 'Ideology and Literary Form in Fielding's *Tom Jones*', in *Ideology and Form*, ed. Richter, 35.

7. For a fuller description of these changes, see Nicholas Hudson, *Samuel Johnson and the Making of Modern England* (Cambridge: Cambridge University Press, 2003), 11–76.

8. Fielding's friend John Harris, cited in Martin C. Battestin, with Ruthe R. Battestin, *Henry Fielding: A Life* (London and New York: Routledge, 1989), 145.

9. See Rawson, *Henry Fielding and the Augustan Ideal under Stress*, 238–9.

10. The depiction of Allworthy's gazing from the summit of Paradise Hall recalls Joseph Andrews's description of 'one *Al_ Al_*', meaning Ralph Allen, who 'hath built up a Stately House', and whose 'Charity is seen farther than his House, tho' it stands on a Hill' (*Joseph Andrews*, 235; III.vi).

11. Black George's ambivalent status is well discussed by Stevenson, *Real History*, 77–101.

12. See Claude Rawson's discussion of this episode in *Order from Confusion Sprung* (London: Allen and Unwin, 1985), 281–2.

13. Martin C. Battestin's note in his edition of *Tom Jones*, 36, n.1. The main lines of debate may traced through Eleanor Hutchens, *Irony in Tom Jones* (University, AL: University of Alabama Press, 1965), 101–18; Glenn W. Hatfield, 'The Serpent and the Dove: Fielding's Irony and the Prudence Theme of *Tom Jones*', *Modern Philology* 65 (1967), 17–32; Martin C. Battestin, *The Providence of Wit: Aspects of Form in Augustan Literature* (Oxford: Clarendon Press, 1974), 164–92; C. J. Rawson, 'Order and Misrule: Eighteenth-Century Literature in the 1970s', *ELH* (1975), 484–90; Frederick G. Ribble, 'Aristotle and the "Prudence" Theme of *Tom Jones*', *Eighteenth-Century Studies* 15 (1981), 26–47.

14. See Eric Rothstein, 'Virtues of Authority in *Tom Jones*', in *Critical Essays on Henry Fielding*, ed. Albert Rivero (New York: Hill, and London: Prentice Hall International, 1998), 152–3.

15. Martin Price, *To the Palace of Wisdom: Studies in Order and Energy from Dryden to Blake* (Garden City, NY: Anchor Books, 1965), 287.

16. See John Preston, *The Created Self: The Reader's Role in Eighteenth-Century Fiction* (New York: Barnes and Noble, 1970), 132.

17. See Bernard Harrison, *Henry Fielding's 'Tom Jones'* (London: Sussex University Press, 1975), 104–12.

18. For discussion of space and landscapes in the novel, see George A. Drake, 'Historical Space in the "History of": Between Public and Private in *Tom Jones*', *ELH* 66 (1999), 707–37.

# 7

PETER SABOR

# *Amelia*

In December 1751, when *Amelia* was first published, Fielding was at the height of his fame, both as the energetic and conscientious Bow Street magistrate for Westminster and Middlesex and as a novelist whose only equal was his great rival, Samuel Richardson. His previous novel, *Tom Jones*, published in February 1749, two months after the final instalment of Richardson's *Clarissa*, had gone through four authorized editions within a year, running to a total of 10,000 copies, and, despite some hostile criticism, had been generally acclaimed. There were Dublin reprints, translations into Dutch, French, and German, and (as with Richardson's best-seller, *Pamela*, ten years earlier), exploitative spin-offs by anonymous hacks, such as *The History of Tom Jones, the Foundling, in his Married State* (1749) and *The History of Charlotte Summers, the Fortunate Parish Girl* (1750). The new novel, which Fielding began writing in autumn 1749, was eagerly awaited. On 29 October 1751, Walter Harte in Bath informed his friend Sir Charles Hanbury Williams in Dresden that 'Fielding is coming out with another work, in the tone and style of his late performances.'[1] Shortly afterwards, on 2 December 1751, Fielding's publisher Andrew Millar placed an advertisement for *Amelia* in *The General Advertiser*, designed to increase interest in the forthcoming novel still further: 'To satisfy the earnest Demand of the Publick, this Work is now printing at four Presses; but the Proprietor notwithstanding finds it impossible to get them bound in Time without spoiling the Beauty of the Impression, and therefore will sell them sew'd at Half a Guinea a Sett.'[2] The four presses, two of which belonged to William Strahan, were working overtime because Millar had ordered the extraordinary number of 5,000 copies for the initial printing of *Amelia*: 1,500 more than the first and second editions of *Tom Jones* combined. Sales were apparently brisk enough for Millar to order a second edition of 3,000 copies almost immediately. But this plan was rapidly abandoned, and the 5,000 copies of the first edition proved to be more than Millar, for all his ingenious advertising, could sell. He still had copies to dispose of in 1759,[3] by which date the 'Beauty of the Impression' must have been somewhat faded. The novel fared better abroad, with two German translations in 1752 and a Dutch translation in 1756, but no French edition was published until 1762, the same year in which a second English edition at last appeared. Richardson, who affected to have read only the first of the novel's four volumes, could announce as early as February 1752 that *Amelia* 'is as dead as if it had been published forty years ago, as to sale'.[4] What went wrong?

As its title announces, *Amelia* differs in one obvious respect from Fielding's previous novels: *Joseph Andrews*, *Jonathan Wild*, and *Tom Jones*. With his eponymous heroine taking centre stage, Fielding was moving into territory associated with Richardson, whose distressed heroines, Pamela and Clarissa, had both captured the imagination of the reading public. Fielding's first prose fiction, *Shamela*, had also recounted the history of a woman, but only in mockery of Richardson: now he was taking the risky step of creating a virtuous and admirable heroine of his own. As several contemporaries remarked, Amelia Booth was modelled on Fielding's beloved first wife, Charlotte, who died in November 1744, while his hero, Captain Booth, devoted to Amelia despite his philandering, was inspired by the author himself, probably with touches of his equally feckless father Edmund (a soldier, like Booth). Fielding's first critics did not object to the new direction that his novel was taking, but they found a plethora of other shortcomings. Perversely, the single most prominent failing was held to be the heroine's lack of a nose.

In Book II of *Amelia*, Captain Booth, confined in Newgate prison, tells his companion Miss Mathews about his wife's unfortunate carriage accident, reminding her of 'The Injury done to her Beauty by the overturning of a Chaise, by which, as you may well remember, her lovely Nose was beat all to pieces' (II.i). When Amelia, a month after the accident, removes a protective mask and shows Booth her injured face, he declares: 'Upon my Soul, Madam, you never appeared to me so lovely as at this Instant'. No mention, however, at least in the first-edition text, is made of surgical repairs to the nose that had been beaten 'all to pieces', and Fielding himself draws attention to his heroine's noselessness. Booth recounts to Miss Mathews the jibes of 'several young Ladies', one of whom had declared that Amelia 'will never more turn up her Nose at her Betters', while another suggests that 'a very proper Match might now be made between *Amelia* and a certain Captain, who had unfortunately received an Injury in the same Part, though from no shameful Cause'. The cause alluded to is syphilis, which has previously been linked to the ravages suffered by another of Booth's fellow-prisoners in Newgate, Blear-Eyed Moll: 'Nose she had none; for *Venus*, envious perhaps at her former Charms, had carried off the gristly Part; and some earthly Damsel,

perhaps from the same Envy, had levelled the Bone with the rest of her Face'
(I.iii). In thus linking his delicate and long-suffering heroine to a hardened
prostitute who stands out even amidst the squalor of Newgate, who 'measured full as much round the middle as from Head to Foot' and whose 'vast
Breasts had long since forsaken their native Home, and settled themselves a
little below the Girdle', Fielding was taking a tremendous risk, forcing Blear-
Eyed Moll and Amelia together in a startling and rebarbative manner. Terry
Castle notes that 'Moll's Goyaesque visage lingers in the mind like a ghastly
souvenir, and one fears the worst: the visible depredation of Amelia's own
"former charms" '.[5] Walter Harte might have expected another comic novel,
'in the tone and style' of *Tom Jones*, but Fielding seemed determined to prove
rumour false by making *Amelia* as different as possible from its celebrated
predecessor.

One of the earliest reviews of *Amelia* rightly seized on its experimental
quality. John Cleland, author of another innovative novel, the notorious
*Memoirs of a Woman of Pleasure* (1748–9), described *Amelia* in the
*Monthly Review* for December 1751 as 'the boldest stroke that has yet
been attempted in this species of writing', noting that in depicting the history
of a marriage, Fielding 'takes up his heroine at the very point at which all his
predecessors have dropped their capital personages'. Even the sympathetic
Cleland, however, believed that parts of the novel 'stand in need of an
apology' and that the characters, 'however exact copies of nature', are
'chosen in too low, and disgustful a range of it'.[6] Other reviewers and readers
went much further, with Amelia's lost nose the most frequent target of their
censure. An anonymous review in the *London Magazine* for December 1751
complained of anachronisms in the novel: it is set in 1733 but takes in recent
phenomena, such as masquerades at Ranelagh, the pleasure gardens opened
in 1742, and the Universal Register Office, a clearinghouse for those seeking
employees or employment and for those with goods to sell or buy, founded
by Fielding and his half-brother John only in February 1750. The review then
turns to another 'imperfection': Fielding 'should have taken care to have had
Amelia's nose so compleatly cured, and set to rights, after its being *beat all
to pieces*, by the help of some eminent surgeon, that not so much as a scar
remained'.[7]

Other writers were quick to follow suit. John Hill, in his 'Inspector'
column of the *London Daily Advertiser* for 8 January 1752, mocked
Fielding's heroine, who could 'charm the World without the Help of a
Nose'.[8] Bonnell Thornton wrote a series of satires of *Amelia* in the *Drury-
Lane Journal*, beginning with the first issue on 16 January 1752, which
contained a spoof advertisement for a novel entitled 'Shamelia' (with 'long
Digressions, polite expletives of Conversation', and 'genteel Dialogues') and

culminating in a witty parody entitled 'A New Chapter in Amelia'. Here, after a drunken Booth belches in Amelia's face: 'what was her consternation, when she found his high-arch'd Roman Nose, that heretofore resembled the bridge of a fiddle, had been beat all to pieces! As herself had before lost the handle to her face, she now truly sympathis'd with him in their mutual want of snout.'[9] Tobias Smollett, who had recently attacked Fielding as a sycophantic scribbler in his novel *Peregrine Pickle* (1751), now had a fresh target for his satire. *A Faithful Narrative of … Habbakkuk Hilding*, a pamphlet published anonymously on 15 January, probably by Smollett, features Fielding astride an ass, 'riding up to a draggle-tailed Bunter, who had lost her Nose in the Exercise of her Occupation' (18). The 'Bunter', who resembles Blear-Eyed Moll in appearance and profession, is nonetheless addressed as 'the adorable *Amelia*' (with a pun on 'adwhoreable' used by Fielding himself in *Jonathan Wild*). These and other attacks on the novel were known to Samuel Johnson, who, despite his general hostility to Fielding, believed that Amelia 'was the most pleasing heroine of all the romances' and regretted that 'that vile broken nose never cured, ruined the sale'.[10]

Fielding was swift to respond to his critics, and the onslaught on Amelia's injured nose was his first concern. As early as 11 January, before Thornton or Smollett had yet held forth, Fielding inserted a paragraph in his periodical *The Covent-Garden Journal*, reporting, with heavy irony, that 'a famous Surgeon, who absolutely cured one Mrs Amelia Booth, of a violent Hurt in her Nose, insomuch, that she had scarce a Scar left on it, intends to bring Actions against several ill-meaning and slanderous People, who have reported that the said Lady had no Nose, merely because the Author of her History, in a Hurry, forgot to inform his Readers of that Particular'.[11] It is, of course, possible that Fielding had somehow forgotten, in the haste of composition, to mention that his heroine's nose had been surgically repaired. It seems more probable, however, that Fielding is here beating a strategic retreat: attributing to an oversight what was a deliberate feature of his novel. There is a striking resemblance between the passage in the *London Magazine* review quoted above and the *Covent-Garden Journal* paragraph: the reviewer's 'some eminent surgeon' becomes 'a famous Surgeon', 'so compleatly cured' becomes 'absolutely cured', 'not so much as a scar remained' becomes 'scarce a Scar left', etc. Fielding, that is, has imaginatively recast the novel to refute the reviewer's criticism, much as Richardson had done, a few months earlier, in *Letters and Passages Restored from the Original Manuscripts of … Clarissa* (1751). (Richardson claimed that these 'restored' passages were not merely a response to his critics but in fact anticipated their objections, having been excised from the first- and second-edition texts of the novel because of its excessive length, when in fact they provided a mixture of new and pre-publication material.)

Two weeks later, in *The Covent-Garden Journal* for 25 January, Fielding published the first of a two-part mock-trial of *Amelia*. Here a long series of complaints against the novel is made by the prosecutor, 'Counsellor Town', whose charges include both objections already raised in print and others devised by Fielding himself. For the gravest charge against the heroine, strident capitals proliferate to insist 'That she is a Beauty WITHOUT A NOSE, I say again, WITHOUT A NOSE'. Withdrawing from the fray at the end of the trial, Fielding, in the persona of a 'grave Man', acknowledged that his novel was not 'entirely free from Faults' while declaring that *Amelia*, 'this poor Girl', was his 'favourite Child', and that he would 'trouble the World no more with any Children of mine by the same Muse'.[12] *Amelia* was, indeed, to be Fielding's last novel; the works of his final years were non-fictional, although his *Journal of a Voyage to Lisbon*, completed shortly before his death in October 1754, has something of the wit of *Tom Jones* and the gravity of *Amelia*. The obsession with Amelia's nose died with Fielding, but Sterne's endless play on noses and their sexual connotations in *Tristram Shandy* (1760–7) surely looks back to a once celebrated debate.

A second edition of *Amelia* was published posthumously in 1762 as part of Millar's collected *Works of Henry Fielding*. The edition came equipped with a prefatory essay by the editor, Arthur Murphy, declaring that '*Amelia*, in this edition, is printed from a copy corrected by the author's own hand. The exceptionable passages, which inadvertency had thrown out, are here retrenched; and the work, upon the whole, will be found nearer perfection than it was in its original state.'[13] Almost all Fielding scholars, with the notable exception of Hugh Amory,[14] have taken Murphy at his word. But the revised edition contains numerous alterations and deletions, and to suggest that all of these were necessitated by Fielding's 'inadvertency' is clearly absurd. A more logical reading of Murphy's claim, as Amory suggests, is that some of the second-edition revisions stem from a copy corrected by Fielding, while others are the result of Murphy's own retrenching. The results, in any case, are of dubious value. Lance Bertelsen has written well on the damage caused to *Amelia* by the systematic removal, in the second edition, of all references to the Universal Register Office;[15] chronologically anachronistic and self-promoting though these passages are, they form part of the fabric of the novel. Other alterations include the deletion of an entire chapter involving a dispute among doctors, the suppression of compliments to individuals, the removal of a passage in praise of the Glastonbury Waters, and the bowdlerization of sexual innuendo and profanity. In addition, and most predictably, several inserted passages ensure that carping readers can no longer claim that the heroine lacks a nose; Booth now admires the 'Surgeon's Skill' (II.i), and there are other references to a 'little Scar' and a 'visible Scar' left by reconstructive surgery (IV.vii, XI.i). These changes, designed to create a smoother, more polished text, are largely counter-productive. The risks that Fielding took in *Amelia* form part of the experience of reading a novel brilliantly successful in parts and a mawkish failure in others. Sir Walter Scott, astonishingly, saw *Amelia* as 'a continuation of *Tom Jones*';[16] it has, however, more in common with the other often bafflingly contradictory works of his final years: *An Enquiry into the Causes of the Late Increase of Robbers* (1751), *Examples of the Interposition of Providence in the Detection and Punishment of Murder* (1752), *A Proposal for making an Effectual Provision for the Poor* (1753), and *The Journal of a Voyage to Lisbon.*

Both *Tom Jones* and *Amelia* have classical epigraphs on their title pages. *Tom Jones* has a well-known line from Horace, accessible to readers with a minimum of Latin education. *Amelia* also has a familiar Horatian quotation, but this is followed by a more remote piece of Greek verse from the *Iambics* of Simonides of Samos. Fielding seems determined not to smooth his readers' way into the novel, and the title-page epigraphs are soon followed by a six-line Latin quotation from Claudian's *In Rufinum* (I.iii). In his defence of *Amelia* in the *Covent-Garden Journal*, Fielding declares that he has followed the rules for the epic with as much care as had Homer and Virgil, and that the 'learned Reader will see that the latter was the noble model, which I made use of on this Occasion'.[17] Here Fielding is inviting readers to revisit his opening chapter, which takes the form of an 'Exordium', a term used in formal analysis of the epic. Like the *Aeneid*, *Amelia* has a twelve-book structure, and the opening books of the novel, set in Newgate, clearly parallel those of Virgil: Booth recounts his life story to Miss Mathews as Aeneas does to Dido, and the week-long adulterous affair between Booth and Miss Mathews parallels the amours of Aeneas and Dido in a Carthaginian cave. Fielding makes the link explicit in a quotation from the *Aeneid*, 'Furens quid Foemina possit' ('what a woman can do in frenzy'); Booth has escaped from Miss Mathews's clutches, and, like Aeneas on abandoning Dido, is fearful of his mistress's rage (IV.v). Even a bailiff comes up with his own version of a Virgilian line, 'dolus an virtus, quis in hoste requirat' ('whether deceit or valour, who would ask in the enemy'), which in the bailiff's garbled rendition, 'Bolus and Virtus, quis in a Hostess equirit', sounds mildly obscene (VIII.i). Virgilian quotations and allusions abound in *Amelia*, and Mrs Bennet, the novel's learned lady, is especially fond of the *Aeneid*. Translations for the Latin and Greek are not always provided; the reader's knowledge of the classics is assumed. Conversely, Fielding does supply glosses for criminal jargon; thus when Blear-Eyed Moll tells Booth that she had thought him 'upon the snaffling Lay', rather than being 'some sneaking Budge Rascal', the 'snaffling Lay' is defined as 'A Cant Term for Robbery on the High-way' and 'Budge' as 'Another Cant Term for Pilfering' (I.iii).

The Virgilian parallels in *Amelia* do something, as Ronald Paulson and others suggest, to dignify the novel, to 'elevate the domestic (marriage) plot and to connect it with public issues of a degenerating society and nation'.[18] But reading *Amelia*, for all of its classical buttresses, is hardly an elevating experience. For Richardson, *Amelia*, like its author, was deplorably low: 'His brawls, his jarrs, his gaols, his spunging-houses, are all drawn from what he has seen and known.' As for the novel's putative Virgilian parallels, Richardson declares that Fielding 'must mean Cotton's Virgil Travestied; where the women are drabs, and the men scoundrels'.[19] Richardson's jibe is typically spiteful, yet it captures something of the strange power of a novel that he claimed not to have read beyond the opening volume. Charles Cotton's *Scarronides: or, Virgil Travestie* (1664–5), a burlesque of the first and fourth books of the *Aeneid*, inspired by the *Virgile travesty* (1648–52)of the French poet, dramatist, and novelist Paul Scarron, could have provided Fielding with a useful model. Many of Fielding's men and women are indeed drabs and scoundrels, and the lowness that so disgusted Richardson in *Amelia* was a favourite target of many hostile critics. Bonnell Thornton's 'New Chapter in Amelia' seizes on the novel's frequent references to homely food and strong drink by having Amelia consume a 'Welch rabbit', while her children are 'knawing each of them an huge luncheon of bread and butter ... strew'd with brown sugar', and Mrs Bennet, who 'had taken too large a sip of the Cherry Brandy bottle', is asleep at the fireside, snoring.[20] Thornton's parody ridicules *Amelia* in much the same way that Fielding's *Shamela* had ridiculed *Pamela*, a novel in which the heroine's healthy appetite comes in for its share of mockery. As Claude Rawson observes, the detailed recording of precise amounts of food and drink consumed in *Amelia* seems 'precisely the kind of Richardsonian "meanness" which Fielding had derided through *Shamela*'.[21]

The two poles of *Amelia*, Virgil and cherry brandy, meet in the person of Mrs Bennet, subsequently Mrs Atkinson after her marriage to Sergeant Atkinson, Booth's loyal friend and Amelia's foster-brother. Together with Booth and Miss Mathews, Mrs Bennet is one of three characters in *Amelia* who recount their own lives. Each of Fielding's novels uses the device of interspersing authorial narrative with first-person accounts: Mr Wilson's story in *Joseph Andrews*, Mrs Heartfree's in *Jonathan Wild*, and both the Man of the Hill's and Mrs Fitzpatrick's in *Tom Jones*. In *Amelia*, however, the three dramatic histories differ significantly from their predecessors.

Instead of briefly interrupting an already established narrative, the histories of Miss Mathews and Booth occupy most of the first three books – about a quarter of the novel – while that of Mrs Bennet is given a subsequent book to itself. We cannot, in this case, speak of digressions, as the dramatic histories in Fielding's other novels are often called: the histories here constitute a major part of the text.

Before Mrs Bennet begins her history, Fielding warns the reader that 'she was desirous of inculcating a good Opinion of herself, from recounting those Transactions where her Conduct was unexceptionable, before she came to the more dangerous and suspicious Part of her Character' (VII.i). Everything that she says in her own defence is questionable, and at many points in her story Fielding seems to be deliberately tantalizing the reader. Her remarkably violent history makes her dangerous to know: her mother is killed by a bizarre fall into a well, clutching a tea-kettle in her hand; there is a deadly antagonism between her and her stepmother; her father ejects her from his house; she is drugged and raped by an unscrupulous lord; she unwittingly poxes her first husband, who in turn throws her to the ground, stamps on her, and then tries to kill himself; her first husband's corpse undergoes a post-mortem; and her friendship with Mrs Ellison turns to bitter enmity. Amelia's sympathetic declaration to her friend, 'you are much too severe a Judge on yourself: For they must have very little Candour, in my Opinion, who look upon your Case with any severe Eye' (VII.x), is too naïve too lull our suspicions. Mrs Bennet's narrative raises more questions about her past than it answers, and her frequent protestations of innocence confirm, rather than removing, our suspicions of her guilt. Like Miss Mathews, Mrs Bennet sees herself as a perpetual victim, oppressed by the wilful cruelty of others. Their recollections both exacerbate and relieve their misery, affording the painful pleasure of scratching an itch or picking a scab.

Mrs Bennet's history of violent victimhood continues after her second marriage. In one of the strangest incidents of the novel, she is attacked in her sleep by her husband, who has had a 'most horrid Dream' that Amelia is being threatened with rape by her admirer, Colonel James. Still befuddled by his dream, Sergeant Atkinson takes his wife for the Colonel and catches her by the throat; this 'rough Treatment immediately roused Mrs *Atkinson* from her Sleep, who no sooner perceived the Position of her Husband … than she gave a violent Shriek, and presently fell into a Fit' (IX.vi). Attempting to revive his wife, Atkinson sprinkles her with what he thinks is water but is in fact the cherry brandy that 'she used to apply for Comfort in all her Afflictions'; Mrs Atkinson thus seems to be weltering in her blood. In a fine analysis of this scene, Jill Campbell suggests that Atkinson's 'confusion of his sleeping wife with a sword- and phallus-brandishing Colonel

James' might suggest the extent to which he 'feels threatened (and emasculated) by his wife's classical "learning," by her more elevated class background, and by her rather fierce and domineering temper'.[22] The attempted strangulation and the dousing with cherry brandy are an assault on Mrs Atkinson's classical studies, as much as on her person; a soldier has defended English manhood from the threat posed by an over-educated woman.

Mrs Atkinson has not only acquired knowledge of the classics from her father; she is also a strong advocate for female intellect and for women's education. After quoting six lines from the *Aeneid* to Amelia and Booth, which she does 'with so strong an Emphasis, that she almost frightened *Amelia* out of her Wits', she comments on 'that great Absurdity, (for so she termed it,) of excluding Women from Learning; for which they were equally qualified with the Men, and in which so many had made so notable a Proficiency' (VI.vii). Neither Amelia nor Booth concurs with such radical views, but their 'Complaisance' towards their friend prevents them from challenging her. No such compunctions, however, deter Dr Harrison, the novel's very fallible wise man (and as such a counterpart to Squire Allworthy in *Tom Jones*), from attacking her at every opportunity. In their initial skirmishes, each is courteous enough. Mrs Atkinson claims that she will not be offended by the Doctor's holding women to be 'incapable of Learning', while deftly quoting a line of Horace against him; he in turn questions 'the Utility of Learning in a young Lady's Education' and suggests that 'if a learned Lady should meet with an unlearned Husband, might she not be apt to despise him?' (X.i). Dr Harrison soon becomes more aggressive, quoting Virgil's notorious adage, 'Varium et mutabile semper Foemina' ('Woman is a various and changeable Thing', in the Doctor's own translation), and at the same time detecting Mrs Atkinson's inability to parse the line correctly. On discovering that Mrs Atkinson reads some Greek, as well as Latin, Dr Harrison quotes three lines from the *Iliad* in which Hector is berating his wife Andromache. Fielding provides a translation in a footnote: 'Go home and mind your own Business. Follow your Spinning, and keep your Maids to their Work' (X.iv). The dispute, not surprisingly, now degenerates, and soon involves Booth, Amelia, and Sergeant Atkinson, as well as the principals. Sergeant Atkinson's attempts to act as peacemaker only fan the flames and lead to an unpleasant marital spat:

'I beg, my dear,' cried she, '*you* will say nothing upon these Subjects. – I hope *you* at least do not despise my Understanding.'

'I assure you, I do not,' said the Serjeant, 'and I hope you will never despise mine; for a Man may have some Understanding, I hope, without Learning.'

(X.iv)

Husband and wife are reconciled, but Dr Harrison is added to Mrs Atkinson's long list of *bêtes noires*; hereafter she considers him 'a conceited Pedant, nor could all of *Amelia*'s Endeavours ever alter her Sentiments'.

Where Fielding stands in all this is far from clear. Mrs Atkinson is hardly a sympathetic character, but Dr Harrison is at least as prone to error as Allworthy and far less congenial than Parson Adams in *Joseph Andrews*. He may not be a 'conceited Pedant', as Mrs Atkinson supposes, but he is certainly subject to 'gross Flattery', as Fielding points out when he is taken in by the repeated compliments of a self-serving elderly acquaintance (x.iv). The Doctor's antifeminist jibes – a learned lady, in his view, being as unnatural as 'a Man's being a fine Performer with a Needle' – seem to heighten the novel's anxieties about gender confusion: anxieties that emerge in the scene of the Sergeant's mistaking his sleeping wife for a man, Colonel James, bent on rape, as well as in the earlier Newgate section of the novel, where the repulsive prostitute Blear-Eyed Moll has been 'taken in the Fact with a very pretty young Fellow' (i.iii) and 'a very pretty Girl', with 'great Innocence in her Countenance', damns Booth's eyes and discharges 'a Volley of Words, every one of which was too indecent to be repeated' (i.iv). But the Doctor's mockery also follows a scene recounted by Booth, in which Colonel Bath, brother-in-law to the predatory Colonel James, is depicted in feminine garb. Booth has found Bath tending his ailing sister, warming a drink for her while wearing 'a Woman's Bed-Gown, and a very dirty Flannel Night-Cap'. Given James's martial disposition and extraordinary height – he is 'a very aukward thin Man near seven Feet high' – the scene might, as Booth observes, 'have formed, in the Opinion of most Men, a very proper Object of Laughter' (iii.viii). For Booth, however, it is not his friend's dressing like a woman that is risible so much as his shame at being detected in what is clearly a benevolent act. The Doctor's strictures on masculine women and feminine men are undermined by an episode in which a masculine man is also feminine, just as Mrs Atkinson hopes to be feminine while still possessing learning. (She tells the Doctor, 'I hate a masculine Woman, an Amazon, as much as you can do; but what is there masculine in Learning?' (x.iv).)

The conflict between Mrs Atkinson and Dr Harrison continues until the final chapter of the novel. Here the Doctor scores points by quoting three lines from the *Iliad*, compelling Mrs Atkinson to admit that she lacks the '*Greek* Ears' to understand them. She also makes the egregious error of referring to a 'Delphin *Homer*'; Fielding expected his readers to know that the famous Delphin classics were editions of Latin texts only. When, however, Amelia is made aware that she has inherited her mother's large estate and that her family's future is thus secure, Mrs Atkinson finds the apt Virgilian quotation to celebrate the occasion, repeating her lines as she 'rose from her Chair, and jumped about the Room for Joy' (XII.viii). Her mannish behaviour resembles that of Parson Adams at the end of *Joseph Andrews*, when Joseph is found to be the son of Mr Wilson and can thus marry his beloved Fanny Andrews after all; the Parson expresses his delight by 'capering, rubbing his Hands, and crying out, *Hic est quem quaeris, inventus est, &c.*' ('Here is the one whom you seek; he is found') (IV.xvi). If Colonel James's feminized masculinity is to be commended, Mrs Atkinson's masculinized femininity need not be deplored. In a letter to Richardson, Anne Donnellan expressed her disdain for the characterization of Fielding's learned lady: 'Must we suppose that if a woman knows a little Greek and Latin she must be a drunkard, and virago?'[23] But Mrs Atkinson is more than a drunkard and a virago, just as Amelia, with her various duplicities and concealments, is not an entirely docile wife. Among Amelia's duplicities, significantly, is her plan of sending Mrs Atkinson to a masquerade at the Haymarket in place of herself. The ruse succeeds because of a remarkable physical similarity between the two women, who are, Fielding tells us, of 'exactly the same Make and Stature', with an additional 'very near Resemblance between their Voices' (X.iii). Thus having earlier been twinned with Blear-Eyed Moll, Amelia is now matched with Mrs Atkinson, an equally problematic pairing.

As he had in *Tom Jones*, Fielding equipped *Amelia* with a concluding chapter in which the characters' afterlives are rapidly rehearsed. Some are straightforward enough: the attorney who cheated Amelia out of her mother's inheritance by fabricating a will 'was at length convicted of Forgery, and was soon afterwards hanged at *Tyburn*', and the noble Lord who plots Amelia's downfall dies from venereal disease, 'by which he was at last become so rotten, that he stunk above Ground' (XII.ix). The case of the novel's Colonels, however, is less simple. Colonel Bath, much the more sympathetic of the two, is made to pay for his obsession with dignity and honour: he 'was killed in a Duel about six Years ago by a Gentleman who told the Colonel he differed from him in Opinion'. But his vicious brother-in-law, Colonel James, lives on. Separated from his wife, he dotes on his mistress Miss Mathews, 'though now very disagreeable in her Person, and immensely fat', to such an extent 'that he submits to be treated by her in the most tyrannical Manner'. The word 'submits' is also used, a few lines later, of Sergeant Atkinson, now promoted to Captain, who 'chearfully submits' to his wife's 'superior Understanding and Knowledge'. That Colonel James should pay, at least to some extent, for his crimes by being saddled with a dictatorial mistress seems reasonable enough, but it is unclear why the always benevolent Atkinson should suffer a similar fate at the hand of his wife.

*Amelia* is replete with minor mysteries, most of which are eventually solved. Writers of forged letters and wills are discovered and punished, impersonations are admitted, and thefts are revealed. But the novel's larger mysteries remain impenetrable. Much the most admired part of *Amelia* is the Newgate section, in which Fielding is clearly at the height of his powers. His portraits of the venal justice Thrasher, who is profoundly ignorant of the law he is supposed to uphold, and the greedy Newgate bailiff, preying on the prisoners under his control, suggest that this will be a reformist novel, in which the corruption of penal institutions will be shown to cause the degradation, not the rehabilitation, of their inmates.[24] But the narrator's shifting stance makes it difficult to read *Amelia* as a proto-Dickensian novel of social protest. Among the more disturbing of the Newgate scenes is one in which Blear-Eyed Moll and her companions seize a 'Man who was committed for certain odious unmanlike Practices, not fit to be named'. They give him 'various Kinds of Discipline, and would probably have put an End to him, had he not been rescued out of their Hands by Authority' (i.iv). The passage can be read in quite different ways. Fielding's horror of the homosexual prisoner's 'unmanlike Practices' could be such that Moll and her companions are to be commended; natural justice has been thwarted only by the meddling of the guards. Alternatively, Fielding the magistrate could be endorsing the controlling hand of 'Authority', which in this instance, at least, has protected a prisoner from the depredations of his fellows.

Mysterious in a different way is the failure of tone in parts of the novel, in which a mawkishness not found in Fielding's previous fiction appears: there is, as J. Paul Hunter observes, a 'betrayal of reader expectations that had been earned and that now seem, cheaply, sold out'.[25] Consider, for example, Booth's account to Miss Mathews of the death of his beloved sister Nancy, who in a delirium has mistaken him for a highwayman:

> 'At last she seemed for a Moment to know me, and cry'd, "Oh Heavens! My dearest Brother!" upon which she fell into immediate Convulsions, and died away in my Arms.'
> Here *Booth* stop'd a Moment, and wip'd his Eyes; and Miss *Mathews*, perhaps out of Complaisance, wip'd hers. (ii.iv)

The writing is astonishingly bad, imbued with the trite sentimentality so effectively mocked by the young Jane Austen in 'Love and Freindship' and her other juvenile writings. In these and other such passages, Fielding is deploying what Rawson aptly terms a 'sub-Richardsonian mode, reminiscent of novelettish imitators'.[26] The influence of *Clarissa*, which Fielding had praised lavishly in a famous letter to Richardson of October 1748, was clearly counter-productive; Fielding's effort to stir his readers' passions in the manner for which Richardson was celebrated seems laboured and artificial.

*Amelia* has been the subject, in recent decades, of many incisive articles and chapters in books; its experimental qualities make it attractive to critics of both the development of the eighteenth-century novel and the trajectory of Fielding's career. Modern readers, however, have shown less enthusiasm for the work. A Penguin paperback, now out of print, was published in 1987, but between 1996 and 1998 it sold only 700 copies, compared with Penguin's sales, in the same period, of 7,200 copies for *Joseph Andrews*, 6,900 for *Tom Jones*, and almost 1,200 for both *A Journal of a Voyage to Lisbon* and *Jonathan Wild*.[27] *Amelia* might never become the 'favourite Child' of Fielding's readers, as it was of Fielding himself. But his last and most problematic novel did not, as he protested with surprising mildness, 'deserve the Rancour with which [it] hath been treated by the Public',[28] and it will reward those approaching it afresh today. Their experience of reading *Amelia* will be richer in the unbowdlerized first-edition text which, for all its flaws, represents Fielding's original conception of the novel and which has been inaccessible for too long.[29] This, after all, is the *Amelia* that provoked early readers, disgusting Richardson while winning the admiration of that odd couple, Cleland and Johnson. And this is the *Amelia* that deserves our attention, rather than the patched-up version of 1762 prepared by Murphy for Millar's collection of Fielding's works: a version that attempts to appease and reassure us, instead of offering a literary challenge.

## NOTES

1. Martin C. Battestin, Intro. to *Amelia* (Oxford: Clarendon Press, 1983), xliii. Battestin's Introduction adds much to previous accounts of the novel's publication and reception, but, for reasons explained below, my quotations are from the first-edition text.

2. Battestin, Intro. to *Amelia*, xlvi.

3. Battestin cites an advertisement for *Amelia* appended to Sarah Fielding's novel *The History of the Countess of Dellwyn* (1759); Intro. to *Amelia*, l, n. 1.

4. Richardson to Anne Donnellan, 22 February 1752; see Ronald Paulson and Thomas Lockwood, eds., *Henry Fielding: The Critical Heritage* (London: Routledge, 1969), 335.

5. Terry Castle, *Masquerade and Civilization: The Carnivalesque in Eighteenth-Century English Culture and Fiction* (London: Methuen, 1986), 179.

6. John Cleland, review of *Amelia*, *Monthly Review* 5 (1751); see *Critical Heritage*, ed. Paulson and Lockwood, 304, 306.

7. Review of *Amelia*, *London Magazine* 20 (1751); see *Critical Heritage*, ed. Paulson and Lockwood, 303. This review would gain more currency by being reprinted in several issues of the *Ladies Magazine* in 1752; see ibid., 288.

8. Frederic T. Blanchard, *Fielding the Novelist: A Study in Historical Criticism* (New Haven: Yale University Press, 1926), 85.

9. Bonnell Thornton, *Drury-Lane Journal*, 16 January, 13 February 1752; see *Critical Heritage*, ed. Paulson and Lockwood, 321, 323.

10. Hester Lynch Piozzi, *Anecdotes of the Late Samuel Johnson* (1786), in ibid., 445. A different version of this anecdote is in *Thraliana*, ed. Katharine C. Balderston, 2nd edn (Oxford: Oxford University Press, 1951), vol. I, 247: 'Amelia had performed all her Wonders with a broken Nose, which Fielding had forgotten to cure, & had broken indeed with no other Reason than to impress himself with an Idea of his favourite Wife, who had once met with a similar Accident ... thus did this oddity spoyl the Sale of one of the first Performances in the World of its Kind'.

11. Fielding, *The Covent-Garden Journal and A Plan of the Universal Register-Office*, ed. Bertrand A. Goldgar (Oxford: Clarendon Press, 1988), 395.

12. Fielding, *Covent-Garden Journal*, 25, 28 January 1752, ed. Goldgar, 58, 65–6.

13. Arthur Murphy, 'An Essay on the Life and Genius of Henry Fielding', in Battestin, Intro. to *Amelia*, lix.

14. Hugh Amory, 'What Murphy Knew: His Interpolations in Fielding's *Works* (1762), and Fielding's Revision of *Amelia*', *Papers of the Bibliographical Society of America* 77 (1983), 133–66.

15. Lance Bertelsen, *Henry Fielding at Work: Magistrate, Businessman, Writer* (Basingstoke: Palgrave, 2000), 80–2.

16. Sir Walter Scott, 'Prefatory Memoir to Fielding' (1824), in *Henry Fielding: A Critical Anthology*, ed. Claude Rawson (Harmondsworth: Penguin, 1973), 236.

17. Fielding, *Covent-Garden Journal*, 28 January 1752, ed. Goldgar, 65.

18. Ronald Paulson, *The Life of Henry Fielding: A Critical Biography* (Oxford: Blackwell, 2000), 294. See also Nancy A. Mace, *Henry Fielding's Novels and the Classical Tradition* (Newark: University of Delaware Press, 1996).

19. Samuel Richardson, letters to Anne Donnellan and Lady Bradshaigh, 22, 23 February 1752; see *Critical Heritage*, ed. Paulson and Lockwood, 335, 336.

20. Bonnell Thornton, *Drury-Lane Journal*, 13 February 1752; see ibid., 321–2.

21. Claude Rawson, *Henry Fielding and the Augustan Ideal under Stress* (London: Routledge and Kegan Paul, 1972), 90.

22. Jill Campbell, *Natural Masques: Gender and Identity in Fielding's Plays and Novels* (Stanford: Stanford University Press, 1995), 209.

23. Anne Donnellan to Richardson, 11 February 1752; see *Critical Heritage*, ed. Paulson and Lockwood, 319.

24. See John Bender's discussion of *Amelia* in *Imagining the Penitentiary: Fiction and the Architecture of Mind in Eighteenth-Century England* (Chicago: University of Chicago Press, 1987), 180–98.

25. J. Paul Hunter, *Occasional Form: Henry Fielding and the Chains of Circumstance* (Baltimore: Johns Hopkins University Press, 1975), 203.

26. Claude Rawson, 'Henry Fielding', in *The Cambridge Companion to the Eighteenth-Century Novel*, ed. John Richetti (Cambridge: Cambridge University Press, 1996), 149. See also T. C. Duncan Eaves, '*Amelia* and *Clarissa*', in *A Provision of Human Nature*, ed. Donald Kay (University: University of Alabama Press, 1977), 95–110.

27. These figures are taken from Allen Michie, *Richardson and Fielding: The Dynamics of a Critical Rivalry* (Lewisburg: Bucknell University Press, 1999), 191.
28. Fielding, *Covent-Garden Journal*, 28 January 1752, ed. Goldgar, 65.
29. A new edition of *Amelia* based on the first-edition text, edited by Linda Bree, is forthcoming from Broadview Press.

# 8

BERTRAND A. GOLDGAR

# Fielding's periodical journalism

Fielding's writings are dotted with signs of his quest for fame and his insecurity about achieving it. Here he is, for example, in a typical moment: 'It is certain that a Man no where meets with such Opposition as in an Attempt to acquire Reputation by Writing, which the World always with-holds from him as long as it is able, and seldom allows him till he is past the Enjoyment of it.'[1] Yet despite this fear of being unrecognized at the court of Prince Posterity, he spent at least three and a half years of his life, off and on, in the ephemeral world of journalism, a genre rooted in the present day and responding to immediate events or interests. For much of the same time, of course, he was seeking the laurel as a novelist, hoping to create something of permanent value that would take him down the avenue of fame and perhaps also the path of wealth. In the prefatory chapter to Book XIII of *Tom Jones*, he invokes 'bright Love of Fame', who inspired Homer, Virgil, and Milton, to fill his 'ravished Fancy with the Hopes of charming Ages yet to come', but then calls on another Goddess, the 'much plumper Dame' of money, com-fort, and solid pudding who presides over bad plays and serial publications. 'Keep back thy Inspiration', Fielding says to this fat deity, 'but hold forth thy tempting Rewards.'[2]

Although Fielding does not cite newspapers among the Grub-street pub-lications inspired by the Goddess of Gain rather than the Love of Fame, he might well have done so. Despite the fact that some of the most famous writers of the eighteenth century, with Addison and Steele as their exemplars, tried their hand at editing or writing periodical journalism (Swift, Pope, Fielding, Johnson, Goldsmith), it was still generally considered hack-work, its practitioners not worthy of citizenship in the Republic of Letters. Pope put 'Journals, Medleys, Merc'ries, Magazines' among the 'Grub-street race' (*Dunciad*, 1.42); and the supercilious *Grub-Street Journal* dismissed all other periodical journals as merely cheap short-cuts to learning, resulting in the proliferation of bad English, false politics, vague morality, and bathetic poetry or criticism, all 'well adapted to the curiosity and capacity of most persons' (1 March 1732). According to Michael Harris, the leading authority on the newspaper press in the first half of the century, the status of newspaper writers was 'peculiarly low', in large part simply because they were writing to order and for cash.[3]

Yet in spite of all that, and in spite too of Fielding's literary ambitions, nurtured by his success as a playwright, between the early 1730s and 1752 he wrote leading essays and in some cases was the principal writer for a wide range of different periodicals. Those we can list with some confidence are *Common Sense* (1738), the *Champion* (1739–40), the *True Patriot* (1745–6), the *Jacobite's Journal* (1747–8), and the *Covent-Garden Journal* (1752), as well perhaps as a short-lived magazine called the *History of Our Own Times* (1741). In addition, some scholars, principally Martin and Ruthe Battestin, have also seen Fielding's hand in contributions to many other periodicals: *Fog's Journal, Mist's Journal*, the *Comedian*, the *Universal Spectator*, the *Gray's Inn Journal*, and especially the *Craftsman* (forty-odd essays in the period 1734–9); since many of these attributions are still under debate, they will not be included in this overview.[4]

Although the canon is thus unsettled, a look at Fielding's first serious venture into journalism, writing extensively for the anti-Walpole *Champion* in 1739–40, may help us understand at least the nature of the newspaper press in the period. Although Fielding was the major contributor in 1739–40 and for a time owned a 2/16 share of this paper, students of the book trade stress that the *Champion* was not *his* paper in any modern sense of either literary or business ownership.[5] Like most other papers of the day, it was a joint venture owned and operated by a group of shareholders, mostly book-sellers, who had a commercial interest in owning newspapers as a way of advertising their books and otherwise controlling the market. Whether Fielding was himself one of the original projectors behind the paper is, how-ever, an open question. The paper's political slant, Harris tells us, would have been no surprise to insiders, since the shareholders were in general associated in particular with that segment of the London book trade producing news-papers opposed to the chief minister Sir Robert Walpole.[6]

When the paper began, Fielding was still preparing for a career in law and, as usual, suffering from lack of money. Despite such circumstances he managed to obtain a 'writer's share' in the partnership – presumably through John Nourse, a retail bookseller for whom Fielding had done some trans-lations from French. As Harris says, the venture was a kind of compro-mise between literary and commercial interests, with Fielding (writing as 'Hercules Vinegar') and his fictional family (other Vinegars) meant to supply a line of gentle Addisonian social satire intermixed with what he called a 'Vein of Wit ... which the Town hath not, lately, seen any Thing equal to'

(*Champion*, 18 December 1739). Sometimes the content of the early essays was completely social or literary, as in the essay of 27 November comparing the success of soldiers and writers in achieving Fame – all very light-hearted on a serious theme, with a few jokes at the expense of his own *Tom Thumb* and a fake legal ruling in law French by Counsellor Vinegar on a literary question.

But from the very beginning there were also political jabs at Walpole, often with the political theme enmeshed in a framework of what seems to be only social or moral or literary commentary. This was by now a time-honoured technique of the literary Opposition to Walpole, dating back to the days of *Mist's Weekly Journal* and its witty successor *Fog's*. The mixture of humour and political bite had also earlier been the hallmark of *Common Sense*, begun in early 1737 and sponsored by two political figures close to Fielding, Lyttelton and Chesterfield, central figures of the new 'Patriot' Opposition to the Walpole government. Although apparently Fielding himself contributed little more than a letter and one essay to *Common Sense*, he obviously recognized that its style made the paper distinctive – witty, cool, urbane, a style and manner uncommon in political writings, as the 'Printer to the Reader' of the first collected volume claims.[7] As the best study of that paper points out, it was 'a medium of political writing for those who, as it were, cared more for writing than politics'.[8] For Henry Fielding, in other words, who began demonstrating the accuracy of that characterization when he started his numerous contributions to the *Champion*.

The political side of the scale took on additional weight in April of 1740 when the *Champion* became an evening paper and simultaneously sharpened the edge and increased the amount of its political satire; by the spring the paper also was featuring leaders by Fielding's friend and fellow-shareholder James Ralph, who under the name 'Lilbourne' wrote more 'serious' anti-Walpole essays. With the increase in political satire, sales rose almost at once, and the paper began to flourish. 'Fair-sexing it', to adapt Swift's phrase about the *Spectator*, was resorted to less and less, as were moral essays with no political subtext. Instead of Addison and Steele as models, the *Champion* and Fielding now took over devices from the early *Craftsman* and other Opposition journals: dream allegories, mock advertisements, constant allusions to Walpole as 'Robin Brass' or 'His Honour' or 'Guts', sarcastic accounts of naval losses, and, of course, straight propagandizing about evil ministers. Fielding delighted too in harping on the old Opposition theme of the decay of letters under the present administration, and there his favorite example in 1740 was the Poet Laureate Colley Cibber, whose *Apology* for his life had appeared in April. Cibber's stellification as the Laureate had all along been viewed by the Opposition as symptomatic of the debasement of literature under Walpole, and his posturing autobiography, which Fielding ridiculed because of its dreadful prose, also contained some comments explicitly pro-Walpole, of which the *Champion* took due notice (29 April, 6–8 May 1740). The more general theme of the administration's neglect of men of letters sometimes aroused Fielding to open indignation. Speaking of Walpole in the leader of 6 September 1740, he wrote: 'when future Writers shall render him that Justice which his Cotemporaries deny him, when he shall be hang'd up, as it were, in History for our Children to stare at, how will they wonder that his Glories never warmed a *Pope*, a *Swift*, a *Young*, a *Gay*, a *Thompson*, to celebrate his Name'. Contemporaries would have laughed at the innuendoes in 'hang'd up' and 'stare at', but they would also have seen the passage as pointed at the neglect of writers whom the state should support – a theme which would come to be of major importance to Fielding as he continued in journalism.

But although the political content of the *Champion* increased in volume, there is no evidence that such a change reflected a corresponding heightening of Fielding's personal dedication to the 'Patriot' cause. It seems very likely that he was telling the truth when he wrote in the *Champion* of 14 February 1740, in response to a supposed complaint that he was not applying himself sufficiently to politics, 'I find I am no Politician.' Indeed, he says, he has read most of the historians and writers on government, but one can't do everything, and he hopes readers will stop asking him questions about policy, because 'I declare for my Part, so far from knowing, I cannot even guess what we are about, or what we intend to do.' This mock-disclaimer is, of course, satiric, but I think it can also be taken seriously, as Fielding revealing his hopes to keep the paper light and witty even while scoring points against the administration. No doubt he had his grievances against Walpole, among them the Licensing Act which pushed him off the stage, but (unlike Ralph) he was not an ideologue, and his motives derived in part from his friends and in part from the desire to be on the side of the clever and witty, not on that of 'Bob, the Poet's Foe'.

The number for 17 May, for example, is sufficiently political to satisfy the most rabid Opposition MP, but it also mingles politics with enough sophisticated and humorous knowledge of the Town to satisfy any coffee-house wit. Here for the first time we find Fielding's 'Court of Censorial Enquiry', in which his persona Hercules Vinegar brings to justice such malefactors as Pope, for aiding and abetting 'one *Forage*, alias *Guts*, alias *Brass*' by not satirizing him; Colley Cibber, for murdering the English language; and even 'Guts' himself, whose trial is deferred, the indictment being so long that 'it would have reached from *Westminster* to the *Tower*'. Readers were also treated to other entertaining features, such as 'Political Amusements Forged in the Mint of the *Daily Advertiser*', 'Home News' with sardonic editorial comments, and a column headed 'Ministerial Puffs'. The leader may be the only thing in the issue that can be attributed to Fielding himself, but the whole four-page paper (which also had genuine news items) constituted a fine mesh of the political, the literary, and the journalistic. Although the *Champion* also had serious numbers, especially four essays called 'An Apology for the Clergy' and another hortatory series late in the year addressed to the 'Electors of Great Britain' (perhaps not Fielding's), on the whole his contributions to the *Champion* are meant to divert by wit, not convert by argument.

After Fielding was called to the Bar (10 June 1740) and began attending the assizes on the Western Circuit in July and August, his contributions to the *Champion* diminished, so that for the rest of the year he wrote fewer than half of the leading articles.[9] Some of his essays in that period and afterwards have apparently not survived; some that have, such as the weak imitations of *Gulliver's Travels* called 'Voyages of Job Vinegar', are only moderately successful. Then late in the year Fielding's attitude toward Walpole became unstable. In a leader of 4 October he pretends to have rejected an offer of a bribe from a quack doctor named 'Roberto' to praise his 'Nostrums', though he admits he once took money from the same source to suppress a book (some think he means an early version of *Jonathan Wild*); the ministerial press was filled with increasing attacks on him in November and December. Although he published two other pieces in January 1741 that were resolutely anti-Walpole, his contributions to the *Champion* had apparently stopped by February 1741, and all his work for the Opposition came to an end early in that year. Pro-ministerial journalists mocked his tendencies to political tergiversation, and hints and accusations abounded in the pro-government *Gazetteer* and elsewhere. Finally in December 1741 Fielding published a pamphlet called *The Opposition: A Vision*, in which, as Frederick Ribble has said, he seems to be reborn as a ministerial propagandist. Scholars have disagreed over the extent to which this allegory was written actually in support of Walpole, but Ribble has recently found clear evidence showing that Fielding did indeed change sides for money.[10]

Fielding's reputation as a turncoat would surface again in connection with his next two political papers. But well before those papers began, in fact at about the same time as he finished with the *Champion*, he apparently tried a brief experiment in another form of journalism, a magazine called the *History of Our Own Times*, published by Charles Corbett (also an early publisher of the *Champion*), which ran only from 15 January to 5 March 1741. According to Thomas Lockwood (whose attribution has not been disputed) Fielding wrote the 'Introduction' which served as the opening leader, and he was perhaps also responsible for some of the other magazine-like features of the new periodical. But perhaps more interesting than what Fielding wrote in this paper is the question of why he wrote in it at all – that is, since the *Champion* was still a successful operation and Fielding was still a friendly shareholder, why did he undertake a role in this different sort of periodical? Lockwood, to whom we owe what knowledge we have of this venture, explains it as 'an attempt by Fielding to enlarge and . . . challenge his *métier* as a writer and journalist', expressing his ambition not as a political commentator or publisher but as 'a professional journalist, an essayist, and a scholar'.[11] Interestingly, Harris sees Fielding's last months on the *Champion* in much the same way, commenting that Fielding's solitary vote in June 1741 against selling the reprint of the collected leading essays to a bookseller may have derived from the triumph of literary over commercial values in an author already thinking of his reputation in posterity.[12]

Fielding did not return to any form of journalism until 5 November 1745, when the world was very different. Walpole was dead, his protégé Henry Pelham was chief minister, the Young Pretender had landed in Scotland and found initial success, and Fielding's friends and connections among the 'Patriot' politicians (Lyttelton, Dodington, Cobham, Chesterfield) now had places of power. Some of those, perhaps Dodington and Lyttelton, presumably worked out an arrangement with publishers for a weekly paper called the *True Patriot*, which had a short life, from 5 November 1745 to 17 June 1746. Yet though its backers can be guessed at, and its alarm at the Jacobite invasion is sounded with apparent sincerity, the motive behind the paper is not clear, nor is it obvious what or who prompted Fielding to lend his hand to guiding and writing it.[13] Though the paper does not seem to have been directly supported by the government, Fielding was nonetheless in the same tricky defensive role as those on Walpole's *Gazetteer* whom he had formerly ridiculed, and the *True Patriot* is accordingly more ineffective more of the time than is typical of Fielding's journalism.

Yet it starts extremely well. The first number shows Fielding at his most arch and humorous, as he sniffs at the styles of other newspapers, makes promises to the readers about his abilities, and throws out hints about his identity, suggesting all those he *might* be (Bolingbroke? Bishop Hoadly? Chesterfield? Fielding?). But the remainder of the first number gives sober and earnest 'Observations on the present Rebellion', and several months go by before readers are treated again to the level of wit Fielding reached so often in the *Champion*. Nor is the guest appearance of Parson Adams in two of the numbers of much help. Possibly Fielding or his backers felt wit to be inappropriate when the nation was in danger, though such a consideration does not seem to apply when Fielding has special reasons to fall back on ridicule, as in No. 16, which quotes from Shakespeare, Buckingham's

*Rehearsal*, and Fielding's own *Tragedy of Tragedies* to laugh at the two-day ministry in February of Bath and Granville, leaders of the Opposition who could find no-one to take office with them. At any rate humour is rare in this journal, and gloomy anti-Jacobite prophecies or exclamations of patriotic sentiment are the rule.

Fielding himself was no doubt seriously alarmed at the Jacobite threat and quite sincere in his sometimes violent anti-Catholic sketches and harangues. Despite the many shifts in his political views throughout his career, he never shows the slightest hint of any sympathy for Pretenders young and old or for any party that could reasonably be thought to support their cause; his many essays here (as well as his several pamphlets published separately) that see the triumph of Jacobitism as the ruin of the nation are, we can assume, heightened versions of his true views. At the same time it is also the case that strong anti-Jacobitism was a useful way for the Patriot politicians to strengthen their hand with the king and defeat the plans of his favourite, Granville.

Almost half-way through, in the *True Patriot* No. 14, Fielding steps out of the journalistic persona to defend his paper and to profess his political impartiality. He is not a 'party writer', he says, for there would be no point in it – the Great Man of the present day (Pelham) 'hath the utmost Indifference for all Writers, and the greatest Contempt for any Good or Harm which they can do him'. Fielding himself, however, takes the occasion in this essay to deliver one of his rare but significant tributes to writers *qua* writers, men who though they do not style themselves as 'of a Profession' deserve praise because they have either 'improved the Understanding, corrected the Will, or entertained the Imagination; such especially as have blended these three Talents together, who have temper'd Instruction and Correction with Humour, and have led Men pleased and smiling thro' the Paths of Knowledge and Virtue'. Nothing is said here about political writers, and Fielding's tendency to set up as an ideal a non-political art of writing will recur as his novels succeed and his political motivation wanes.

The *True Patriot* changed its tack somewhat after No. 17 (25 February). 'The Present History of Great Britain', a regular feature which had been merely an account of the rebellion and excerpts from other papers, became after this number a vehicle for serious essays on Patriot politics, perhaps written by James Ralph. Fielding's own leaders went back to occasional social commentary on hoop petticoats and the like, intermixed with panegyrics on the Royal Family and other forms of 'Broad Bottom' propaganda – all in all a feeble finale to Fielding's most feeble effort in journalism, writing essays which have not 'improved the Understanding, corrected the Will, or entertained the Imagination'.

His next effort began, at least, on a more lively note, though it too degenerated into routine praise of political friends and anathematization of journalistic enemies. The *Jacobite's Journal* appeared first on 5 December 1747 as a four-page weekly in the usual format (leading editorial essay, followed by departments such as foreign affairs and domestic news reprinted from other papers, sometimes with satirical comments). The booksellers connected with it were mostly those with whom Fielding had had earlier dealings. No records of payment are extant, but it was assumed by Fielding's enemies at the time, and has recently been demonstrated, that he got a governmental subsidy for writing it, and that several thousand papers were taken off by the government each week for free distribution. It is thus not surprising that this paper was the only one supporting the Pelham administration in 1747–8 and that its editor took care to single out for praise both Pelham and his other patrons in the government (Lyttelton, Hardwicke, and Bedford), but not two earlier patrons who were no longer on good terms with the administration, Chesterfield and Dodington.[14] Moreover, by the time the paper ended (5 November 1748), Fielding, now finishing *Tom Jones*, had finally received his reward from the Great Men he flattered, an appointment as Justice of the Peace for Westminster.

Fielding's backers for this paper may have been surprised by the way the enterprise began. The persona, 'John Trott-Plaid', is an unrepentant Jacobite who explains to the readers the doctrines and creed of his politics. England was at war, but no longer with invading Jacobites, who had received their decisive defeat in April 1746; thus one must look to domestic issues, not foreign affairs, to fathom the reason for this ironic pose, which continues for the first sixteen numbers. There were, to be sure, riots and signs of popular discontent laid to the door of Jacobites, and some in the administration were truly concerned over the possibility of new risings. But Fielding perhaps exaggerates the danger, as part of his stance in favour of the administration. As one historian points out, since Tories were no longer any threat, the Whigs in government needed Jacobites to attack, so that Opposition politicians could be stigmatized as the enemies of king and country.[15] Trott-Plaid's irony is meant to lay bare the perniciousness of whatever is left of the Jacobite movement, but the irony often seems forced and cumbersome: 'It hath been conceived impossible, that I should in Earnest hold the Principles I have asserted; and this for no other Reason, but because they are directly repugnant to common Sense.'[16] The usual deftness of Fielding's irony is missing, possibly because he tries here to be ironic and yet simultaneously to convey a politically 'true' meaning. An unusually high proportion of letters from (supposed) readers suggests that Fielding was himself unhappy about the way his irony was not working.

Fortunately, other aspects of the essays of the first four months are more entertaining than the creaky ironic frame. Fielding seemingly tries to destroy the enemy by pseudo-pedantry, a genre he loved: we get learned essays on the 'esoteric' and 'exoteric' mysteries of Jacobitism (the mystery of passive obedience, for instance, or the unfathomable belief that a Popish prince can defend a Protestant Church); and he applies to the Jacobite movement the euhemerist explanations of myths in Abbé Banier's *Mythology and Fables of the Ancients Explain'd* (recently published by his friend and publisher Andrew Millar). But all this effort to combine politics with good pedantic fun is abandoned in No. 17 (26 March 1748), when Fielding decides to 'pull off the Masque' and drop his effort at irony. Remarkably, this decision is accompanied by his rejection of irony itself as a possibly dangerous and certainly unpopular form of wit, unsuited especially to the present times, since Popish traitors and Jacobite principles are not proper subjects for ridicule. Satire gives way to straightforward essays putting the Pelhamite case on a host of issues, from the very local (e.g. moving the summer assizes from Aylesbury to Buckingham) to the international (culmination of the peace efforts with the treaty signed at Aix-la-Chapelle). But the presentation is not unremittingly political, for Fielding intersperses in most of the numbers his 'Court of Criticism', in which he metes out blame and praise to literary, journalistic, and theatrical figures and works, including Richardson's *Clarissa* and Thomson's *Castle of Indolence*.

Fielding was identified early on as the author of this ministerial organ and to his distress was subjected to enormous personal abuse in the Opposition press. He fought back in the *Journal* as best he could, pointing to the illiteracy and meanness of his individual attackers and in several essays addressing Slander as a general theme. One of his opponents was his former coadjutor on the *Champion*, James Ralph, now the editor of the *Remembrancer*, chief organ of the Prince of Wales's Opposition party. Rather than taking Ralph to task for changing allegiances, Fielding in No. 17 (26 March), the somewhat bitter essay in which he drops his mask of irony, looks at the whole question of the literary man forced to deal with a political world and reaches a conclusion that throws some light on his own political twists and turns: 'In a Country where there is no public Provision for Men of Genius, and in an Age when no Literary Productions are encouraged, or indeed read, but such as are season'd with Scandal against the Great', in such a time and place, he says, the temptation for a hungry man to feed himself by a little calumny is too hard to resist, and if one set of men deny him encouragement, he reasonably seeks it from another – after all, the worst that could happen is a change of a ministry. Of course Fielding hurries to explain that he doesn't mean this to apply to the present time, since the nation is threatened by Jacobites, and so on; but it's difficult not to see behind these pronouncements Fielding himself, at the last stage of composing his masterpiece, and eager to exchange the constraints of the political writer for the fame accorded to 'Men of Genius'.

A little over three years later Fielding had the opportunity to show what he could do in a sustained journalistic enterprise which had no political strings attached. Now a magistrate for Westminster and Middlesex and holding court in the notoriously disreputable neighbourhood of Covent Garden, he began a new periodical, the *Covent-Garden Journal*, which came out (initially) twice a week as a four-page paper edited by 'Sir Alexander Drawcansir, Knight Censor of Great Britain'. Although there was now no political connection, Fielding did have a commercial motive; the new paper was intended to advertise and publicize the Universal Register Office, a sort of combination employment office, real estate agency, and curiosity shop in which he and his half-brother John were partners. Andrew Millar, who published Fielding's main novels, may have owned shares in the enterprise, since his books are constantly puffed; other backers besides the Fieldings are unknown.[17] In form this paper is much like his others: in each number the leading essay or letter from a contributor is followed first by a smaller column called 'Covent Garden', commenting on the cases which had just come before him in court; this in turn is followed by selections of news items from other papers, often with ironic commentary, and again (in seventeen of the seventy-two numbers) by a Court of Censorial Enquiry, similar to the 'courts' he had included in the *Champion* and the *Jacobite's Journal*. Of these features, the 'Covent Garden' column is the most notable, especially when Fielding himself comments on the individual cases. He seems, in fact, to have viewed this aspect of the *Journal* as a way of creating a favourable image of himself as a Justice of the Peace and as a place for editorializing about current issues of criminal justice.

But Fielding is not only the Justice here, he is also the Censor, and though his pseudonym 'Drawcansir' (from Buckingham's the *Rehearsal*) suggests mock-heroic bravado, he seems to have taken the role more seriously now than in his previous journals; here, the censorial mission moves beyond the Court columns and into many of the leaders as well. Instead of taking Addison's *Freeholder* as his model, as he had for his narrowly political papers, Fielding now looks back to the wider range of the *Tatler* and *Spectator* and to a concern with the social and moral health of the whole body politic. But his general reflections are rooted in the concrete details of everyday life, in notable contrast to, say, Johnson's *Rambler*, which was still appearing early in this same year. Frequently, in fact, Fielding's leading essays grow out of the specific events reported in the news or 'Covent Garden' columns. A particular case in his court, for example, produces two essays on the law's inadequacy to punish adultery; the murder trial of the parricide Mary Blandy occasions an essay on false gallantry; a new law to suppress bawdy houses leads both Fielding and a correspondent to discuss how to handle prostitution; and his problems coping with insane defendants produces a biting parody of the restrictive rules for admission to St Luke's Hospital. The main focus of the *Journal* is thus moral and very broadly political, with essays on the problems of the poor, on confusing liberty with mob rule, and on the mistaken political notions of the illiterate members of a heterodox debating society. His main weapon is Swiftian irony, despite the scepticism about its efficacy voiced in the *Jacobite's Journal*. Although the leaders are on moral or social issues, literary and theatrical themes dominate the 'Court' columns; even so they take up less than a third of the space over the life of the paper.

All this sounds quite consonant with his statement of purpose announced in No. 5, 'However vain or romantic the Attempt may seem, I am sanguine enough to aim at serving the noble Interests of Religion, Virtue, and good Sense, by these my Lucubrations.' But he began his lucubrations on a note far less elevated, by deliberately provoking a 'paper war' between himself, as standard bearer of the Republic of Letters, and the united forces of Grub Street. This device, aimed at increasing circulation, was a bad miscalculation, since some readers who thought themselves attacked (including Smollett) responded with abuse. In particular he began a fight with John Hill, a flamboyant and pompous writer of a column called 'The Inspector' in the *London Daily Advertiser*; only five numbers later could Fielding extricate himself, and not with glory. The paper's later themes, however, are usually serious-minded, despite their frequent irony and occasional humour. This is not the Fielding of *Joseph Andrews* but of *Amelia*, of the *Enquiry* and other major social pamphlets, a Fielding in poor health and somber mood, suffering considerable dejection brought on in part by 'the Sight of all those Wretches who are brought before him' at his court in Bow Street (*Journal* No. 16, 25 February).

By midsummer, however, it seemed clear that circulation was dropping. On 4 July the paper became a weekly; in its final months advertising dwindled, and the 'Covent Garden' column became merely a report of actions taken in court. With No. 72 (25 November) Fielding announced the end, saying that he no longer had the inclination or leisure to continue, that his 'graver Friends' had 'chid' him for undertaking it at all since he could employ his pen 'much more to the Honour of myself, and to the Good of the Public', presumably in social tracts and pamphlets. And so he declares that 'unless in revising my former Works, I have at present no Intention to hold any further Correspondence with the gayer Muses'.

In the two years remaining to him the 'former Works' he revised were *Jonathan Wild*, *Amelia*, and – surprisingly – the *Covent-Garden Journal*, surprisingly because it suggests that Fielding, with his eye on posterity and his hopes for lasting fame, nonetheless thought these pieces of ephemeral journalism, grounded in the circumstantial and the topical, worthy of inclusion in some future edition of his works, along with *Tom Jones* and *Amelia*. As far as we know he never considered any of his other periodical writing as worthy of revision, certainly not the two thoroughly political journals. We have no idea what he thought of the collected edition of the *Champion* or why he opposed the sale of those volumes to another bookseller, and we can only speculate why he found his last periodical worthy of revision.[18] My own guess is that his choice reflects the seriousness with which he took his mission as 'Knight Censor'; given his grave frame of mind as he began contemplating his previous writings, we may easily imagine that he thought the overriding social and moral themes in his final effort in lowly journalism worth revising and preserving along with his 'high' works of literary art, to be read by 'those who never knew nor saw me, and whom I shall neither know nor see' (*Tom Jones*, [683]; XIII.i).

## NOTES

1. Henry Fielding, *Contributions to the Champion and Related Writings*, ed. W. B. Coley (Oxford: Clarendon Press, 2003), 212 (1 March 1739/40). Quotations from the *Champion* will be from this edition.
2. Henry Fielding, *The History of Tom Jones: A Foundling*, ed. Martin C. Battestin and Fredson Bowers (Oxford: Clarendon Press, 1974; paperback edn 1983), 684–5; XIII.i. Quotations will be from this edition.
3. Michael Harris, 'Journalism as a Profession or Trade in the Eighteenth Century', in *Author / Publisher Relations during the Eighteenth and Nineteenth Centuries*, ed. Robin Myers and Michael Harris (Oxford: Oxford Polytechnic Press, 1983), 56–7.
4. For texts and discussion of the attributed essays, see Martin C. Battestin, *New Essays by Henry Fielding* (Charlottesville: University of Virginia Press, 1989).
5. Michael Harris, 'Literature and Commerce in Eighteenth-Century London: The Making of the *Champion*', in *Telling People What to Think*, ed. J. A. Downie and Thomas N. Corns (London: Frank Cass, 1993), 103–10. For a full account of the way newspapers were operated in the period, see Harris's *London Newspapers in the Age of Walpole* (London and Toronto: Associated University Presses, 1987).
6. Harris, 'Literature and Commerce', 99.
7. *Common Sense* (London, 1738), vol. I, sig. [A3v].
8. Thomas Lockwood, 'The Life and Death of *Common Sense*', in *Telling People What to Think*, ed. Downie and Corns, 90.
9. Martin C. Battestin with Ruthe Battestin, *Henry Fielding: A Life* (London: Routledge, 1989), 271; Thomas Lockwood, 'New Facts and Writings from an Unknown Magazine by Henry Fielding, *The History of Our Own Times*', *Review of English Studies*, new series 35 (1984), 465.

10. Frederick G. Ribble, 'Fielding's Rapprochement with Walpole in Late 1741', *Philological Quarterly* 80 (2001), 71–81. On Fielding's shifts of political loyalties, see my essay, 'Fielding, Politics, and "Men of Genius"', in *Henry Fielding, Novelist, Playwright, Journalist, Magistrate (1707–1754)*, ed. Claude Rawson (Newark: University of Delaware Press, 2007).

11. Lockwood, 'New Facts and Writings', 492–3; see also his facsimile edition of the magazine (Delmar, NY: Scholars' Facsimiles and Reprints, 1985).

12. Harris, 'Literature and Commerce', 107; but cf. Battestin, *Henry Fielding*, 308, giving a political motive.

13. See Battestin, *Henry Fielding*, 400–3, and W. B. Coley, ed., *'The True Patriot' and Related Writings* (Oxford: Clarendon Press, 1987), lxv–lxxi. Quotations from the *True Patriot* will be from this edition.

14. Battestin, *Henry Fielding*, 426. For evidence of government subsidy, see Frederick G. Ribble, 'New Light on Henry Fielding from the Malmesbury Papers', *Modern Philology* 103 (2005), 86.

15. John Brewer, *Party Ideology and Popular Politics at the Accession of George III* (Cambridge: Cambridge University Press, 1981), 46.

16. Fielding, *The Jacobite's Journal and Related Writings*, ed. W. B. Coley (Oxford: Clarendon Press, 1974), 163 (20 Feb. 1748, No. 12); quotations will be from this edition.

17. Fielding, *'The Covent-Garden Journal' and 'A Plan of the Universal Register-Office'*, ed. Bertrand A. Goldgar (Oxford: Clarendon Press, 1988), xxii–xxviii. Quotations will be from this edition.

18. For details and discussion, see *Covent-Garden Journal*, ed. Goldgar, Appendix viii; Hugh Amory, 'Fielding's Copy of the *Covent-Garden Journal*', *Bodleian Library Record* 11 (1983), 126–8; and Goldgar, 'Fielding, Periodicals, and the Idea of Literary Fame', *Journal of Newspaper and Periodical History* 2 (Winter 1985), 2–9.

# 9

JANE SPENCER

# Fielding and female authority

When Henry Fielding, his second wife Mary, and Fielding's daughter Harriet set off for Lisbon in 1754, they were accompanied by Margaret Collier. The voyage did not improve his relationship with this old family friend. In the final weeks of his life Fielding was troubled by his wife's desire to return to England, and Collier, in his view, encouraged her 'Folly'. Moreover, Collier was behaving ridiculously, he thought, acting the 'fine young Lady of Portugal, a Toast of Lisbon', and trying to attract Mr Williamson, the English minister. 'He is smitten', reported Fielding, 'and she would succeed, if I did not prevent it. She is indeed the most artful wicked B – in the world'.[1] After Fielding's death Collier wrote to the novelist's great rival Samuel Richardson, mentioning Fielding, if less rudely than he had written of her, still in implicitly hostile terms. People, she complained, were attributing the *Journal of a Voyage to Lisbon* to her on the grounds that it was inferior to Fielding's other works and must have been written by his female companion: 'This is the disadvantageous light poor women are held in, by the ill-nature of the world'. She appealed for sympathy to Richardson 'as the only candid man, I believe, with regard to women's understandings; and indeed their only champion, and protector, I may say, in your writings; for you write of angels, instead of women'.[2]

Collier's flattery of Richardson implies criticism of his rival, presumably not generous about women's intelligence and no friend to women in his writing. This was already a familiar contrast between the two novelists, at least from Richardson's point of view. Richardson had made his name as a novelist rewarding the virtue of the militantly chaste servant *Pamela*, and had gone on to create in Clarissa the century's great tragic heroine; Fielding had begun his career as a novelist exposing the hypocrisy of female claims to virtue in *Shamela* and in *Joseph Andrews*. Though the parodist of *Pamela* had later responded admiringly to *Clarissa*, Richardson remained scornful of Fielding's work, especially his depiction of women: he dismissed the heroine of *Tom Jones* as 'the weak, the insipid, the Runaway, the Inn-frequenting

Sophia'.[3] Richardson evidently felt that in praising virtuous women Fielding was encroaching on his own territory.

The trend of seeing the author of *Clarissa* as a writer for women, the author of *Tom Jones* as a man's writer, has continued. Johnson's famous pronouncement about Fielding as the observer of the dial-plate of the watch while Richardson understood the inner movements,[4] and Coleridge's contrast between the 'cheerful, sunshiny, breezy spirit' of *Tom Jones* and 'the close, hot, day-dreamy continuity of Richardson',[5] have been interpreted in gendered terms, as indicating that Richardson, with his interest in subjective interiority, was a feminine writer, and Fielding, with his concern for objective evidence and externality, essentially a masculine one. The two men indeed have seemed neatly to provide the English novel with a two-sex inheritance, without any need to take the contribution of women themselves into account.

The relative reputations of these gendered rivals have fluctuated according to shifts in the critical evaluation of masculinity and femininity in writing. W. B. Carnochan recalls 'being taught to dislike Richardson' in the Harvard of the 1950s by a 'rather pugnacious (he actually had been a boxer) professor' who evidently found Fielding's masculinity more congenial than Richardson's femininity, and considered that '*Shamela* on *Pamela* provided a fair critical commentary'. In this critical climate, he notes, Ian Watt's favourable estimation of Richardson's interiority came as something of a shock.[6] In the 1950s Robert Etheridge Moore found Fielding 'virile and forthright', Richardson 'fussy and hesitating'. He considered that Johnson's puzzling preference for Richardson over Fielding must have been some kind of mistake: because of the affinity of their shared masculinity, Johnson must actually have liked Fielding more than he thought he did. 'Johnson, like Fielding, is a man, and what is more, a man's man ... Richardson may be called, in all seriousness, one of our great women'.[7] Conversely, in the early wave of feminist literary criticism in the 1970s, Richardson as woman, or at least as woman's man, was revalued. Katharine M. Rogers praised Richardson for an understanding of women's social disadvantages and an insight into their feelings that amounted to 'sensitive feminism', while Fielding was capable only of 'conventional sympathy' with women.[8] The wheel had come full circle, returning Richardson to the position of women's champion that he had been accorded by contemporaries like Margaret Collier.

The crude division of the two novelists on gender lines has been challenged in various ways from the 1980s onwards. Angela Smallwood argued that the ultra-masculine Fielding was a creation of selective biographies in the early twentieth century, and urged the 'abolition of the Richardson–Fielding polarity'.[9] Placing Fielding's work in the context of eighteenth-century shifts in political and gender discourse, she showed Fielding's interest in contemporary discussions of women's nature and role, and found him generally supportive of the ideas of female moral equality and the ideal of marriage based on friendship rather than the husband's authority. In *Tom Jones*, she argued, the attack on Jacobite tyranny was made through a criticism of Squire Western's arbitrary government of his daughter. Smallwood presents a Fielding who attacks the double standard of sexual morality and seeks a humane morality in which male and female qualities are not sharply differentiated.[10] Fielding's easy acceptance of the sexual desires of women, even heroines, has been noted in his favour by many critics; here the Richardson–Fielding contrast slips in again, for Fielding is strong on precisely the point where Richardsonian feminism, with its investment in female purity, is weak. Tiffany Potter argues that Fielding's more relaxed attitude to female sexuality is part of a complex of ideas she calls 'Georgian libertinism' – a kinder version of the Restoration variety, encouraging freedom where others are not harmed. As a result of this, he writes favourably of women seeking self-determination.[11] While work like Smallwood's and Potter's tends to play down the element of traditional misogyny in Fielding's representations of aggression in women, it is very valuable for restoring to critical sight the woman-friendly aspects of the writer. With a rather different emphasis, Jill Campbell has also challenged the Richardson–Fielding polarity, suggesting that we turn from the differences between the writers to an analysis of the 'differences within' them.[12] Her own discussion of the differences within Fielding draws attention to his interest in the blurring of gender distinctions, shown in the cross-gender casting of his plays, his treatment of male impersonation in *The Female Husband*, and in his movement from burlesque treatment of a woman in the hero's role in *Tom Thumb* to the serious development of an 'ideal of female heroism' in *Amelia*.[13] In this last novel she finds a recurring ambivalence, as Fielding moves between older codes of masculine honour and new sentimental conceptions of manhood, between allegiance to a new ideal of domestic femininity and fear of the independent female authority that might issue from it.[14]

A mixture of responses to female authority is indeed one key to Fielding. He wrote during a period when female cultural power was visible, highly contested, and especially associated with both the theatre, home of his early work, and the novel, the genre he did so much to develop. He began his life as an author in the late 1720s, during a period which Emma Clery has described as characterized by a resurgence of misogynist attitudes centred on an association of the new commercial economy with a debilitating feminization of culture.[15] The literary world was dominated by Alexander Pope, whose recently published *Dunciad* mocked Grub Street hacks as the sons of the Goddess Dulness, herself a hideous warning of the dangers of feminization. In fact one of Fielding's early pieces (never published) was a mock-epic attack on Pope; but he shared many literary attitudes with Pope and the Scriblerian writers, and the classical satirical tradition that influenced him and them exerted its pull in the direction of anti-feminism. At the same time a pragmatic acceptance of the cultural influence of particular women in the theatrical world – and close friendship with one of them – meant not only that he praised women as well as satirizing them, but that in his plays he created especially attractive comic female roles. His new career as a novelist in the 1740s began as a response to a particular deployment of the authority of femininity – Richardson's creation of the virtuous heroine, Pamela, who converts a rake to goodness through the power of her writing as much as her resistance to his advances. Although the polarization of Richardson and Fielding is misleading, the rivalry between them does not go away, and Fielding's later heroines, Sophia and Amelia, are framed in complex dialogue with Richardson's paragon, Clarissa.

All men writing in the mid-eighteenth-century period had to deal in some way with the fact that the world of letters was increasingly a mixed-sex world. Two of them, Samuel Richardson and Samuel Johnson, have been especially noticed for the professional help and encouragement they offered to a number of women writers. Henry Fielding did this too, but his experience of working with women differed from theirs in significant ways. His early career was marked by patronage from a socially powerful woman; he worked in association with actresses and women writers in the theatre; and he worked closely at times with his own sister, the novelist Sarah Fielding, whose relation to him rendered literal the nascent metaphor of the sister-author. An examination of Fielding's relations with Lady Mary Wortley Montagu, Catherine Clive, Eliza Haywood, Charlotte Charke, and Charlotte Lennox, as well as with Sarah Fielding, will show how he responded to various kinds of women's public cultural activity.

Lady Mary Wortley Montagu (1689–1762) was Fielding's second cousin. A woman of wealth and noble rank, well known for her learning, her Eastern travels and subsequent campaign to introduce smallpox inoculation to Britain, and her support for Walpole's ministry, Lady Mary was potentially a powerful patron for her younger, poorer, less well-connected relative. She gave him some help with his first play, *Love in Several Masques*, and he printed it with a dedication to her. As befitted the protégé of a woman famed for learning, he defended women's right to the life of the mind, telling her, 'You are capable of instructing the Pedant, and are at once a living Confutation of those morose Schoolmen who wou'd confine Knowledge to the Male Part of the Species, and a shining Instance of all those Perfections and softer Graces which Nature has confin'd to the Female.'[16] Fielding's mock-epic attack on the *Dunciad* was followed in 1733 by a further poem against Pope, this time in direct response to the poet's treatment of Lady Mary in *The First Satire of the Second Book of Horace*. In his 'Epistle to Mr Lyttleton', Fielding's praise of Lady Mary's wit is generalized into a feminist defence of women's intelligence:

> Man claims o'er Woman, by O'erbearing Might,
> A Pow'r which nature never meant his Right.
> If partial, She to either Sex inclin'd,
> With partial Care, she form'ed the female Mind.
> To greater Wisdom Men make false Pretence
> Nature with Beauty gave Superiour Sense.[17]

Fielding's praise for an intellectual woman was strategic; it contrasts with the more facetious treatment of this standard satirical target in *Tom Jones*, where Mrs Western's learning and 'masculine Person' combine to keep men away from her,[18] and *Amelia*, where Mr Atkinson just about manages to live happily with his learned wife, 'though he hath been sometimes obliged to pay proper Homage to her superior Understanding and Knowledge'.[19]

Fielding's theatrical career was marked by a strong association with one actress in particular, Catherine Clive, née Raftor, known as Kitty (1711–85). She began her stage career young and was a hit with Drury Lane audiences from the 1728–9 season onwards, excelling in comic roles and as a singer: Fielding claimed to have been one of the first to recognize her talents. She acted in many of Fielding's plays and he wrote a number of roles for her: hoydenish but innocent young women, scheming chambermaids. For the revived production of *The Author's Farce* in 1734, he expanded the part of Harriot with her talents in mind, giving the character a more ironic tone and adding songs to her repertoire.[20] She played the maid Lappet in his *The Miser* (1733), and in the same year he wrote a ballad opera, *Deborah: or a Wife for You All* to be performed as an afterpiece to *The Miser* on her benefit night: she took the title role, which was designed to display her singing.[21] *The Intriguing Chambermaid* (1734), another afterpiece, based on Jean François Regnard's *Le Retour Imprévu*, shows in its adaptation of its source her influence on his dramatic practice. Regnard's play features a clever valet; in Fielding's, his part is taken by the chambermaid Lettice.

This turn from male to female as centre of the action has been shown to be typical of Fielding's plays in general, and is attributed partly to the influence of Hogarth's prints, especially *The Harlot's Progress*, and partly to his interest in Clive's acting.[22] Clive inspired Fielding to create strong roles for young women. He dedicated *The Intriguing Chambermaid* to her, and continued to praise her acting long after he had left the stage himself. He appreciated how much her skill could improve an author's work: 'as she has a prodigious Fund of natural Spirit and Humour off the Stage, she makes the most of the Poet's on it. Nothing, though ever so barren, even though it exceeds the Limits of Nature, can be flat in her Hands'.[23] He considered her 'the best Actress of this, and perhaps of any preceeding Age'.[24] His praise not only elevated her among actresses but also elevated the profession of the actress itself, defining it in terms more often associated with male artists when he praised 'the vast Genius of Mrs *Clive*',[25] and placing her alongside Shakespeare and Hogarth, with Shakespeare representing the best of writing, Hogarth of painting, and Clive of acting.[26] He also, more conventionally, praised her for private feminine virtues, important for an actress's reputation at a time when the theatrical profession was moving towards respectability. Singling out especially her financial 'Support of an aged Father', he hailed her as acting, in real life, the parts of 'the best Wife, the best Daughter, the best Sister, and the best Friend'.[27]

Clive's combination of acting genius with the approved mode of femininity was not achieved by all actresses. Fielding also worked with Charlotte Charke (1713–60), who was to make her own signal failure to be 'the best Daughter' the centre of her 1755 autobiography; and he provided her with the opportunity for an extraordinary public display of an unusual father-daughter rivalry. Youngest daughter of Colley Cibber, Charke began her stage career early. Charke specialized in male roles, a common practice for many eighteenth-century actresses, but in her case evidently linked to personally felt concerns about gender identity. According to her autobiography she began dressing in men's clothes at the age of four when she borrowed her father's coat and wig. In later life she passed as a man for considerable periods, and as Charles Brown had a long-term relationship with a woman who went by the name of Mrs Brown. Fielding himself wrote about a similar case in *The Female Husband* (1746), based on the story of Mary Hamilton, who was tried and convicted for passing as a man and marrying a woman. In this text, Fielding's attitude to the male impersonation is clear and hostile. Charke's apparently similar transgression, in Kristina Straub's view, escaped prosecution and public condemnation through its ambiguity: it could be read as an actress's performance rather than an actionable fraud.[28] However, during Charke's association with Fielding, in 1734–6, the question of Charke as 'female husband' had not yet arisen. At issue was her impersonation of men on stage: a very different matter, and one that could be exploited to humiliate her father.

Charke's association with Fielding began after a stormy early career which included joining her brother Theophilus's rebellion against the Drury Lane management, returning to Drury Lane, quarrelling with its then manager, Fleetwood, founding her own short-lived company of players, and writing a satire on Fleetwood for them to perform.[29] Returning once more to Drury Lane after her father's intercession with Fleetwood, she soon left again to join Fielding, at this time opening his own company at the Haymarket. His first play there was *Pasquin*, featuring a satirical treatment of Colley Cibber, now poet laureate, as Lord Place. At one point, Place remarks that he doesn't know what an ode is, 'but I know you may be qualified for the Place [of poet laureate] without being a Poet'.[30] Originally played by Richard Yates, the role of Lord Place was given to Charlotte Charke as her company debut, on the eleventh night of the play's run. As she relates the incident, 'Mr *Fielding* begged the Favour of [Yates] . . . to make room for me': evidently he was keen to secure the daughter's services in sharpening the mockery of her father.[31] According to Cibber's biographer, it was this impersonation that precipitated the final break between father and daughter. Cibber never spoke to Charke again.[32] Charke continued with Fielding at the Haymarket, appearing in various roles. In 1737 she played in *The Historical Register* as Christopher Hen (based on the auctioneer Christopher Cock). It was said that she also sang the song 'Ode to the New Year' in the person of Medley – another send-up of Cibber.[33]

Charke's mimicry of her father had earlier precedents in her life, as the autobiography's early dressing-up incident shows. *A Narrative of the Life of Mrs Charlotte Charke* became a further act of mimicry, recalling as it does her father's own *Apology for the Life of Mr Colley Cibber*: her work is a strange mixture of parody, reproach, and unsuccessful reconciliation attempt. Here, too, there is a connection with Fielding, whose spoof autobiography of her brother Theophilus had been an earlier use of Cibber's autobiographical mode (and of his undutiful children) against him. For Charke, her connection with Fielding allowed for public display of her mingled hostility to and wish to emulate her father. For Fielding, she was a useful weapon in his satirical armoury against Cibber. The playwright who praised Kitty Clive as a loving daughter to her father was not above exploiting Charlotte Charke's fraught relationship with hers.

Another actress who worked at Fielding's Haymarket theatre was Eliza Haywood (1693?–1756), who played Mrs Screen in *The Historical Register* and the Muse in *Eurydice Hiss'd*.[34] The final performance of these plays before Fielding closed the theatre, on 23 May 1737, was a benefit performance for Haywood, billed as 'Mrs Haywood the Muse, Author of Love in Excess, and many other entertaining Pieces'.[35] Haywood was, in fact, much better known as an author than as an actress. She had written several plays (none of them very successful) and in collaboration with William Hatchett had written *The Opera of Operas*, an adaptation of Fielding's *Tragedy of Tragedies* with music and songs, which had a successful run in 1733. She was best known, though, as a novelist, whose popular early work *Love in Excess* (1719) had been followed by a string of short fictions in the 1720s. Detractors and admirers alike placed Haywood in a female line of amatory fiction, following Aphra Behn and Delarivier Manley. It was as a novelist that Haywood was first noticed by Fielding. In *The Author's Farce* (1730) she is satirized as Mrs Novel, one of the popular authors and entertainers who appear in an underworld setting in Luckless's puppet show. Mrs Novel pretends to be a maiden who has (like Violetta in *Love in Excess*) died for love, but it turns out that she died in childbed after suffering (like many Haywood heroines) seduction and desertion. She is reunited in death with her lover, Signior Opera. Though these digs at Haywood's romantic plots are mingled with a glance at her personal reputation, the treatment of Mrs Novel was nowhere near as nasty as Pope's presentation of Haywood in Book II of the *Dunciad*, where she was featured as the prize in a pissing contest between Curll and Chetwood.[36] Indeed, the most significant thing about the identification of Haywood as Mrs Novel is probably that it shows how Haywood's prominence as a novelist in the 1720s had consolidated the general understanding of the novel as a woman writer's genre. While other forms of entertainment – tragedy, comedy, opera, oratory, and pantomime – are represented in the play by male figures, Mrs Novel indicates women's place in the trade of authorship.

When he created Mrs Novel, Fielding had no thought of being a novelist himself. A decade later, in his new guise as fictional historian, he gave more serious attention to delineating the faults of the popular novel, and though he did not name Haywood in his critical pronouncements, J. R. Elwood has shown how many of them could be understood as containing a reference to her.[37] Writing *Joseph Andrews*, he was careful to distinguish his own fictional enterprise both from the Richardsonian novel of heroinely virtue and the Behn-Manley-Haywood tradition of women's romantic/scandalous fiction that Richardson himself repudiated. His famous claim to be writing a 'comic Epic-Poem in Prose' provided his fiction with a classical literary heritage, his imitation of Cervantes with a more recent one.[38] Defending such fictional writers as Cervantes and Le Sage, who may make factual mistakes but whose understanding of human nature is to be trusted, he specifically excluded from his encomium 'those Persons of surprising Genius, the Authors of immense Romances, or the modern novel and *Atalantis* Writers; who without any Assistance from Nature or History, record Persons who never were, or will be, and Facts which never did nor possibly can happen: Whose Heroes are of their own Creation, and their Brains the Chaos whence all their Materials are collected'.[39] Haywood, one of the best-known modern novel writers and often associated with Manley, author of the *New Atalantis*, is among Fielding's targets here. In *Tom Jones*, written after Haywood had responded to the narrative blossoming of the 1740s with new narrative experiments of her own, there is a sharper attempt to sort good fiction from bad. In a chapter entitled 'Of those who lawfully may, and of those who may not write such Histories as this', Fielding points to his own practice of writing introductory critical chapters as a mark distinguishing genuine work from false, a mark made necessary in an age threatened with 'a Swarm of foolish Novels, and monstrous Romances'; and he compares himself 'the ingenious Author of the Spectator' who, he claims, included Greek and Latin mottoes on the same principal of distinguishing himself from inferior imitators, talentless writers who might nevertheless 'assume the same Titles with the greatest Genius'.[40] This seems to glance at Haywood's recent writing – she had had a successful run with her periodical *The Female Spectator* from 1744 to 1746 – and perhaps to imply that the unworthy imitator of the *Spectator* is equally unworthy as a fictional historian.

Haywood, by this time author of *The Fortunate Foundlings* (1744) and *Life's Progress Through the Passions* (1747), may well have understood this passage in *Tom Jones* as intended to shut her out from those who 'lawfully may' write the new fictional history. If she did, she was not deterred. Her next novel, *The History of Miss Betsy Thoughtless* (1751), is 'a Fieldingesque exercise in social/moral commentary'[41] which specifically follows and revises *Tom Jones* in its choice of an imprudent but good-hearted heroine, instead of hero, as the centre of a series of comic adventures. Far from acknowledging Fielding as her mentor here, Haywood sets her scene in the mid-1730s and takes the opportunity to refer disparagingly to 'the little theatre in the Hay-market, then known by the name of F–g's scandal shop', thus ignoring Fielding as novelist and placing him as mere antiministerial dramatist who later managed to 'wriggle himself into favour'.[42] Fielding perhaps responded to Haywood's attack on him by calling B–T– (probably Betsy Thoughtless) to account in the *Covent-Garden Journal*, accused of dullness. Acquitted, on the grounds that as a citizen of Grub Street she is rightfully dull, B–T– is neatly placed in the world of the *Dunciad*, where Haywood herself had been lampooned.[43]

Fielding's comments on foolish modern novels and romances served to distinguish by contrast a learned tradition of fictional history for which male writers like himself would set the standard. Reviewers followed his lead, seeing Fielding himself, Smollett, and other men as the best exemplars of fictional practice, to the detriment of women novelists' reputations. For instance, his recommendation of the introductory chapter as a mark of good fiction was adopted by the *Monthly* reviewer who criticized *Betsy Thoughtless* for failing to provide such chapters, 'which distinguish the work of a Fielding, a Smollett, or the author of Pompey the little'.[44] This is not to say that Fielding wished to keep good writing as a male preserve. His disparagement of modern novel and *Atalantis* writers was matched by support for a younger generation of women novelists whose work he recognized as taking part in the prestigious fictional tradition he himself had named. The *Covent-Garden Journal* remarks on B– T– say nothing about Betsy beyond that she is dull. By contrast, a few weeks later the journal ran a detailed appraisal of another recent novel, *The Female Quixote* (1752) by Charlotte Lennox (1729/30?–1804). This was an imitation of *Don Quixote* with a female protagonist, misled by the feminocentric seventeenth-century romances instead of by the adventures of chivalry. Thus Lennox joined Fielding as an imitator of Cervantes and joined a tradition of fiction as parody of romance. There was considerable significance in a female author's writing of a female Quixote. Where women novelists like Behn, Manley, and Haywood, in Fielding's view, offered merely debased versions of feminocentric romance, a woman who parodied romance crossed the line to join a more knowing, learned, comic, and implicitly masculine tradition. By laughing at a romance-obsessed heroine, she offered a critique of female behaviour that seemed all the more valid for coming from a female authority.

Fielding accords Lennox's novel the dignity of direct comparison with *Don Quixote*, and if he pronounced Cervantes the superior author as an original, as a sharper satirist of existing follies, and as creating better characters, he found Lennox his equal in blending affection for the characters with exposure of their folly, and superior to him in realism, regularity of design, and the creation of an endearing central character.[45] Both the superiority and the inferiority of Lennox's novel are linked to the gender of its protagonist. Cervantes's male protagonist offers greater scope for action and hence comic situations; on the other hand it is more plausible for a young woman than an old man to have a head turned by romances, and young women are more attractive and endearing than old men. Lennox clearly represents for Fielding a particular kind of female authority: not, as in the popular understanding of Behn, Manley, and Haywood, an erotic authority based on unrealistic plot and sensational treatment of character, but an authority that came of sharing male tradition and offering a complementary version of it. An important part of the woman writer's contribution is her critique of women: Lennox 'hath taken such Care throughout her Work, to expose all those Vices and Follies in her Sex which are chiefly predominant in our days, that it will afford very useful Lessons to all those young Ladies who will peruse it with proper Attention'.[46]

This kind of acceptable female authority was best exemplified for Fielding by the work of his own sister. Sarah Fielding (1710–68) had begun her writing career by working with her brother in the early 1740s, providing pieces written in a woman's voice to add to his works; later, he provided prefatory material and contributed letters to some of hers. Her first publication is generally agreed to be the letter from Leonora to Horatio inserted in *Joseph Andrews* as 'written by a young Lady'.[47] She also probably wrote, or part-wrote, the narrative of Anna Boleyn's life in *Journey from this World to the Next*. J. F. Burrows, using stylometric analysis, concludes that both brother and sister contributed to this chapter, with Henry supplying beginning and ending, and Sarah the middle.[48] Henry Fielding himself explained this narrative as 'writ in a Woman's Hand: and tho' the Observations in it are, I think, as excellent as any in the whole Volume, there seems to be a Difference in Style between this and the preceeding Chapters; and as it is the Character of a Woman which is related, I am inclined to fancy it was really written by one of that Sex'.[49] Here, a woman's writing is seen as complementary to a man's, different in style and showing special understanding of female character. Soon after this Sarah Fielding published her first novel, *The Adventures of David Simple* (1744), centring on a male protagonist, and offering an early analysis of the man of feeling and his relationship to an unfeeling world. Her brother, however, treated it as a woman's commentary on women. Citing a 'Lady of very high Rank' (probably Lady Mary Wortley Montagu) who claimed that *David Simple* 'could not have been written by a Man', he explained that this was because only a woman could understand a woman's conduct: women are educated 'in Constraint of, nay, in direct Opposition to, Truth and Nature' and are therefore bound to deceive men.[50] Sarah Fielding, he claimed, had exposed in *David Simple* 'some of these nicer Female Foibles, which have escaped most other Writers', and she may be subject to 'the resentment of her own lovely Sex ... for having betrayed the Secrets of the Society'.[51]

There are two aspects to Fielding's praise of women's writing, which tend to pull against each other. On the one hand, there is respect for a different, specifically feminine viewpoint. Only women can truly understand women, so their writing offers something a man's cannot: if Fielding wants to express the views of a Leonora or an Anna Boleyn, he turns to his sister for help. On the other hand, this distinctive viewpoint is best employed in satire upon women by those who best understand their follies. In Henry Fielding's praise, Lennox's and Sarah Fielding's work are both absorbed into a satiric masculine tradition. He describes *David Simple* as a comic epic like *Joseph Andrews*, and classes it with Butler's *Hudibras* and Cervantes's *Don Quixote* as an epic of serial action.[52] These two aspects are united by being deployed as weapons in Fielding's rivalry with Richardson and his critique of Richardsonian writing. In his Preface to Sarah Fielding's *Familiar Letters*, her brother notes that some men disagree that women are the best authorities on women: they are men 'who are not only absolute Masters of some poor Woman's Person, but likewise of her Thoughts'.[53] This glances at Richardson, famous for his presentation of Pamela's voice and innermost thoughts, and characterizes the Richardsonian claim of insight into the female heart as a form of male tyranny. Equally, the stress on both Sarah Fielding and Charlotte Lennox as satirists in his own tradition pointedly ignores the connections of both novelists with Richardson: Sarah Fielding's interest in the analysis of human motivation already linked her early work with Richardson's, while Lennox included high praise of *Clarissa* in her *Female Quixote*. Henry Fielding's praise of these women novelists serves, in part, to further his own rivalry with Richardson.

Henry Fielding worked variously with women who were taking on cultural authority in Georgian England. For Eliza Haywood, whom, despite the changes to her work, he treated as a representative of the amatory fiction he and other mid-century authors had rendered decisively outmoded, he had only mockery. Charlotte Charke's striking attempts to undermine or take over her father's authority he encouraged for his own satirical purposes. The kind of public female authority he really approved of, though, was the sort he believed to be exemplified by Kitty Clive, Sarah Fielding, and Charlotte Lennox – an authority based on the use of acting or writing talents to reveal female character in a way men could not. Clive's ability to display female folly on stage, Sarah Fielding's and Lennox's to expose it in narrative, drew his admiration. In this way women as actresses or writers could be assimilated into the prestigious, male-dominated tradition of satire, while remaining in a separate, clearly complementary role. If this is a limited and limiting role for women, it should also be recognized that Fielding was willing to be influenced by female authority, from creating lively comic roles for women because he could envisage what Clive would make of them, to using ideas from his sister's fiction. Here, indeed, he tacitly acknowledged that her contribution was not confined to satire on women: in *Tom Jones* he developed the situation of rivalry between a good-hearted and a malevolent brother that she had made the starting point for *David Simple*.

The women discussed here were unusual in their creation of female public authority in an age when women were supposed to shine in private life alone. A word should also be said about Fielding's debt to a woman whose virtue in private life was in tune with the growing ideology of domesticity: his first wife, Charlotte Cradock, the inspiration for Sophia Western and Amelia Booth. On one occasion, writing publicly of her, he abandoned the idea of satire as the touchstone for female authority and allowed for the authority of feeling. In an essay 'Of the Remedy of Affliction for the Loss of our Friends', he recollected her words on their daughter Charlotte:

> I remember the most excellent of Women, and tenderest of Mothers, when, after a painful and dangerous Delivery, she was told she had a Daughter, answering; *Good God! I have produced a Creature who is to undergo what I have suffered!* Some Years afterwards, I heard the same Woman, on the Death of that very Child, then one of the loveliest Creatures ever seen, comforting herself with reflecting, that *her Child could never know what it was to feel such a Loss as she then lamented.*[54]

Charlotte Cradock Fielding is here given a rare public voice, not to expose the follies of her sex, but to lament women's vulnerability in childbirth and as mothers. Her exemplary philosophy in the face of loss highlights the poignancy of that vulnerability. The authority of the loving, suffering, domestic woman is deployed here by her husband to combine stoic and Christian consolation with an expression of his own grief.

## NOTES

1. Martin C. Battestin and Clive T. Probyn, eds., *The Correspondence of Henry and Sarah Fielding* (Oxford: Clarendon Press, 1993), 111.
2. A. L. Barbauld, ed., *The Correspondence of Samuel Richardson*, 6 vols. (London: Richard Philips, 1804), vol. II, 77–8.
3. J. Carroll, ed., *Selected Letters of Samuel Richardson* (Oxford: Clarendon Press, 1964), 143.
4. James Boswell, *Life of Johnson*, ed. R. W. Chapman, corr. J. D. Fleeman (Oxford: Oxford University Press, 1970), 389.
5. Samuel Taylor Coleridge, *Marginalia*, vol. II ed. George Whalley (Princeton, NJ: Princeton University Press, 1984), 693.
6. W. B. Carnochan, 'A Matter *Discutable*: The Rise of the Novel', *Eighteenth-Century Fiction* 12:2–3, *Reconsidering the Rise of the Novel* (2000), 166, 178.
7. Robert Etheridge Moore, 'Dr Johnson on Fielding and Richardson', *PMLA* 66:2 (1951), 172.
8. Katharine M. Rogers, 'Sensitive Feminism vs. Conventional Sympathy: Richardson and Fielding on Women', *Novel: A Forum on Fiction* 9:3 (1976), 256–70.
9. Angela J. Smallwood, *Fielding and the Woman Question: The Novels of Henry Fielding and Feminist Debate 1700–1750* (Hemel Hempstead: Harvester Wheatsheaf, 1989), 3.
10. Ibid., 69, 88.
11. Tiffany Potter, *Honest Sins: Georgian Libertinism and the Plays and Novels of Henry Fielding* (Montreal and Kingston: McGill-Queen's University Press, 1999), 11, 135.
12. Jill Campbell, *Natural Masques: Gender and Identity in Fielding's Plays and Novels* (Stanford, CA: Stanford University Press, 1995), 9.
13. Ibid., 2.
14. Ibid., 212–13.

15. Emma J. Clery, *The Feminization Debate in Eighteenth-Century England: Literature, Commerce and Luxury* (Basingstoke: Palgrave Macmillan, 2004), 51–73.
16. Henry Fielding, *Plays*, volume I, ed. Thomas Lockwood (Oxford: Clarendon Press, 2004), 19.
17. Isobel Grundy, 'New Verse by Henry Fielding', *PMLA* 87:2 (1972), 240–1.
18. Henry Fielding, *The History of Tom Jones*, ed. Martin C. Battestin and Fredson Bowers (Oxford: Clarendon Press, 1974), 273; VI.ii.
19. Henry Fielding, *Amelia*, ed. Martin C. Battestin (Oxford: Clarendon Press, 1983), 533; XII. ix.
20. Henry Fielding, *Plays*, vol. I, 200–1.
21. Martin C. Battestin with Ruthe R. Battestin, *Henry Fielding: A Life* (London and New York: Routledge, 1989), 164–5.
22. Ronald Paulson, *The Life of Henry Fielding: A Critical Biography* (Oxford: Blackwell, 2000), 95.
23. [Henry Fielding,] *Apology for the Life of Theophilus Cibber*, cited in P. H. Highfill, K. A. Burnim, and E. A. Langhans, *A Biographical Dictionary of Actors, Actresses, Musicians, Dancers, Managers and Other Stage Personnel in London, 1660–1800* (Carbondale and Edwardsville: Southern Illinois University Press, 1975), vol. III, 359.
24. *The Champion*, 15 March 1739–40, in *Contributions to 'The Champion' and Related Writings*, ed. W. B. Coley (Oxford: Clarendon Press, 2003), 237.
25. This praise is given by the character Valentine in one of the letters Fielding contributed to his sister's second novel. Sarah Fielding, *Familiar Letters between the Characters in 'David Simple'* (London: A. Millar, 1747), vol. II, 30.
26. In *Amelia*, 43; I.vi, describing Miss Mathews, he writes: 'Such indeed was her Image, that neither could *Shakespeare* describe, nor *Hogarth* paint, nor *Clive* act a Fury in higher Perfection.'
27. Fielding, 'An Epistle to Mrs Clive', in *The Intriguing Chambermaid* (London, 1734), n.pag.
28. Kristina Straub, 'The Guilty Pleasures of Female Theatrical Cross-Dressing and the Autobiography of Charlotte Charke', in *Body Guards: The Cultural Politics of Gender Ambiguity*, ed. Julia Epstein and Kristina Straub (New York: Routledge, 1991), 158–60.
29. For Charke's career see Fidelis Morgan, *The Well-Known Troublemaker: A Life of Charlotte Charke* (London: Faber, 1988) and Highfill, Burnim, and Langhans, *A Biographical Dictionary*, vol. III, 167–78.
30. Henry Fielding, *Pasquin: A Dramatick Satire on the Times* (London: J. Watts, 1746), 19.
31. Charlotte Charke, *A Narrative of the Life of Mrs Charlotte Charke* (1755; Gainesville, FL: Scholars' Facsimiles and Reprints, 1969), 63.
32. Helene Koon, *Colley Cibber: A Biography* (Lexington: University Press of Kentucky, 1986), 141.
33. Battestin, *Henry Fielding*, 219.
34. For Haywood's biography see Christine Blouch, 'Eliza Haywood and the Romance of Obscurity', *Studies in English Literature 1500–1900* 31:3 (1991), 535–52.
35. Marcia Heinemann, 'Eliza Haywood's Career in the Theatre', *Notes and Queries* 218 (1973), 13.

36. John Butt, ed., *The Dunciad*, in *The Poems of Alexander Pope* (London: Methuen, 1963), 385; II.153–9.
37. John R. Elwood, 'Henry Fielding and Eliza Haywood: A Twenty Year War', *Albion* 5:3 (1973), 184–92.
38. Henry Fielding, *Joseph Andrews*, ed. Martin C. Battestin (Oxford: Clarendon Press, 1967), 4; Preface.
39. Ibid., 187; III.i.
40. Fielding, *Tom Jones*, 486–7; IX.i.
41. John Richetti, 'Histories by Eliza Haywood and Henry Fielding: Imitation and Adaptation', in *The Passionate Fictions of Eliza Haywood: Essays on Her Life and Work*, ed. Kirsten T. Saxton and Rebecca P. Bocchicchio (Lexington: University of Kentucky Press, 2000), 249.
42. Eliza Haywood, *The History of Miss Betsy Thoughtless*, ed. Beth Fowkes Tobin (Oxford: Oxford University Press, 1997), 45–6; I.viii.
43. Henry Fielding, *'The Covent-Garden Journal' and 'A Plan of the Universal Register-Office'*, ed. Bertrand A. Goldgar (Oxford: Clarendon Press, 1988), 109–12.
44. Elwood, 'Henry Fielding and Eliza Haywood', 189.
45. Fielding, *The Covent-Garden Journal*, 159–61.
46. Ibid., 161.
47. Fielding, *Joseph Andrews*, 106; II.iv.
48. J. F. Burrows and A. J. Hassall, 'Anna Boleyn and the Authenticity of Fielding's Feminine Narratives', *Eighteenth-Century Studies* 21 (1988), 444.
49. *Miscellanies by Henry Fielding, Esq.*, vol. II, ed. Hugh Amory (Oxford: Clarendon Press, 1993), 111.
50. Henry Fielding, Preface to Sarah Fielding, *Familiar Letters*, vol. I, xvi–xvii.
51. Ibid., xix–xx, xix.
52. Henry Fielding, Preface to 2nd edn, in Sarah Fielding, *The Adventures of David Simple, and The Adventures of David Simple, Volume the Last*, ed. Peter Sabor (Lexington: University Press of Kentucky, 1998), 345–6.
53. Sarah Fielding, *Familiar Letters*, vol. I, xviii–xix.
54. *Miscellanies by Henry Fielding, Esq.*, vol. I, ed. Henry Knight Miller (Oxford: Clarendon Press, 1972), 224.

# 10

PAT ROGERS

# Fielding on society, crime, and the law

Fielding established himself as a writer before he embarked on his legal studies, and he had achieved success in the novel before he became a magistrate. Nevertheless, issues related to crime and the law underlay his entire career as an author, even in his earlier days as a dramatist and journalist. For much of the 1730s, he had practised the often reviled trade of a professional scribbler, and on several occasions found himself in the line of ministerial fire because of his Oppositional broadsides against officialdom. At the end of the decade his social position was more respectable, even though his finances remained on a precarious footing and his debts brought him into the courtroom as a defendant rather than an advocate. By the time *Tom Jones* was published, he held a central position in the judicial system of London, as chief magistrate for Westminster. This may look like a sudden swerve, but it was not altogether an unpredictable development. His family background, for one thing, included distinguished jurists. Nevertheless, his ancestry also embraced a number of soldiers, and Fielding did not join the army; it also covered some notable churchmen, and he did not enter holy orders. Some explanation is called for, since a variety of personal and political factors must have gone into his decision to switch the course of his life.

As soon as Fielding was appointed to the magistracy, he naturally took a central role in the national discourse regarding legal and social affairs. The area of his responsibility covered some of the most notorious blackspots in the entire country, with a thriving criminal subculture and a pattern of unrest marked by frequent riots. In addition, Fielding did more than serve as a proactive Justice of the Peace in the capital. He wrote widely on matters of public policy, as they were affected by the law and by the institutions which supported its implementation: pamphlets, charges to the jury, and articles in the press flowed from his pen during the brief tenure of his magistracy. Of course, his novels deal centrally with some of the same issues, as they had done from the start. Equally, his comic masterpiece, *Jonathan Wild*, touches (albeit with satiric obliquity) on authentic issues regarding crime in London which had not disappeared since the real-life Wild stalked the streets a generation earlier.

Most of Fielding's pronouncements relate to topical circumstances, such as an apparent wave of violent robberies, a riot in the streets, or a controversial 'missing persons' case. However, the cast of mind underlying the writing of these works is philosophic as well as pragmatic. While Fielding was a practical reformer and active participant in day-to-day controversial discourse, he was also a deeply reflective man, with a fuller knowledge of humane learning – history, literature ancient and modern, and political theory – than almost all of his colleagues on the bench. Even if he had never written his plays or his fiction, his remaining oeuvre would still interest students of early Hanoverian England, because it discusses the controversies of the time through the prism of a thoughtful attitude towards society and a well-stocked mind. One other complicating factor enters into the equation. The failed Jacobite rebellion led by Prince Charles Edward Stuart ('Bonny Prince Charlie') in 1745–6 was not primarily a legal phenomenon: its roots lay in nationalist and constitutional affairs and in religious divisions. However, the means by which the regime defended itself from invasion, the way in which it put down the rising, and the manner in which captured Jacobites were tried and punished did excite general debate. Fielding had something to say on these issues, as he did on so many subjects related to crime and punishment – prisons, the state of the poor, charity, the problem of gin abuse, the game laws, and much else.

This chapter will explore many of the topics just mentioned, in the light both of what Fielding wrote and of what he did as a serving magistrate. Firstly, it is necessary for a full understanding of the issues at stake to have some knowledge of the historical context of crime, an area of study revolutionized in the past twenty-five years.[1] Secondly, we must look in detail at Fielding's substantive contributions to penology, that is the non-fictional texts he produced as a Justice of the Peace for Westminster and Middlesex. These discussions should help to illuminate his practice in major 'literary' works.

## Criminal justice in London

In the early Hanoverian age it was widely thought that crime had reached a new pitch of intensity: people in most ages have felt the same. Yet there were rational grounds for believing that social unrest posed an increasing threat, especially in the capital. Even if the crime waves Fielding wrote about were in some measure a matter of perception rather than objective reality (the statistics do not show a simple graph of upward progression), there was enough reality in them to warrant serious concern. For one thing, a polite and commercial nation could no longer endure some of the blatant evils which had gone on more or less unchecked in earlier centuries. For another, demographic changes had outrun the administrative capacity of a system based on medieval and Tudor institutions. Thirdly, sheer growth meant that the law encountered a different scale, if not always a different kind, of problems in its operations.

Fielding's purview as a magistrate incorporated one of the most troublesome regions in the country, although it covered only a matter of a few square miles. It excluded the historic city within the walls, as well as the city 'without the walls', including well-known parts of the town such as the area around Fleet Street – that is the district of Farringdon Ward Without, which had its own abundant share of crime. The parishes on the south side of the Thames, in Surrey, also lay outside the magistrate's writ. Sometimes this demarcation of responsibility caused practical problems, as constables in the act of hot pursuit could hardly expect their quarries to give themselves up when the chase reached Temple Bar. But Fielding had enough problems on his hands with the regions over which he did preside. Metropolitan Middlesex stretched out north and east of the historic city. A motley collection of settlements reached further eastwards along the river: the formerly sprawling parish of Stepney had been split into a number of smaller units in the first four decades of the eighteenth century, without easing their varied social problems very directly. Closer to Fielding's base lay half a dozen out-parishes belonging to Middlesex, of which the most notable included St Giles's in the Fields, St Andrew's Holborn, and St Botolph's – a ring of densely inhabited neighbourhoods with a cluster of criminal ghettoes in their midst.

As for Westminster, this contained just nine parishes (disregarding a number of small 'liberties' attached to places like historic churches and palaces), but among them were growing areas with a high crime rate. Some of these were situated near the present-day palace of Westminster and Whitehall: others occupied what would later become known as the West End, and adjoined the trouble-spots of Middlesex. Here, the inhabitants of St Martin's in the Fields, St Clement Dane, and St Paul's, Covent Garden, by themselves brewed up business that could have filled the hours of a whole panel of fulltime magistrates, never mind that of a single dedicated justice. Some amusingly stylized vignettes of low life in the red-light district appear in Fielding's mock-heroic play *The Covent-Garden Tragedy* (1732), set in the brothel of Mother Punchbowl. The author's second cousin, and one-time collaborator on a mock-*Dunciad*, Lady Mary Wortley Montagu, had these very quarters of the town in mind when she wrote of his having lived in his days of struggle 'sometimes in a wretched garret without necessaries; not to speak of the sponging-houses and hiding-places where he was occasionally to be found'. (She added that 'the highest of his preferment' extended to no more than 'raking in the lowest sinks of vice and misery'.) Now it would be Fielding's job to seek out wrongdoers in just the same environment.[2] He had of course moved also among the wealthy and well connected: but though this was a necessary condition of the social span of his novels, it mattered much less for the magistrate, as crime was then defined and regulated.

Before the Industrial Revolution, the growth of urban community posed problems unique to London. It contained about a tenth of the national population, and almost half the wealth as measured by the value of its building stock. Thus the city became a place where it was easy to aspire to riches and easy to fall into abject poverty. By comparison with cities elsewhere in Britain, the capital had a very large proportion of immigrants from other parts of the country and from abroad. Additionally, more of the residents were young and unmarried, and within this cohort there was an unusually high ratio of males to females. All these factors conspired to turn London into a fertile breeding ground for crime, as well as a dynamic agent of economic growth, as 'rich and poor, landed and landless, apprentices and servants, flooded to the capital in pursuit of power, social standing, trade, employment and stimulation of the intellectual, aesthetic, and bodily kinds'.[3] Many of the dilemmas which Fielding encountered on the bench, and which he wrote about in his pamphlets, stemmed from these aspects of the sociology of London.

According to conventional wisdom, the scale of lawlessness was determined less by structural factors than by the moral standing of the criminal classes, that is to say the poor. One bugbear took the form of 'luxury', otherwise the tendency, among labouring people especially, to indulge in licentious pastimes such as gambling and drinking. Even Fielding, not averse to the pursuit of pleasure, was sucked into this favourite area of homily, and unlike his contemporary Samuel Johnson he gave credit to the notion that 'idleness' was the prevailing vice of the masses, with the corollary that sensible public policy should be designed to support the 'industrious' poor at the expense of their workshy brethren. Shading into this debate was the problem of the abuse of gin-drinking. Ever since the 1720s, it had become apparent that heavy consumption of gin was localized in particular regions, with a marked concentration of spirit-shops in the parts of London where other nuisances such as alehouses, gambling dens, and prostitution flourished. With some confusion of cause and effect, a campaign was led by the Middlesex justices to expunge the evil from their territory: they led the movement for parliamentary legislation, passed in 1729, 1736, and 1743.

Some measures attempted to stifle demand, some to control supply; but neither kind worked. The impetus for change had been accelerated by social unrest: the measure of 1736 had been made inoperable by riots, or the threat of riots, with mock-funerals to celebrate 'Madam Geneva's lying-in state'. Illicit stills went on producing, as they did during Prohibition in America; those who informed were ruthlessly eliminated; and the magistrates found themselves powerless in the face of widespread intimidation. It occasions no surprise to find that the 'mob' controlling this resistance had a strong base in the precise corners of the town where Fielding would soon come to exercise his authority. More rioting followed in 1743. Finally, in 1751 a more radical measure went through parliament (24 Geo. II, c. 40), which attempted to put into practice the magistrate's own aim, that is to drive gin 'beyond the Reach of the Vulgar' (*Enquiry* 91). This legislation proved more effective, though Fielding did not live long enough to witness many of its effects at first hand.

Fielding was not alone in making genuine attempts to deal with the very real problems afflicting London. Many such efforts at reform, control, or suppression foundered on the rock of corruption. In a system where patronage was endemic, and where appointments to the bench (like Fielding's own) went to politically approved candidates, the magistracy could not be expected to act with totally clean hands. Many believed that Fielding's predecessor Sir Thomas de Veil (1684–1746) had kept his finger in a nutritious pie by taking hush-money, questionable fees, and downright bribes. Among his profitable sinecures was the post of Inspector-General of Imports and Exports. He certainly received payments out of the royal bounty, effectively the secret service funds, and his work as a gang-buster earned him a government subsidy. If so, he got further up the ladder of promotion than Fielding ever did. De Veil became a Colonel of the Westminster Militia, he held office as a Justice of the Peace in four counties besides Westminster, and he regularly sat with the judges in the Old Bailey: finally in 1744 he gained a knighthood. Perhaps he deserved as much, for his stand against those exploiting the cravings of gin-dependent masses, a course of action which required physical courage on many occasions. One of the organizations he destroyed was the Black Boy Alley gang, a collection of men and women in the vicinity of Smithfield with names straight from *The Beggar's Opera* like Gentleman Harry, Barefoot, and Captain Poney: they presented as serious a threat as any group Fielding would face. But it is unlikely that de Veil kept his hands totally clean, when members of the government had their own share of kick-backs. Fielding never held a lucrative sinecure: he earned his keep as a magistrate and working writer. Of course, despite his considerable legal knowledge and years of hands-on experience, he would not reach the upper ranks of the judiciary, nor did he receive a knighthood.

Lower down the pecking order, corruption was more obvious if not more rife. The post of the City Marshal generally went to persons without many scruples, as in the case of Charles Hitchen (*c.* 1675–1727), a one-time associate of Jonathan Wild whose semi-criminal activities must have been known to Fielding when he wrote his mock-biography. Wild was only the most prominent in a wide array of thief-takers, many located in the vicinity of Drury Lane: these were men who arranged for crimes to be committed and then sold the perpetrators to law enforcement for blood money. Court proceedings were suborned by 'knights of the post', and delayed by mysteriously absent witnesses, while justice was derailed by the limited range of options open to defendants (which did not in general include a right to counsel). And corruption spread even as far as juries, to whom all paid lip-service as a bastion of English liberties, since the panel could be rigged or loaded with sympathizers.

Some historians have interpreted the entire system as a ruling-class conspiracy masquerading as a genuine operation of criminal justice. The view has not been accepted by the majority of scholars, who have pointed to the checks and balances by which some of the rigours of the law could be mitigated, and by which the court-room could provide a relatively level playing-field, granted the inequalities which prevailed outside the compass of law in the wider society. Fuller investigation of the day-to-day workings of legal institutions has shown that the system contained many fair-minded and hard-working people, who attempted to carry out their duties honourably in the face of huge social problems presented by the new urbanized environment. Justice Thrasher in *Amelia* displays no such urge to deal equitably with the men and women who come before him, and he was not alone in this (as I argue below). But in his magisterial capacity Fielding himself met the best standards of the time, even if his conduct does not stand up to meticulous scrutiny on every occasion (whose would?), and his judicial philosophy lagged behind the most advanced thinking of the Enlightenment.

Most scholars have reached the conclusion that from about 1750 the quality of life improved, gradually and hesitantly, for most Londoners. There was some modest progress in lighting and sanitation, public drunkenness declined after the 1751 Gin Act, and though there would be street riots on political issues in years to come, one common occasion for such disturbances (the divide over the Jacobite claimant to the throne) had been removed for good in 1746. Most important, a serious effort had been made to get to grips with organized crime. Where advances in social and penal matters occurred, Fielding generally had a leading share in bringing them about. The resources available to him were limited, both financially and institutionally. As regards the punishments he could mete out from the bench, he still had a pitifully narrow range of options: virtually no custodial sentences, and instead an array of blunt instruments – hanging, transportation, the pillory, whipping through the streets, 'corrective' labour in Bridewell, and so on. Most felonies were potentially hanging offences. Few of these sanctions proved effective deterrents, and none had a serious reformative purpose. Moreover, Fielding had to implement some laws which were controversial at the time and have remained so, notably the Riot Act of 1714 (1 Geo. I, c. 2, s. 5), as used in the Penlez episode, and the Black Act of 1723 (9 Geo. I, c. 22), a catch-all provision imposing severe penalties for offences against persons or property which may appear quite small today. Most of those who have undertaken a careful study of the way in which he dispensed the law conclude that he emerges with credit. As has often been said, Fielding was fully prepared to send a rogue to the gallows, but always ready to look for reasons why an accused man or woman might be spared. We could not say as much for everyone who occupied the bench at that date.

### Enquiries and proposals

The formal contributions Fielding made to discourse about crime are limited in number, but they include some of the most articulate and knowledgeable published in his lifetime. They relate chiefly to conditions in London, for obvious reasons: but he had a full acquaintance with the situation more generally, either through early brushes with the law, through his work on the Western circuit, or through his efforts to combat the smugglers in Sussex. Comments on legal affairs are sprinkled through his journalism, and fitfully in his plays; pamphlets such as his *Plan of the Universal Register-Office* (1751) reveal many of his social attitudes. In the final section of this chapter I shall discuss the light which his novels throw on some of the issues explored here.

This leaves six items directly concerned with crime. Of these the least important is probably the short pamphlet called *Examples of the Interpositions of Providence* (1752), distributed free from the house in Bow Street. It is a response to a spike in the murder rate during the previous winter. Fielding aims, as an advertisement put it, to 'raise just Sentiments of Horror at this most heinous Sin' (*Enquiry* lxxxvii). To this end he collects over thirty cautionary tales, ending with the current hot news story. This involved Mary Blandy, an educated young woman convicted in March 1752 for poisoning her father with arsenic supplied by her lover, a married soldier. Many thought that she had been deceived and manipulated by the lover, and there was an outburst of sympathy after she was executed at Oxford gaol. Elsewhere Fielding wrote with compassion about the case, though like others he may have been influenced by her refined manners and genteel bearing in court. Most of the *Examples* elicit less pity, as they are designed to ram home the traditional message concerning a watchful Providence which intervened in the affairs of men to cause 'the Detection and Punishment of Murder'. The work belongs in the time-honoured line of providential literature relating stories of God's revenge against the wicked, rather than in contemporary penology.

The *Charge to the Grand Jury* which Fielding delivered soon after his elevation to the bench also fits into an established genre. Such charges were an expression of the power of the chairman to set the agenda for the session to come. Fielding's most important predecessor here was Sir John Gonson, an expert two decades earlier in the hortatory and 'performative' manner of instructing the jury. For his part Fielding reaches back into the history of the jury system with the aid of numerous legal authorities and texts. He offers a fairly orthodox analysis of evils currently abounding in the city, although there seems to be a special fervour in his denunciation of blasphemy, cursing, and the commission of an 'open Act of Lewdness and Indecency in public' (*Enquiry* 21): the Restoration poet and rake Sir Charles Sedley provides his instance here. He reserves some of his greatest scorn for fashionable entertainments:

> Gentlemen, our News-papers, from the Top of the Page to the Bottom, the Corners of our Streets up to the very Eves of our Houses, present us with nothing but a View of Masquerades, Balls, and Assemblies of various Kinds, Fairs, Wells, Gardens, &c. tending to promote Idleness, Extravagance and Immorality, among all Sorts of People. (*Enquiry* 25)

The explanation for this moralistic zeal has been suggested earlier. Although Fielding was no killjoy, he distrusted the new forms of commercial entertainment burgeoning in the rapidly growing economy of the capital. What he feared was the capacity of such diversions to turn harmless and industrious people – especially among the poorer classes – into a group of wastrels, who would be dependent for the means to satisfy their cravings on public welfare or in the last resort crime.

Not long afterwards came *The Case of Bosavern Penlez*, which was published in November 1749, a month after the 'unfortunate' victim (as he was widely known) went to the gallows. The episode grew out of a brawl in the preceding June at a brothel near the church of St Mary le Strand. This stood in a zone long notorious for sundry vices – Pope locates some of the games of his Dunces in the immediate vicinity, which had once housed the shop of the notorious publisher Edmund Curll, a target several times of Fielding's satire. Next day some of the sailors caught up in the fight had returned to wreck the bawdy house, and troops had to be called out to quell the riot. The following day a larger complement of seamen descended on the Strand, targeting the many brothels in this quarter: again military forces had to be summoned to stem the tide of destruction and disorder. Fielding had been out of town and the early measures of containment were the responsibility of his deputy Saunders Welch. From this point the magistrate took control, and reacted with a vigour born of his belief that 'upwards of 3000 Sailors now in Arms' were poised to march into central London.[4] However, the riots petered out and Fielding now had to deal with some of those who had been caught up in the affrays and taken into custody. Only two prisoners were eventually found guilty by the Middlesex jury under the terms of the Riot Act, and one obtained a reprieve. Only Bosavern Penlez, a hapless young man from the West Country, ended up on the gallows in October. The affair was already intensely politicized for a number of reasons, and there were fears that one of the dreaded 'Tyburn riots' would break out when Penlez went to his execution. Luckily this was averted, though disturbances took place during the forthcoming election for Westminster, always the scene of the liveliest campaign in England.

The account of this episode which Fielding now published serves plainly as a justification for his conduct. It is impossible now to assess all the rights and wrongs, centrally on the question as to whether Penlez had actually taken part in the riots, or was merely a sneak-thief who had done some opportunistic looting. Political opponents accused Fielding of trying to defend the bawdy houses because they were protected by the government candidate in the elections, Lord Trentham, who was doubly suspect because of his support of a French troupe of actors. Fielding bore the brunt of much of the Opposition's hostility, real or synthetic, and he had to face charges including an undue readiness to call out the military and accepting perjured evidence from one of the brothel-owners. Most people looking into the matter have concluded that Fielding gave a reasonably accurate narrative of the main lines of the episode, whilst obviously seeking to defend his own actions. However, in the 1970s Peter Linebaugh attacked the *Case* as a nakedly partisan document, which was designed to influence voters in the Westminster election, and to conceal Fielding's panicky reaction to events and his possibly corrupt bending of the law to favour his protectors.[5] Linebaugh was unable to substantiate charges that the magistrate took bribes from the pimps to leave their establishments unmolested, but he does accept most of the accusations made by the Opposition. Underlying this argument is the view that the moral economy of the population at large favoured the sailors, held the brothel-keepers in low esteem, and distrusted the political elite. Viewed in this light, Fielding's actions become an expression of class justice. On these matters the jury is still out, as the Penlez case raises a variety of factual as well as interpretative issues. However, contemporary reappraisals of eighteenth-century attitudes to law and order have certainly made pamphlets such as the *Case of Penlez* appear even more central to the social discourse of Fielding's time.

If this work offers itself as no more than an occasional piece, then Fielding's next production represents something much more substantial. *An Enquiry into the Causes of the Late Increase of Robbers*, published in January 1751, constitutes an extended essay on the causes and remedies of criminal behaviour. Many of Fielding's day-to-day operations at Bow Street related to comparatively minor breaches of the law, and in these instances the magistrate sometimes found ways not to exact the supreme penalty even when it was technically applicable. When Welch brought a group described as 'wretches' before him, he sent one who was suffering from the itch (a contagious form of scabies) to the care of the overseers of the poor law, while another who appeared guilty of no crime but poverty had money given to her so that she could carry on her work as a market trader. Some of the graver offences, especially those with a direct political bearing on matters of state, usually involved remand to Newgate prison and trial at the Old Bailey with one of the foremost judges presiding. However, a proportion of the cases which came before Fielding in 1750 testify to a phenomenon others had observed, that is an increase in serious offences apparently instigated by a network of organized crime. Such organizations had certainly existed in the time of Jonathan Wild, as Fielding knew well, and he evidently had set views on the issue: for example, he disapproved of large rewards offered by the government for the capture of prominent suspects (these included the renegade 'Thomas Jones', who had been sprung from gaol). These experiences inform the argument of the *Enquiry*, with its concrete and constructive ideas on the best way to solve the massive problems confronting the metropolis.

Seated in his house on the west side of Bow Street, Fielding did not have to look far to see the evidence of what was going on. When first appointed to the magistracy, he had briefly taken a house in the neighbourhood, at Brownlow Street, off Drury Lane. From this site he could have taken a five-minute stroll and assembled a hundred career criminals, if they had been willing to show themselves. Close by squatted the fearsome 'rookeries' of St Giles, a byword for poverty, disease, and crime for another century, and a model for the slum Tom-all-alone's which Dickens later created in *Bleak House*. In the *Enquiry* Fielding quotes reports that he had received from Saunders Welch, and observes that 'in the Parish of St *Giles's* there are great Numbers of Houses set apart for the Reception of idle Persons and Vagabonds, who have their Lodgings there for Twopence a Night'. Such dwellings were 'all properly accommodated with miserable Beds from the Cellars to the Garret'. Moreover, 'as these Places are thus adapted to Whoredom, so are they no less provided for Drunkenness, Gin being sold in them all for a Penny a Quartern [a quarter of a pint, the usual unit of sale]; so that the smallest Sum of Money serves for Intoxication'. When Welch exercised a search warrant here, he found a collection of inmates 'numbered 58 Persons of both Sexes, the Stench of whom was so intolerable, that it compelled him in a very short time to quit the Place' (*Enquiry* 143). Quite apart from the health risks, such slum quarters obviously were ripe to become nurseries of crime, and the *Enquiry* explores in some depth the interaction between poverty and lawlessness.

The work delves into many of the darkest corners of life in the capital. It is pervaded by a sense of indignation, which does not preclude historical references or rational analysis. The issues canvassed range widely from matters such as the poor law to the mechanisms of arrest and trial, houses of correction to the award of pardons as a kind of plea-deal, the constitutional guarantees of liberty to the scourge of receivers of stolen goods. Perhaps the most eloquent passage comes near the end, where Fielding inveighs against the undue prominence given to public executions – another topic on which he disagreed with Samuel Johnson. He vividly evokes the carnivalesque triumph of the hanged man:

> The Day appointed by Law for the Thief's Shame is the Day of Glory in his own Opinion. His Procession to *Tyburn*, and his last Moments there, are all triumphant; attended with the Compassion of the meek and tender-hearted, and with the Applause, Admiration, and Envy of all the bold and hardened ... And if he has Sense enough to temper his Boldness with any Degree of Decency, his Death is spoke of by many with Honour, by most with Pity, and by all with Approbation ... I will appeal to any Man who hath seen an Execution, or a Procession to an Execution: let him tell me when he hath beheld a poor Wretch, bound in a Cart, just on the Verge of Eternity, all pale and trembling with this approaching Fate, whether the Idea of Shame hath ever intruded on his Mind?
>
> (*Enquiry* 167–8)

Because he considered these occasions provided a recruiting-ground for criminals, Fielding counselled his readers to avoid false compassion, as damaging an attitude as its reverse, savage cruelty.

The *Enquiry* provides an unflinching examination of the law, both as regards the principles that should underlie its drafting and the methods by which it should be implemented. While his advocacy may not have directly inspired the Gin Act of 1751, which had other roots, that measure certainly took steps in the direction recommended in the pamphlet. All in all, the work is irradiated by intelligence, humanity, and practical good sense. Its qualities have been well outlined by Malvin R. Zirker in his 'General Introduction' to the *Enquiry*:

> For over two years Fielding had observed the spectrum of criminal life and had taken note of the varieties of poverty and human desperation and misery. He was intimate with the ploys of habitual criminals ... and alert to the inadequacies and misdirections of the traditional machinery that was to control them. Much more than practical expertise, however, went into the writing of the *Enquiry*. To it Fielding also brought the sophistication of a man of letters, the knowledge of a historian, and the perspective of an accomplished student of English law and legal precedents.                                    (*Enquiry* lix)

Another way of putting this would be to say that Fielding had been preparing for the task for most of his life. No-one else alive in England could have combined the qualities which went to make this work, with its great rhetorical skills underpinning the theoretical and empirical understanding of crime at its heart.

While it retains considerable interest, Fielding's next social tract, *A Proposal for Making an Effectual Provision for the Poor*, published in January 1753, has a more narrow focus. He had put a related proposal to the prime minister, Henry Pelham, in 1751, but had evidently amended his scheme in the meantime. He had decided that the poor laws could not be tinkered into just or effective working without a radical overhaul, since they had become a wilderness 'intersected' and 'perplexed with Mazes and Confusion'. Most people, especially among the leisured classes, simply did not understand the depth of the problem of poverty in London: 'The Sufferings of the Poor are indeed less observed than their Misdeeds.' Once more Fielding takes us into a world where the poor 'starve, and freeze, and rot among themselves; but they beg, and steal, and rob among their Betters'. There is not, he claims, 'a Parish in the Liberty of *Westminster* which doth not raise Thousands annually for the Poor, and there is not a Street in that Liberty which does not swarm all Day with Beggars, and all Night with Thieves' (*Enquiry* 229–31).

The remedy which follows consists of a detailed plan for a county workhouse to take in up to five thousand paupers in Middlesex, to be set up notionally at Acton Common on the western edge of the county. Fielding drafts meticulous regulations covering the organization and administration of the workhouse, followed by equally precise 'arguments' in favour of adopting the plan. The rules laid down were clear and explicit, for example Fielding was adamant that men and women should be housed separately: 'Our present Houses of Correction, for Want of this Regulation, are

Places of the most infamous and profligate Debauchery' (*Enquiry* 261). Architectural plans were also drawn up, and the entire project carefully costed, to show that it would be cheaper than the existing system of poor relief, in view of the value of the inmates' labour (Fielding calculated that the 'impotent', i.e. those incapacitated from work, made up only a very small proportion of the poor at large). He had consulted many earlier proposals along similar lines, and indeed his own scheme was unusual only in the amount of detailed planning and organization it sets forth. The idea was not put into practice, although large workhouses of this kind began to appear in other parts of the country shortly after Fielding's death. Within a generation social reformers had moved on to notions such as Bentham's Panopticon, and posterity chose to shelve both the scheme and the tract by Fielding.

The last pamphlet Fielding produced is entitled *A Clear State of the Case of Elizabeth Canning*, which appeared in March 1753. It concerns the mysterious disappearance of a servant named Elizabeth Canning, who had vanished from her master's house on the northern edge of the City at the start of the year. She reappeared a month later, claiming that she had been kidnapped and taken to a house of ill repute in the village of Enfield, eight miles from the centre of London. After suffering harsh treatment, she had escaped from her prison in an attic and found her way home. A complaint was made to the magistrates, the principal suspects arrested, and then Fielding brought in a number of witnesses. As a result two women were tried in front of the Lord Mayor in late February, including a gypsy named Mary Squires. A conflict of evidence occurred when the defendant Squires claimed that she had been in far-off Dorset: witnesses were brought up all the way to London as corroboration. Despite this, both women were found guilty, and Squires received the death sentence. But further enquiry yielded fresh doubts, when the main prosecution witness recanted her testimony. Newspaper commentaries exacerbated a growing feeling of unease about the safety of the convictions, and Fielding became entangled in a battle with an old adversary, the writer and quack John Hill. It became necessary to institute a full review of the case by the law officers of the crown; their report in May vindicated the two women who had been convicted, and laid the blame on Canning's party. She was charged with perjury and sentenced to transportation.

The story has an obvious appeal as an unsolved mystery, and one of the books to which it gave rise is the well-known thriller by Josephine Tey, *The Franchise Affair* (1949). We still have no certainty on some of the crucial points: aside from a few diehards, most people believe Canning to have been caught in a deception, but the motives remain unclear. The widespread prejudice against gypsies may have made her case more persuasive. In some ways the narrative Elizabeth presented bears a likeness to abduction tales of a more recent vintage. As for Fielding's part in the episode, the best that can be said is that he entered the affair at a late stage, when the two original suspects had already been taken into custody, and he was not involved in the trial itself. All the same, he does seem to have made serious mistakes, notably his over-credulous attitude towards Elizabeth and his willingness to cut too much slack to a solicitor acting for the supposed victim. It is clear that over time he came to regret his rush to judgement and his hasty pamphlet on behalf of the Canning side. By the time he wrote to the Secretary of State in April, he was visibly hedging his bets. It follows that the *Clear State* represents only a provisional assessment, which would later be superseded in the light of fuller evidence.

## The fictional response

The novels are the supreme expression of Fielding's genius, and they touch on many of the questions he would confront as a magistrate. However, they dramatize rather than analyse legal matters, and it would be unwise to read off his views in too direct a fashion. Thus, *Jonathan Wild* holds obvious interest, as it takes its subject from the career of the best-known criminal of Fielding's lifetime. But the book is a moral satire, not a serious enquiry into the causes of crime in the 1720s: it deals with the problem of evil partly in a playful way, and partly in terms of political grandees such as Walpole, whose rise and fall Fielding allegorizes as a timeless exemplum. The narrative proceeds by way of a succession of caricatures and vignettes, often suggesting the manner of *Candide* (1759). Its stylized progression brings with it a mode of almost abstract quality. The book does not give us the Newgate to which the authorities dispatched Penlez, or even for that matter the prison in which Booth finds himself at the start of *Amelia*.

The opening sections of that novel contain some mordant passages on the state of the criminal system, and shades of the prison-house soon begin to close on the plot as it develops. Much of *Amelia* clearly draws on Fielding's experience in the hard days he endured before achieving his eminent position on the bench. Most of the action revolves around the quarter of London that Fielding knew best, in parishes such as St Martin's and St Clement's. But more important than any literal allusions are the pervading images of enclosure, confinement, exile: the book portrays the capital as a forest of gaols and sponging-houses. By comparison *Joseph Andrews* has a lighter touch in its handling of the perils of crime. Two such innocents as

Joseph and Parson Adams are always likely to fall foul of some powerful interest, and the titular hero risks losing his liberty as well as his job when he resists the advances of his mistress. But the language is always less menacing in its overtones than it will become in *Amelia*. The outcome here is a happier one, and the impact of judicial inadequacy on rural society is made to seem, implausibly in some ways, less baneful than is the case in London.

*Tom Jones* remains the most complex and fully articulated of Fielding's novels, and as such it conducts a more elaborate interrogation of crime than his other fiction. It embodies Fielding's most comprehensive survey of the human comedy. As was the case with his later tenure as a magistrate and his legal writings, it draws on a lifetime's experience of the myriad ways in which human beings interact with crime and the law, as victims, perpetrators, witnesses, and innocent bystanders. If the novelist ultimately bequeathed a more lasting legacy, it could be argued that his contemporaries had equal cause to value him for his energetic and sometimes heroic efforts to cope with the immediate problems thrown up by a society barely able to contain the pressures of modern living.[6]

## NOTES

For the fullest presentation of the issues, see Malvin R. Zirker's 'General Introduction' to his edition of Fielding's *'An Enquiry into the Causes of the Late Increase of Robbers', and Related Writings* (Oxford: Clarendon Press, 1988). Subsequent references to the *Enquiry* will appear parenthetically in the text.

1. Among the large body of important works in this area, the most relevant for a student of Fielding include J. M. Beattie, *Policing and Punishment in London 1660–1750: Urban Crime and the Limits of Terror* (Oxford: Oxford University Press, 2001); and Peter Linebaugh, *The London Hanged: Crime and Civil Society in the Eighteenth Century* (Cambridge: Cambridge University Press, 1992).
2. Letter to Lady Bute, 22 September 1755, in *The Selected Letters of Lady Mary Wortley Montagu*, ed. Robert Halsband (Harmondsworth: Penguin, 1986), 66. The cases which came before the magistrate during the course of 1752 are helpfully tabulated in Lance Bertelsen, *Henry Fielding at Work: Magistrate, Businessman, Writer* (Basingstoke: Palgrave, 2000), Appendix 1, 'Fielding's Bow Street Clientele, January 3–November 24, 1752', 149–76.
3. Craig Spence, *London in the 1690s: A Social Atlas* (London: Institute of Historical Research, 2000), 2. Spence is writing about the situation in the years just before 1700, but his words apply equally well fifty years later.
4. Martin C. Battestin and Clive T. Probyn, eds., *The Correspondence of Henry and Sarah Fielding* (Oxford: Clarendon Press, 1993), 83.
5. Peter Linebaugh, 'The Tyburn Riot against the Surgeons', in *Albion's Fatal Tree: Crime and Society in Eighteenth-Century England* (New York: Pantheon, 1975), 89–102.

# 11

CLAUDE RAWSON

# Fielding's style

At the beginning of Fielding's last novel, *Amelia* (1751), there is an extended account of life in Newgate Prison.[1] It is one of his most unusual and powerful writings, creating a new voice, which, had he lived to write novels again, might have given an additional dimension to Fielding's already considerable influence on the future of the English novel. This early part portrays a scabrous sub-world of prison inmates and guardians, including not only criminals, but criminalized unfortunates, either guilty of petty offences or more or less innocent. Fielding had dealt with such material before, notably in *Jonathan Wild* (1743), but without the vivid engagement or the pained intensity of bafflement which mark the opening of this late novel.

The narrative exposes, among other things, the injustices of a legal system personified by the vicious and corrupt magistrate Mr Thrasher, 'who was never indifferent in a Cause, but when he could get nothing on either Side' (*A* I.ii; *W* 21). This stingingly conclusive summation belongs to a type not uncommon in Fielding's prose or that of his contemporaries. It shares features with, or perhaps emulates, the satirical portraiture of the great verse satirists we sometimes speak of as 'Augustan'. Thus Dryden wrote, in *Absalom and Achitophel* (1681), of a prominent nobleman, the Duke of Buckingham (Zimri), as one for whom 'Nothing went unrewarded, but Desert' (line 560). This is part of a virtuoso portrayal of self-destructive instability, but the individual line captures a moral perversity similar to that of Thrasher, in a similarly ordered definitional style, in which the second half of the description reverses norms or expectations evoked by the first. Pope's *Rape of the Lock* (1714) offers another example, describing what happens when judges are in a hurry for lunch, and 'Wretches hang that Jury-men may Dine' (III. 22).

This style, in verse and prose, was a received manner among late-seventeenth- and eighteenth-century writers, reflecting cultural aspirations, even in defeat, to notional ideals of order, elegance, and discipline. Fielding's version has its distinctive form of urbane acerbity or playfulness, and its own flavour of relationship with the verse couplet, sometimes called 'heroic' or valued for 'correctness', which was the dominant idiom of English poetry in Fielding's lifetime. Its masters were John Dryden (1631–1700), and especially Alexander Pope (1688–1744), with whom Fielding was personally acquainted. This style, crisp, antithetical, and conclusive, has its most concentrated expression in the verse couplet, as perfected by Pope, where each line not only develops a startling or paradoxical sting, but is then capped by the next, as in Pope's *Epistle to a Lady* (1735):

> Who purchase Pain with all that Joy can give,
> And die of nothing but a Rage to live.          (lines 99–100)

The woman portrayed in these lines, like Dryden's Zimri, is volatile and contradictory, and her instabilities are paraded in an almost triumphalist display of summary definition and containment. Each line has its own aphoristic conclusiveness, to which the closure of the couplet adds a further dimension, often compounded throughout a verse paragraph or entire poem, which in turn generate further finalities of their own. The orchestration of symmetries and antitheses, and their air of definitional control over unruly forces, creates a corresponding release from the coercive grip of disorder. Seldom has a metrical convention worked so emphatically to intimate the orderly arrangement of disorder, or reflected, on a cultural scale, the impulse to display authorial mastery over recalcitrant energies. This should not be taken to imply 'an age of prose and reason', more stable or orderly than any other, or a 'peace of the Augustans'.

Sometimes, however, this style of masterful summation has an opposite effect, creating an atmosphere not of release, but of enveloping viciousness. The finalities suggest entrapment, a readerly bind, rather than reassuring containment. The biting acerbity of the sentence about Justice Thrasher gives the impression that the fitness of things is being violated. The words have an imprisoning aura, in its way not inappropriate in a Newgate setting, whose effect is to close off for the reader any relief from a sense of unbearable and unnatural injustice, of which the system of justice itself is a part. The Newgate scenes in this novel create a closed world of outlandishly strange behaviours and happenings, which are both the consequence of Thrasher's judgements and expressions of a no-way-out quality in Fielding's perspective on the subject.

In this darker manner, Fielding sometimes approaches Swift, a more persistent practitioner of the harsher modes of stylistic impasse. *Gulliver's Travels* (1726) includes, a quarter of a century before Justice Thrasher, monarchs who never promote on merit except by mistake or through treachery (*GT* III.viii.199), and judges who exceed even Thrasher in never ruling in favour of a just cause, even when the righteous party offers the biggest bribe (IV.v.249).[2] Such things, which are part of a sustained atmosphere in Swift's writings, are unusual in Fielding, and generally appear in short bursts. Fielding admired Swift among his greatest satirical masters, and Swift said that one of his only two lifetime experiences of laughing was at a (misremembered) scene from Fielding's play *Tom Thumb*.[3] The two writers were, however, generally of very different temperament and style. Even in the account of Thrasher, where Fielding perhaps come closest to Swift, Swift's tart acknowledgement of a habitual human depravity differs from the uncomprehending indignation, compassionate and pained, of Fielding's account.

Fielding was at that time a magistrate himself, a believer in law and order, and by no means soft on crime. Like many of his contemporaries, for example, he defended the death penalty for felonies that might consist of no more than the theft of 'a few Shillings', and denounced 'false Compassion' and 'ill grounded Clemency' in such matters.[4] This was not an extreme position, or exceptionally hard-line in the culture of the time. He held generally humane views on social and legal issues. In his novels, free from the constraints of administering the law, he was strenuously ready to present the full human case, the character or circumstances of, for example, a good man driven to theft by dire poverty and a duty to feed his family. He was equally aware, as far back as *Jonathan Wild*, of the full villainy of hardened and exploitative criminals, and of the squalor and sleaze of prisons and prison life.

In *Jonathan Wild*, however, for all its bleakness, the satirical buoyancy sustains a version of Fielding's usual atmosphere of confidence. The wicked, with some fanfare, get their just deserts in the end, but even the upside-down irony, professing to admire the wicked and despise the good, has a strenuous energy in its inverted affirmation of the book's underlying values. Even if the legal system is corrupt, the book makes sure that poetic justice, reflecting a moral fitness in the order of things, is not only respected, but grandly celebrated. The hero's public hanging is triumphally orchestrated, giving full honours to a conclusion (Wild's execution) which, according to the author, ought to follow in all such cases, even if it doesn't in fact (or in the ending of Gay's *Beggar's Opera* (1728), where the villain is reprieved). Fielding makes a great point of the fact that the proper outcome occurs in his own book, and constantly reminds us that he is seeing to it. An atmosphere of authorial mastery informs all of Fielding's novels before *Amelia*. In *Joseph Andrews* (1742) and *Tom Jones* (1749), it is accompanied by a geniality necessarily absent from *Jonathan Wild* (perhaps his first novel, though published after *Joseph Andrews* in 1743), as well as from *Amelia* (his last). But the grimness of *Amelia* is of a different order, offering neither the schematic feeling of control of *Jonathan Wild*, nor the more supple and urbane authority of the two more famous novels.

*Amelia* however offers instead a series of injustices which remain uncorrected, as in the case of an innocent woman, who had been sent to fetch a midwife for her pregnant employer, and was arrested for prostitution (I.ii; W 22), or the war-crippled soldier, found not guilty of 'stealing three Herrings', who is back in prison (where 'he hath lain ever since'), for being unable to pay the fee for his discharge, though innocent prisoners were entitled to be discharged without a fee (I.iv; W 35). These cases are of basic injustice, but that of the soldier takes a further cruel turn, and we are left to wonder about the fate of the pregnant woman deprived of a midwife. Both reflect a perversity in the judge or the system. Thrasher's judgements are the product of a mind locked in its own compulsive depravity. But they are also accompanied by gratuitous cruelties of circumstance. An even harsher superogation of disaster occurs in the case of the prisoner 'committed for a small Felony' and now in 'the highest Disorder of Mind', because his pregnant wife 'had thrown herself from a Window . . ., by which means he had, in all Probability, lost both her and his Child' (I.iv; W 32).

Such appalling outcomes, though inherent in the system, and as it were notionally unsurprising, actually defeat natural expectation. The vicious circles of circumstance are a nightmarish reflection of those of Thrasher's moral character, of which they are partly the consequence. But it is at the same time a signature of *Amelia* to suggest a radical inexplicability in the order of things. A convicted whore called Blear-Eyed Moll appears before the hero Booth, himself unjustly in prison for assault and without money to bribe his way out (I.ii; W 24–5):

> The first Person who accosted him was called *Blear-Eyed Moll*; a Woman of no very comely Appearance. Her Eye (for she had but one) whence she derived her Nick-name was such, as that Nick-name bespoke; for first, as if Nature had been careful to provide for her own Defect, it constantly looked towards her blind Side; and secondly, the Ball consisted almost entirely of white, or rather yellow, with a little grey Spot in the Corner, so small that it was scarce discernible. Nose she had none; for *Venus*, envious perhaps at her former Charms, had carried off the gristly Part; and some earthly Damsel, perhaps from the same Envy, had levelled the Bone with the rest of her Face: Indeed it was far beneath the Bones of her Cheeks, which rose proportionally higher than is usual. About half a dozen ebeny Teeth fortified that large and long Canal, which Nature had cut from Ear to Ear, at the Bottom of which was a Chin, preposterously short, Nature having turned up the Bottom, instead of suffering it to grow to its due Length.

> Her Body was well adapted to her Face; she measured full as much round the middle as from Head to Foot; for besides the extreme Breadth of her Back, her vast Breasts had long since forsaken their native Home, and settled themselves a little below the Girdle. (*A* I.iii; *W* 27–8)

This portrait belongs to a long line of descriptions of old or ugly women, to which had been added the more recent predilection for viewing raw data in a frame of couplet-like symmetries.[5] Fielding had assimilated this couplet style by the time of his first published novel, *Joseph Andrews*, which contains an earlier analogue of Moll in Lady Booby's maid Slipslop, who, like her mistress, lusts after the hero Joseph:

> She was a Maiden Gentlewoman of about Forty-five Years of Age, who having made a small Slip in her Youth had continued a good Maid ever since. She was not at this time remarkably handsome; being very short, and rather too corpulent in Body, and somewhat red, with the Addition of Pimples in the Face. Her Nose was likewise too large, and her Eyes too little; nor did she resemble a Cow so much in her Breath, as in two brown Globes which she carried before her; one of her Legs was also a little shorter than the other, which occasioned her to limp as she walked. (*JA* I.vi; *W* 32)[6]

Both portraits differ from traditional accounts of hags or bawds, variously presented as randomly and overflowingly misshapen. In Fielding's descriptions, shapelessness and deformity seem instead to be continually reaching out to, or else defying, some normative ideal of symmetry and harmonious balance: Moll's good eye straining for concordance with the blind eye, 'Nature' being 'careful to provide for her own Defect'; her syphilitically curtailed nose balanced, again thanks to Nature, by an abnormally shortened chin (a further fearful symmetry unfolds, whether by design or not, when we later discover that the heroine Amelia has a broken nose, a fact which occasioned hostile ribaldry at the time); her 'Body ... well adapted to her Face', and measuring 'full as much round the middle as from Head to Foot'; her 'vast Breasts' symmetrically overspilling their natural proportions. It is as though the overflowing physical grotesquerie mirrored the whole character's resistance to containment, in a style usually equipped to impose order on excess and contradiction.

The earlier portrait of Mrs Slipslop shows a similar emphasis, more concisely formulated, and more sharply highlighting violated symmetries in the language of symmetry. Mismatches are registered in the habitual couplet-evoking arrangement: 'Her Nose was ... too large, and her Eyes too little'. What might be thought of as random or cumulative details of deformity are pointedly represented as mismatches: her 'two brown Globes' resembling the udders of a cow; her legs, like Moll's eyes, uneven, one 'a little shorter than the other', making her 'limp as she walked'. Such descriptive ordering is not restricted to fat women, like Slipslop and Moll, with their aura of over-flowing and excess. In *Joseph Andrews*, it is extended to the inn-keeper's wife, Mrs Tow-wouse, who 'was short, thin, and crooked', and to the diminutive dandy Beau Didapper, whose effeminate appearance and manner suggest reversed sexual characteristics (*JA* I.xiv, IV.ix; *W* 61–2, 312–13). Mrs Western in *Tom Jones*, whose 'masculine Person, ... near six Foot high' makes her their opposite in size, is also Didapper's symmetrical obverse in her contravention of gender norms (*TJ* IV.ii; *W* 273–4).

These examples show once again the underlying likeness, in style of perception and thought, between Fielding's prose and Pope's couplets. Fielding's description of the bisexual Didapper is a replay of Pope's Sporus, a caricature of the same real-life nobleman, Lord Hervey, who is described, in the *Epistle to Dr Arbuthnot* (1735), as an 'Amphibious Thing',

> Now high, now low, now Master up, now Miss,
> And he himself one vile Antithesis.   (lines 305–34, esp. 324–6)

Even more strikingly, because the resemblance is more fortuitous, the eyes and legs of Slipslop and Moll may be compared with Pope's description of the foul-speaking Homeric rogue Thersites:

> His Figure such as might his Soul proclaim;
> One Eye was blinking, and one Leg was lame:
> His Mountain-Shoulders half his Breast o'erspread,
> Thin Hairs bestrew'd his long mis-shapen Head.

These lines are not from a satire, but from Pope's translation of a section of the *Iliad* (1720) which some critics regarded as incompatible with epic dignity, and which Pope himself thought of as giving a taste of Homer's lost work of '*Satyric* or *Comic* Poetry'.[7] If Pope's portrait resembles or anticipates those of Fielding's Moll or Slipslop, it is precisely in details which Pope added to his Homeric original. This reads, in Richmond Lattimore's very close translation:

> He was
> bandy-legged and went lame of one foot, with shoulders
> stooped and drawn together over his chest, and above this
> his skull went up to a point with the wool grown sparsely upon it.[8]

The two translations share the lameness and the balding head, but are otherwise very unlike. Even Homer's bent shoulders, which are merely a continuing detail in a portrait of ugliness, receive a grandiose transformation in Pope. 'His Mountain-Shoulders half his Breast o'erspread' adds, without any warrant from the Homeric original, the Augustanizing signature of a strong, metrically enforced finality, and the ironically 'heroic' inflation, which also became a feature of Fielding's style.

Such calculated inflation does not occur, for example, in Swift's mock-heroic application of the Thersites portrait to the pedant Bentley, in the *Battle of the Books* (1704).[9] His account of the 'crooked Leg, and hump Shoulder' imitates Homer's unstylized notation, without the mock-aggrandisements of Pope's or Fielding's patterned summations. Swift was himself, in other places, a master of such patterned summations, but usually in their most stingingly imprisoning mode discussed above. He did not normally share Pope's or Fielding's impulse to submit the particularities of raw observation to a triumphalist definitional order, least of all with grandiose accoutrements.

The emphasis on a perverse or shocking conformity to 'Nature', in Pope's line 'His Figure such as might his Soul proclaim', which was ironically replicated in a hostile squib describing Pope's own hump as 'the Emblem of thy crooked Mind',[10] shows a stylistic predisposition similar to Fielding's account of Nature's ministrations in the matter of Moll's eyes, nose, and chin, but not present in Swift's Thersites episode. Ironies of unnaturalness are common in Swift, but with little of the residual allure of the original violated norm. Pope introduces a further offended symmetry by adding an eye not in Homer: 'One Eye was blinking, and one Leg was lame', a symmetrical deployment of two separate asymmetries, prefiguring Moll's bad eye and Slipslop's uneven legs.

A fixation on female breasts, in descriptions of women in all periods, was traditional.[11] It readily turns, in these two writers and some contemporaries, to norms of balanced equilibrium, or their violation, as in the grotesque asymmetry of Moll's breasts, or the account of Slipslop, which combines anomalies in her eyes, breasts, and legs, all within a single sentence.

> Her Nose was likewise too large, and her Eyes too little; nor did she resemble a Cow so much in her Breath, as in two brown Globes which she carried before her; one of her Legs was also a little shorter than the other.     (*JA* I.vi; *W* 32)

Such portraits differ sharply from Richardson's near contemporary description of Mrs Jewkes as seen by the heroine Pamela: 'She is a broad, squat, pursy, fat Thing, quite ugly ... Her Nose is flat and crooked ... a dead, spiteful, grey, goggling Eye, to be sure she has. And her Face is flat and broad.'[12] The details are often similar, but they come in an unstylized sequence, as ugly empirical facts rather than aberrant departures from confidently accepted patterns. Jewkes's 'hoarse man-like Voice' evokes a hot-house atmosphere of lesbian overtures, rather than, like Lord Didapper's or Mrs Western's similarly contrary sexual characteristics, mainly a comic disarrangement of the fitness of things. The words have the stamp of the heroine's, not the author's, voice, as in her comment about Jewkes's saltpetre complexion, with its immediacy of spite ('I dare say she drinks'), which Fielding would have converted into a stylish narrative knowingness.

Jewkes was probably the original of Slipslop. But the contrast between her and both Slipslop and Moll could not be more marked. All are misshapen women, but as against Richardson's fraught factuality, Fielding's portraits come in paired arrangements self-consciously evoking the patterns they contravene. Even the nose, which does not come in pairs, has to be paired and balanced with another part of the face (eyes in Slipslop, chin in Moll). The resemblance of Slipslop's 'two brown Globes' to the udders of a cow belongs with Pope's nearly contemporaneous portrait of the writer Eliza Haywood as a 'Juno of majestic size,/With cow-like udders, and with ox-like Eyes'. The latter image recycles a frequent Homeric epithet about the goddess Hera's (Juno's) 'ox-like eyes' (*Iliad*, 1.551 etc.), which comes without any of Fielding's or Pope's elaborate montage. Pope's lines appeared in all versions of the *Dunciad* between 1728 and 1743, i.e. both before and shortly after the publication of *Joseph Andrews* in 1742.[13]

'Nature', in such contexts, means something like the 'natural order of things', rather than the raw facts or spontaneous impulses a modern reader might think of as 'natural'. It implies an ideal 'normality' in which the proportion and balance of human eyes, breasts, or limbs are taken for granted, and whose disfigurement we speak of as 'abnormal', just as an infringement of customary moral values might be called 'unnatural' (as in an 'unnatural' crime, however spontaneously committed). An accompanying assumption, familiar from the earliest poetry and fiction, is that moral worth is reflected in physical beauty, so that the strongest hero, or the ideal heroine, tend also to be supremely beautiful in body. In many couplet styles, notably in Fielding and Pope, this takes the form of an unusually strong preoccupation not only with the notional harmonies and contradictions of moral character or the physical body, but also with the correlation between the two.

The cultural aspirations of eighteenth-century England did not usually include a literal belief in such congruences, but they did involve an accentuated feeling for order and the 'fitness' of things. That Pope added a crisply definitional irony about Thersites' 'Figure' being 'such as might his Soul proclaim' reflects an impulse to emphasize the bad or unnatural not as mere facts of circumstance, but in a presumed relation to a violated or ironic norm.

Fielding's prose has a more relaxed version of this feature, supplemented by Fielding's habitual display of narrative management. *Joseph Andrews* and

*Tom Jones* offer a witty parade of the narrator's right to proceed in any way he pleases, his manipulation of the events and his commentaries about them, his discursive 'introductory' chapters, and his frequent conversations with the reader. Proceeding which way the author pleases is a directly opposite claim to that in which a narrator's self-expression purported to be guided by his pen rather than the other way round. Sterne's Tristram Shandy, and indeed Sterne himself, were to say some years later that their pen 'governs me, – I govern not it' (*Tristram Shandy*).[14] Richardson similarly addressed his pen as though it were an autonomous being, a pretension Swift saw as peculiarly 'modern', and mocked in advance when his narrator at the end of *A Tale of a Tub* (1704), having nothing more to say, announces his determination 'to let the Pen still move on'.[15]

Fielding's novels provide the earliest major challenge to an alternative and almost equally recent novelistic tradition, which prides itself on effacing the author and neutralizing the impression that what we are reading 'is only a story'. Its early master was Richardson (1689–1761), Fielding's older contemporary and rival, whose novels are narrated by the characters in their letters. Richardson preened himself on the fact that his novels were sometimes taken for real, an objective that was later professed by the French novelist Gustave Flaubert (1821–80), and some English followers, including Ford Madox Ford (1873–1939). Ford was to deplore Fielding's authorial intrusions as symptoms of an unprofessional preference for displaying himself as a gentleman at the expense of his fiction.[16] Fielding viewed Richardson's manner as an abdication of selection and authority, and as an ill-bred failure to keep his distance. His own manner was designed to show the reader that he was not overwhelmed by the flow of events, or by intimate emotional immediacies. His contempt for Richardson's boasts of conveying his characters' emotions in their own words and 'to the Moment' had more than a touch of patrician scorn for what Fielding saw as Richardson's vulgar and unselective surrender to the raw data of circumstance and sentiment. Richardson's hot-house immediacies in the matter of his heroines' sexual appeal, and their suitors' lustful cravings, repelled Fielding as a literary equivalent of indecent exposure.

These attitudes are already visible as early as *Shamela* (1741), an exuberant parody of Richardson's *Pamela* (1740). *Shamela* was not only Fielding's debut as an author of prose fiction, but the beginning of a lifetime of novel-writing in which the novels of Richardson were a persistent focus of Fielding's ironic attention. This is true even of *Amelia*, written after Fielding had expressed generous admiration of Richardson's second novel, *Clarissa* (1747–8), and in emulation of which *Amelia* was partly undertaken.[17] Fielding's fictions exhibit an almost obsessive awareness of

Richardson, as does his last prose work, the non-fictional *Journal of a Voyage to Lisbon* (1755). This is not to say that Fielding's novels are all parodies, like *Shamela*. But they define themselves self-consciously as holding an adversarial and partly mocking view of Richardson's fictional style, and of what Fielding represented as his prudential and hypocritical morality.

These characteristics Fielding regarded, in a patrician way, as 'low', a description Richardson applied to Fielding himself on different grounds, namely that Fielding's novels dealt with low life and were improperly tolerant of sexual misconduct. Fielding was more relaxed about sexual indiscretions, and accorded them an affectionate respect if they were expressions of an honourable and generous nature. He derided what he saw as Richardson's burgherly pseudo-proprieties, while Richardson was outraged at Fielding's lordly defiance of these. Fielding's attitude reflects a traditional symbiosis between the lordly and low, a more mundane or desublimated version of Yeats's 'dream of the noble and the beggar-man',[18] from which the middle ranks of society tend to be excluded, and which purported to share a certain openness and freedom in social and sexual matters. By the same token, Richardson nourished a burgherly distrust of the aristocracy, and was quick to pounce on lordly vulgarities.

In Fielding's derisive dealings with Richardson, sexual behaviour, including love, affection, and lust, as well as Richardson's censorious prurience, inevitably play a dominant role. It was not the sexual content as such that Fielding was objecting to, but Richardson's sex-obsessed and sanctimonious particularity in depicting behaviour of which he professed to disapprove. A well-bred writer, as Fielding ostentatiously implies, would accept sexual intimacies as natural, private, and not to be gone into in writing. Several scenes in Fielding's novels bring us to the brink of an amorous consummation, only to be interrupted by the observation that the reader knows perfectly well what usually happens, and that the author has no intention to pry, or to cater for readers whose 'Devotion to the Fair Sex . . . wants to be raised by the Help of Pictures' (*TJ* XIII.ix; W 722).

These inflections have much in common with the putdowns which many eighteenth-century writers (including Pope, Swift, and even Samuel Johnson) applied to the objects of their contempt, without themselves making any claim to aristocratic connections, though Fielding himself did have such connections. The manner goes back to a literary tradition of Restoration wits and their contemptuous treatment of the merchant classes or 'cits', a species of class warfare which later became to some extent uncoupled from, and sometimes disapproving of, real-life jealousies and antagonisms of rank. This style implies that bad behaviour or character, even in lords, is itself 'low', and that this is true of a nasty and foolish arrogance of rank. The phenomenon extends as much to a 'Lady, of no greater Dignity in the order of Beings than a Cat', who expresses 'Contempt to a Woman who was an Honour to her Sex',[19] as to the airs of Mrs Western's maid in *Tom Jones*, who 'claimed Great Superiority over Mrs *Honour*' because 'her Birth was higher: For her great Grand-mother by the Mother's Side was Cousin, not far removed, to an *Irish* Peer' (*TJ* VII.viii; *W* 354). Fielding's nuanced way of being uppish about uppishness is brought out in the 'Dissertation concerning high People and low People', which makes the point that the two categories are fluctuating, so that 'the lowest of the High, and the highest of the Low' keep changing places, often in the course of a single day, depending on place and time (*JA* II.xiii; *W* 156, 157).

It was part of a standard literary idiom to be uppish about vices and follies, including uppishness itself. This manner achieved its most fervid expression a few years earlier (1733) in these often-quoted lines by Pope, which use lordly accents to denounce bad behaviour in lords:

> And who unknown defame me, let them be
> Scriblers or Peers, alike are *Mob* to me.[20]

The style was developed into a characteristic signature of Augustan writers, and in particular of the coterie known as the Scriblerus Club, the circle of Swift, Pope, Gay, Arbuthnot, and Thomas Parnell, which set, or refined, the tone of much of the satirical writing of the time. Fielding was not at all times in personal or political sympathy with these writers, but he felt himself to belong to their tradition, signing himself as Scriblerus Secundus in some of his early works.

The style is broadly characterized by a classical and patrician ethos, and an urbanely stinging exploitation of the obliquities of irony. It adopts the accents of an elite, implying a collective superiority to the crowd, which rubs off, in a more or less playfully personalized way, not only on the reader, but on the writers whose manner or quality places them outside the circle of acceptability. It is a signature, as well as expression, of Fielding's difference from Richardson, marking the antithesis of Richardson's purportedly unguarded literalness, his suspicion of irony, his heavy-handed ambivalence about lordly behaviour, and the disapproving awkwardness of his dealings with the classical heritage. Fielding's adoption of a Scriblerian manner would in itself have acted as a stylistic rebuke to Richardson, even if Fielding had had no specific occasion or impulse to score off this hostile rival's writings. Richardson was as necessary to Fielding's novels as the Dunces were to Pope's satires of the 1730s and 1740s, culminating in the *Dunciad* (1728–43).

Fielding was not free from attachments of his own to the minutiae of social rank. In the *Journal of a Voyage to Lisbon* (1 July), he reports his dressing down of a customs officer, who, he said, 'could be no gentleman' because he failed to remove his hat in 'the presence of a lady' (Fielding's wife). When the officer blamed his mate for not informing him that they were persons of distinction, Fielding told him 'he might guess by our appearance ... that he was before a gentleman and lady, which should teach him to be very civil in his behaviour, tho' we should not happen to be of that number which the world calls people of fashion and distinction'. Fielding confides to the reader that the claim to a distinguished appearance was, in his sick and disorderly state, 'more than could be said with the strictest adherence to truth'. An ill-tempered comedy ensues, in which Fielding loftily permits the man 'to put his hat on again', which he unsurprisingly 'refused with some degree of surliness'. This persuades Fielding 'that, if I should condescend to become more gentle, he would soon grow more rude' (V 36–7).

For all its gloomy comedy, the account shows Fielding to be not altogether disengaged from an obsession with his own proper status among high and low people. A few days earlier, on 27 June, he described the rather flamboyant captain of his ship as having 'taken it into his head that he was a gentleman, from those very reasons that proved he was not one; and to shew himself a gentleman, by a behaviour which seemed to insinuate he had never seen one' (V 29). On the previous day, 26 June, at the start of his journey, Fielding, in his crippled state, had been jeered at by sailors and watermen, and reflected on the role of a polite upbringing in refining manners, and purging the natural malevolence of human beings (V 23). The 'barbarous' behaviour of sailors continued to exercise him, especially because he otherwise thought them 'the bravest fellows upon earth' (30 June, V 36). The thought that a polite upbringing had a role in mitigating such things suggests that, even in this late and depressed stage, Fielding was wishfully attached to the idea that virtue and class were not separate, and that nobility of behaviour had a notional, and perhaps more than notional, though not always actual, connection with nobility of rank.

Half-ironic claims of caste were also for Fielding a rhetoric reinforcing his self-projection as a masterful story-teller. He shared with the satirists an ironic attachment to high styles, in which the heightened rhetoric of epic poetry served to show off a cultivated knowingness while guarding against inflated pretensions. This 'Drollery in Style', consisting of burlesque transpositions of high and low, occurs 'in the Descriptions of the Battles, and some other Places, not necessary to be pointed out to the Classical Reader; for whose Entertainment those Parodies ... are chiefly calculated', as he says in the Preface to *Joseph Andrews*. He claims this is a sort of superior extra, restricted to 'his Diction only', and quite distinct from the definition 'comic Epic-Poem in Prose', which he applied to his novel, for whose substance if not style he claimed to offer the unadorned truth, or an 'exactest copying of Nature' (*JA* Preface; W 4–6).[21]

The latter claim might come more readily from Richardson, as Fielding must already have been aware. The less patrician practitioners of a new realist fiction, Defoe and Richardson, purported to present a reality unadorned with classical flourishes, and both spoke of epic with disapproval, as the art of a warrior class not attuned to popular or female readership and as promoting an immoral celebration of war.[22] Fielding aspired to a comparable realism, but was mindful of Richardson's distasteful example, and found it hard to sustain with a straight face. His flights of mock-heroic, which he professed to regard as incidental, in the sense that 'Diction . . . is the Dress of Poetry', not its substance (*JA* Preface; W 5), serve in effect as a protective cover in the management of bare fact or naked feeling, and thus as a token of his authority.[23]

Here is the central, informative part of his description of Sophia Western, one of his most attractive heroines, a passage where an impulse to plain realism is perceptible:

> *Sophia*, then, the only daughter of Mr *Western*, was a middle-sized Woman; but rather inclining to tall. Her Shape was not only exact, but extremely delicate; and the nice Proportion of her Arms promised the truest Symmetry in her Limbs. Her Hair, which was black, was so luxuriant, that it reached her Middle, before she cut it, . . . If Envy could find any Part of the Face which demanded less Commendation than the rest, it might possibly think her Forehead might have been higher without Prejudice to her. Her Eye-brows were full, even, and arched beyond the Power of Art to imitate. Her black Eyes had a Lustre in them, which all her Softness could not extinguish. Her Nose was exactly regular . . .
>
> Such was the Outside of *Sophia*; nor was this beautiful Frame disgraced by an Inhabitant unworthy of her. Her Mind was every way equal to her Person.
>
> (*TJ* IV.ii; W 156–7)

This portrait is not satirical, like those of Moll, Slipslop, and the others, though it has the same concern with symmetries of both subject and presentation (and similarly invokes Envy as officiously meddlesome in matters of disproportion). The object is to present a supremely lovely heroine in the traditional hyperbolic style, but with some concession of minor imperfections ('rather inclining to tall', 'her Forehead might have been higher') in the name of 'exactest copying'.

Even these small gestures of uninflated precision, however, are laced with mock-pompous periphrasis ('nor was this beautiful Frame disgraced'), itself an ironic guard against the lofty style which is simultaneously being

exploited, and the whole passage is ushered in by an operatic display bordering on rant. The chapter begins with 'Hushed be every ruder Breath. May the
Heathen Ruler of the Winds confine in Iron Chains the boisterous Limbs of
noisy *Boreas*.' This shades into some lyrical or pastoral evocations, followed
by high-flown comparisons with famous beauties and supporting quotations
from love poets. This fuss is designed, not to undermine Sophia, but to
indicate that the loyal and loving narrator is in control of the situation,
not really taken in by the gesturing he simulates, while staunchly conveying
that the heroine is fully worthy of honours elsewhere inappropriately
bestowed. A sign of his control of this warm tribute is that he is able to risk
an allusion to a 'rude Answer which Lord *Rochester* once gave to a Man,
who had seen many Things', which was, if the reader cared to search for it, 'If
you have seen all this, then kiss mine *Arse*' (*TJ* IV.ii; *W* 155–6).[24] It is here that
a mock-heroic allusiveness, to heroic romances, high-falutin love poetry, a
fairground mixture of lofty rant and coarse humour, perform a stylizing
function which affirms the narrator's own poise and command.

The mock-heroic which helps to sustain the bossy manner of *Joseph
Andrews* and *Tom Jones* takes a different form in *Jonathan Wild*, possibly
written before *Joseph Andrews*, though not published until 1743. The mock-
heroic in this work is not sporadic but an integral part of the fabric. It
depends not on parody of epic routines but on a linguistic reversal in which
the wicked are called heroic and the virtuous low. The story is told from an
ironic point of view, adopting values which are the opposite of the author's
or reader's, and is thus unusual in not projecting a version of the author's
'real' voice. It is also untypical in its rasping intensity of focus on the twin-
criminalities of crooks and politicians. It has an alternative relation to Pope,
not primarily stylistic, in that its mock-heroic character seems in various
ways to be in dialogue with the evolving publication of the *Dunciad*, which
appeared in successive versions from 1728, and whose final version appeared
in 1743, the same year as Fielding's work. *Jonathan Wild* also stands out
as being extensively preoccupied by the sleazy world of gangsterism and
protection-racketeering, and is partly set, like his last novel *Amelia*, in the
grim environment of Newgate prison.

This uneven but brilliant work is out of step with the familiar Fielding of
the other fictions of the 1740s. It prefigures the Newgate chapters of *Amelia*,
also an uneven novel, but one whose early chapters open up a fiction of
London's dark underside comparable to Dickens, Gissing, and Brecht's
*Threepenny Novel* (1933), the latter a work with particularly close similar-
ities to *Jonathan Wild*. *Amelia* also adopts a primarily unmocking relation to
Virgil's *Aeneid*, which has sometimes been seen as an anticipation of Joyce's
use of Homer's *Odyssey* in *Ulysses* (1922).

The affair of Booth and Miss Mathews in prison is a studied throwback to the story of Dido and Aeneas in their cave in Virgil's *Aeneid*, which Fielding called his 'noble model'.[25] The parallel sustains a relationship with the epic which might be called 'mock-heroic', without the element of parody. It is unlike the mock-heroic flourishes of the earlier novels, in that it points to parallels of past and present without any pointed jokerie at the disproportion. It seems fitting that in this last grim novel, Fielding should have held on to an epic attachment, while dropping the playfulness that normally went with it. The Virgilian parallel underpins the early chapters of *Amelia* in something like the way the Homeric parallel underpins Joyce's novel. Fielding seems not to have known how to sustain or develop this parallel beyond the early chapters. It seems to support them in the way the mock-heroic high spirits of *Joseph Andrews* and *Tom Jones* supported his authority as a narrator throughout, but in a darker mode, without the buoyancy. At all events, the sentimental prosiness of the main story of Amelia and Booth takes over at the point when Fielding lets go of the structuring precedent offered by his Virgilian model.

But *Amelia* marks an important change in Fielding's tone and outlook. The fact that there seems to be no formal set-piece describing the heroine (as there had been for Sophia, and other characters both good and bad) may be an indication of this. She is first described by Booth in II.i, when Booth summarily reports that he 'knew her in the first Dawn of her Beauty', and says he thought her 'absolutely out of my Reach' before the accident in which her nose was broken. Though subsequently repaired, in a posthumous second edition, in response to much critical ribaldry, the injury is noted as disfiguring enough to deprive her of many former suitors. It also 'gave me an Assurance that the Woman who had been so much adored for the charms of her Person, deserved a much higher Adoration to be paid to her Mind' (*A* II.i).[26] This latter body-mind imbalance is redeemed by the surcharge of praise, but the sense of a blemish remains, later somewhat modulated by embarrassed reflections by the narrator, and the foolish Mrs James, as to whether the resulting scar increased her physical loveliness or left the nose well-proportioned or not (*A* IV.vii, XI.i; *W* 184, 454).

Mrs James's observation occurs in an extravagant tirade:

'In the first Place,' cries Mrs *James*, 'her Eyes are too large; and she hath a Look with them that I don't know how to describe; but I know I don't like it. Then her Eyebrows are too large; therefore indeed she doth all in her Power to remedy this with her Pincers: for if it was not for those, her Eyebrows would be preposterous. – Then her Nose, as well proportioned as it is, hath a visible

Scar on one Side. – Her Neck likewise is too protuberant for the genteel Size, especially as she laces herself: for no Woman in my Opinion can be genteel who is not entirely flat before. And lastly, she is both too short and too tall . . . I mean that she is too tall for a pretty Woman, and too short for a fine Woman.

(*A* XI.iv; *W* 454)

This description by a foolish speaker, which seems incidentally to have suggested a similar speech in Jane Austen's *Pride and Prejudice* ((1813), III.iii), is obviously an overturning of the panegyric portrayals, and reads as though some demon had turned Amelia into a Slipslop.[27] But the parody of the formal portrait may remind us that a non-parodic version is not available in the novel, though there are celebrations of Amelia's beauty at II.i, and later, when, for example, she appears in 'a Blaze of Beauty' in VI.i. Lyrical celebration is offered, as with Sophia, through quotations from admired English poets (in this case Milton, Waller, and Suckling), which in both cases also bring out a special vibrancy and glow in the heroines' appearance (VI.i; *W* 230).

That some of the warmest praise of both heroines comes through the mediation of admired poets, may suggest that Fielding could not fully surrender himself to such panegyrics in his own name. But Amelia does not get the obverse of this proxy praise, in which part of the compliment to Sophia is conversely filtered through ridicule of other high styles, as though Fielding in the later novel were no longer prepared to take stylistic risks which once signalled his narrative supremacy. The chapter is headed 'Panegyricks on Beauty, with other grave Matters', a recurrent vestige of the manner of *Tom Jones*. But there is none of the blowsy rococo of the description of Sophia, which plays mockingly with the conventions while honouring them in spirit, and which dares the indignities of rant and coarseness without surrendering any part of the affectionate celebration.

There seem in fact to be few or no formal set-pieces in the old manner in *Amelia*, outside the vignette style of the Newgate chapters, with its account of Blear-Eyed Moll, itself as much an overturning of the panegyric proprieties as Mrs James's denigration of *Amelia*, but, as I have suggested, with some disturbing overtones of its own. Both are framed within Fielding's habitual style of definitional mastery, but Mrs James is being maliciously silly, and there is also a sense that the actual grotesquerie of Moll's size, shape, and deformities painfully exceeds the boundaries of definition, and defies expression. In his usual manner, Fielding says that 'For the Sake of our squeamish Reader, we shall not descend to Particulars' (*A* I.iii; *W* 28). For once, this is not the urbane refusal to enumerate trivialities or describe things which every reader knows about, or which don't deserve his notice. It is also more than Fielding's usual way of subjecting his reader to a fictive contempt, at once genial and superior. Here, the reader has a right to be squeamish: 'Let it suffice to say, nothing more ragged, or more dirty, was ever emptied out of the Round-house at St *Giles*'s'. What is unspoken is, for once, not too trivial to mention, but actually unspeakable.

This marks a defeat, in which reality defies stylistic comprehension, just as the earlier details of the portrait have a heaving enormity that seems to bulge against the limits of orderly description. Moll cannot be contained in a style whose nature typically suggests containment. There are two further surprises: 'this unlovely Creature was taken in the Fact with a very pretty young Fellow', and 'she was one of the merriest Persons in the whole Prison'. These details are not so remarkable for their ostensibly cheerful and lusty nature as for the surprise they create, exacerbating rather than easing an atmosphere of tension and discomfort. They generate bafflement or incomprehension in which even the cheerfulness has a shocking inexplicability, like a motiveless shriek of laughter. In a rare reversal, the ugly portrait has an upbeat payoff, but this seems even more disconcerting than the 'unspoken' revelation of unspeakable squalor.

The note is unusual in Fielding, even in his late style, though it is probably only to be found there. Fielding's writings are often playful on the subject of what he leaves out on grounds of mundane triviality or unpleasantness, and as a sign of authorial good manners. As late as the *Voyage to Lisbon* (1755), the phrase 'Nothing worth notice pass'd' (30 June; V 30) occurs as in the novels, though less jauntily. In the Preface to that last painful and very personal book, he writes that an author is under an obligation not to report everything, and to overlook 'much of what he has seen'. Something of the caustic hauteur of *Tom Jones* survives when Fielding rebukes writers who record 'things and facts of so common a kind, that they challenge no other right of being remembered, than as they had the honour of having happened to the author, to whom nothing seems trivial that in any manner happens to himself' (Preface; V 5, 9). When such admonitions occur in *Tom Jones*, however, the dominant note is of high-spirited bossiness, not nagging dejection. The flat harping on what he expects authors not to do is more apparent than Fielding's actual resort to the formula of 'Nothing worth noting pass'd'. This in itself suggests some surrender of the old urbanity. The formula has become a nervous tic. Fielding's willingness in the *Voyage* to record the details of his debilitated and crippled body, his medical treatments, and the jeering of sailors and watermen at his diseased appearance (26 June; V 22–3) seems as remarkable as his pretended reticence on the subject of Blear-Eyed Moll's looks.

Both kinds of description occur in contexts of purported reticence, somewhat tensely proclaimed within the residual gestures of stylistic assurance. When the narrative resumes after the portrait of Moll in *Amelia*, Moll is seen assaulting the hero Booth with 'a Volley of dreadful Oaths, interlarded with some Language, not proper to be repeated here' (IV.iii; W 29). This refusal to report the language again replays the earlier note of worldly control over what he will not say. Moll reappears in the next chapter, where she 'and several of her Companions' are seen beating up 'a Man who was committed for certain odious unmanlike Practices, not fit to be named' (A I.iv; W 33). 'Not fit to be named' is not an expression of loss of mastery. It is a matter of politeness, not prudery. One doesn't, Fielding implies, mention such things.

There is, however, a new dimension of unpleasantness in this episode. The group would have killed the man if the authorities hadn't intervened. Fielding had no admiration for murderous violence, and the scene is a painful description of prison cruelties. This does not, as a present-day reader might expect, express any special plea for persecuted homosexuals. His attitude probably did not differ greatly from the jeering jokerie about homosexuals found in other novels of the time, including John Cleland's *Memoirs of a Woman of Pleasure* (1748–9), or Smollett's *Peregrine Pickle* (1751, the same year as *Amelia*), in which the hero's 'just detestation for all such abominable practices' is more or less comically reported.[28] Homosexuality was punishable by the pillory and sometimes by execution, and did not often evoke publicly expressed sympathy.[29] But the brief passage in *Amelia* reaches beyond the customary harsh ribaldry about 'unmanlike Practices', into an unsettling atmosphere of cruel inconsequence. The episode of collective bullying is gratuitous. Its brief sudden appearance is hard to account for either as a casual happening, or for any moral it might enforce. Its eruptive and momentary cruelty emerges as one of the surprises of life, unpredictable, unexplained, and outside the range of explanation, not least because its central participant is 'one of the merriest Persons in the whole Prison'.

Moll's merriment does not conform to the stereotype of roguish good fellowship registered, for example, in the Newgate scenes of Defoe's novel *Moll Flanders* (1722) or Gay's *Beggar's Opera*. This stereotype even appears briefly in *Amelia* itself, whose inmates 'instead of wailing and repining at their Condition, were laughing, singing and diverting themselves with various kinds of Sports and Gambols' (I.iii; W 27). The latter is a more conventional jolliness lacking the harsh illogic of Blear-Eyed Moll's merriment or her lusty sexuality, reported later in the same chapter. In the next chapter there is a glimpse of a 'very pretty Girl, ... whose Beauty Mr *Booth* could not help admiring ...', declaring ... he thought she had great Innocence in her Countenance', only to be told she was an 'idle and disorderly Person, and a common Street-walker'. Then, in language that recycles the account of Moll a few pages earlier, she 'discharged a Volley of Words, every one of which was too indecent to be repeated' (A I.iv; W 33).

The repetition (there is another at I.iv; W 47, as well as analogous 'Vollies of ... Abuse' from Justice Thrasher, A I.ii; W 25) may suggest flagging energies, and the multiple harping on unmentionability acquires an aura of obsessiveness. This comes in the middle of some of Fielding's most vivid writing, but it seems to reflect the habitual gesturing of a worldliness in defeat. That Fielding retains the gesture, as he held on to the forms of couplet prose, suggests a tension between the surviving manner and a sense that it is no longer in control.

The shock of a beautiful and sometimes innocent-looking female bursting out with a startling obscenity or unexpected aggression occurs in writers as diverse as Swift and Ian McEwan. In McEwan's *The Child in Time* (1987), the main character gives generously to a girl beggar who looks like his long-lost abducted daughter, to which she replies 'Fuck you, mister'.[30] The situation is similar to Fielding's but adds the personal sadness of a highly individualized case. Fielding gives his example an exemplary or fabular form, intimating that such things, however outlandish, are also habitual. This feature is even more marked in Swift's late pamphlet, *A Proposal for Giving Badges to the Beggars* (1737). When Swift reports that 'not a few' of the beggars he met with spoke to him 'in very injurious Terms, particularly the Females', the last three words are disconcerting, but with an intimation of 'What do you expect?'[31]

Fielding's innocent-looking woman, unlike McEwan's, is without a personal history. The event comes over as a cruelty of the Absurd, with the reservation that Absurdist writers, as it were programmatically, offer such things as normal in a world in which shocking inconsequence is taken for granted and invites no comment. Fielding's story, on the other hand, cries out for comment, and Fielding offers none. The episode ostensibly belongs to a favourite type in his writings. He gives several other, outwardly similar, short glimpses of beautiful or innocent women, with a reversal or sting at the end, several of them in his earlier works. In his periodical *The Champion* (24 May 1740; W 338) a 'beautiful young Creature of about 15' appears pregnant (first shock) but loses 'her big Belly' when she takes off her clothes (second shock). The situation is then explained by her wearing a hoop petticoat, a dress fashion of the time. As early as 1735, Fielding had remarked, in the play *Miss Lucy in Town*, on the fine ladies who 'spoil their Shapes, to appear big with Child because it's the Fashion' (scene ii). A different fabular reversal occurs in the *Journey from this World to the Next* (I.vii; W 32), where 'a very beautiful Spirit indeed' seeks admission to Elysium by making eyes at Minos and boasting that she had remained chaste by refusing 'a great Number of Lovers'. Minos turns her away, telling her 'she had not refused enow yet'.

All these early passages are fables with a moral, ridiculing fashion or rebuking a prude. Such simple payoffs are not the usual stuff of Fielding's novels, where moral ironies and overturnings occur in a more broadly and fluidly animated context. When the mood of some episodes (sad cases of good people victimized for small felonies carried out in circumstances of poverty or need, for example) runs counter to Fielding's discursively expressed views (on the death penalty for petty theft, and on law and order generally), one senses that the full human context resists any schematic reduction to an expected moral conclusion.

*Amelia*, on the other hand, sometimes reaches a contrary point, where humane understanding gives way to human incomprehension. The opening chapters return to a mode of fabular vignette more readily found in early non-novelistic writings. In *Amelia*, such episodes lack a clarifying point, rather than challenging or contradicting one that is on offer. The episode of the whore has no such payoff, unless its lack of a payoff is itself a payoff. Its implication is that the only response is surprise, not understanding. Though not a pervasive feature of Fielding's later writing, or perhaps even of *Amelia*, such episodes belong to a darkening outlook mainly glimpsed in Fielding's last years. The bewildering snapshots in *Amelia* may be set alongside the painful scene from *An Enquiry into the Causes of the Late Increase of Robbers* (1751), published the same year as *Amelia*. Fielding is describing cheap overcrowded housing, which is said to foster immorality and drunkenness. He then adds the case of 'one of the prettiest Girls I had ever seen, who had been carried off by an *Irishman*, to consummate her Marriage on her Wedding-night, in a Room where several others were in Bed at the same time' (sect. vi; W 143). In this passage, no one commits wrongdoing, but the words generate a sense that cruelties of circumstance, the general indecorum of things, is of an order of painfulness quite different from that normally exhibited in Fielding's work.

Such things, including the whole character and situation of Moll, her merriment and grotesque amours as well as her participation in the tribal cruelties of prison life, display a kind of hysteria of circumstance. Their strident and grating inappropriateness reflects not only the unpredictability of events, but an unhinged comportment in the course of things. It is as if the whole nature of things had become indecorous, in the sense of offending against both order and politeness, as when Yeats speaks of 'that discourtesy of death', but without the elegiac grandeurs of nostalgia.[32]

## NOTES

The following abbreviations of works are used in this chapter. For publication details, see 'Guide to further reading'. *A Amelia; CGJ Covent-Garden Journal; Ch Champion; Corr Correspondence; Enq Enquiry into the Causes of the Late Increase of Robbers; JA Joseph Andrews; JJ Jacobite's Journal; JW Jonathan Wild; M1 Miscellanies*, vol. I; *M2 Miscellanies*, vol. II; *M3 Miscellanies*, vol. III; *Pl 1 Plays*, vol. I; *TJ Tom Jones; TP True Patriot; V Voyage to Lisbon; W Wesleyan Edition.*

1. The prison is not actually named, but is commonly assumed to be Newgate. It is referred to as Bridewell (I.ii, v; *W* 22–3, 38), presumably in the generic sense of a house of correction, not the original Bridewell Hospital built in 1720 (*W* 22–3 n. 3).

2. References are to book, chapter, and page of *Gulliver's Travels*, in *The Prose Writings of Jonathan Swift*, ed. Herbert Davis, 16 vols. (Oxford: Blackwell, 1939–74), vol. XI.

3. Fielding, *TP* No. 1, 5 November 1745, *W* 336 (obituary of Swift), *TJ* XIII.i *W* 686, *A* VIII.v *W* 324–5, *CGJ*, nos. 10, 52 (4 February, 30 June 1752), *W* 74 and n. 2, 286 and n. 5, also xliv and n. 1; A. C. Elias, Jr, ed., *Memoirs of Laetitia Pilkington* (Athens, GA: University of Georgia Press, 1997), vol. I, 312, vol. II, 703 n.

4. See *An Enquiry into the Causes of the Late Increase of Robbers* (1751), section x (*W* 164, 166), and sections viii–x *passim*; Tom Keymer, ed., Introduction to *Journal of a Voyage to Lisbon* (1755; London: Penguin, 1996), 16.

5. See further, Claude Rawson, *Henry Fielding and the Augustan Ideal under Stress* (London: Routledge and Kegan Paul, 1972; corrected edn Atlantic Highlands NJ: Humanities Press, 1991), 77 ff.

6. See ibid., 53, for this and other examples.

7. Alexander Pope, *Iliad* (1720), II.263–6 (Homer II.216–19), in the Twickenham Edition of *The Works of Alexander Pope*, ed. John Butt, Maynard Mack, et al., 11 vols. in 12 (London: Methuen, 1939–69), vol. VII, 140, 139 n. 255.

8. Homer, *Iliad*, II.216–19, trans. Richmond Lattimore (Chicago: University of Chicago Press, 1951), 82.

9. Swift, *Battle of the Books* (1704), in *Tale of a Tub, Prose Writings*, vol. I, 160.

10. Lady Mary Wortley Montagu, 'Verses Address'd to the Imitator of ... Horace' (1733), Line 110, in her *Essays and Poems*, ed. Robert Halsband and Isobel Grundy (Oxford: Clarendon Press, 1977), 270.

11. For an extensive account of Fielding's treatment, see Nina Prytula, ' "Great-Breasted and Fierce": Fielding's Amazonian Heroines', *Eighteenth-Century Studies* 35 (2002), 173–93.

12. Richardson, *Pamela* (1740), Letter xxxii, ed. Thomas Keymer and Alice Wakely (Oxford: Oxford University Press, 2001), 114. Discussed in Rawson, *Henry Fielding and the Augustan Ideal under Stress*, 58–62.

13. Pope, *Dunciad* (1728), II.144–5; (1729), II.155–6; *Dunciad, in Four Books* (1743), II.163–4.

14. Laurence Sterne, *Tristram Shandy* (1759–67), VI.vi; Sterne, 'To Sir W.', 19 September 1767.

15. Samuel Richardson, letter to Lady Bradshaigh, *c.* 1 October 1755, in *Selected Letters of Samuel Richardson*, ed. John Carroll (Oxford: Clarendon Press, 1964), 323; see also Richardson, *Sir Charles Grandison* (1754), VI.xxv; Swift, *Tale of a Tub* (1704), Conclusion.

16. For Ford's comments on Fielding, see Claude Rawson, ed., *Henry Fielding: A Critical Anthology* (Harmondsworth: Penguin, 1973), 332, 345–9, 353–66.

17. Fielding on *Clarissa*, *JJ*, No. 5 (2 January 1748), W 119–20; letter to Richardson, *c.* 15 October 1748; both in Rawson, ed., *Henry Fielding: A Critical Anthology*, 71–4.
18. W. B. Yeats, 'The Municipal Gallery Revisited' (1937), vi.
19. Fielding, 'An Essay on Conversation', in *MI* (1743), W 141.
20. Pope, *The First Satire of the Second Book of Horace Imitated* (1733), lines 139–40, in Butt, ed., *Works of Pope*, vol. IV, 19.
21. See W. L. Renwick, 'Comic Epic in Prose', (1946), in Rawson, ed., *Critical Anthology*, 464–8; Claude Rawson, *Satire and Sentiment 1660–1830*, 146–7, 152–3.
22. Ian Watt, *The Rise of the Novel* (London: Chatto and Windus, 1957), 240–8.
23. Rawson, *Satire and Sentiment 1660–1830*, 146–7, 152–3.
24. Rawson, *Henry Fielding*, Profiles in Literature (London: Routledge, 1968), 32–3 and n. 20; 'To all curious Criticks and Admirers of Meeter' (1680), line 16, probably not by Rochester, see *Works*, ed. Harold Love, (Oxford: Oxford University Press, 1999), 270, 490 n.
25. Fielding, *CGJ*, No. 8 (28 January 1752), W 65.
26. For the second-edition adjustment, see *A* II.i; W 66 and n.1, 68.
27. For Fielding's general influence on Jane Austen, see Rawson, *Satire and Sentiment 1660–1830*, 277–95, and Jo Alyson Parker, *The Author's Inheritance: Henry Fielding, Jane Austen, and the Establishment of the Novel* (Dekalb, IL: Northern Illinois University Press, 1998).
28. John Cleland, *Memoirs of a Woman of Pleasure*, ed. Peter Sabor (Oxford: Oxford University Press, 1985), 156–60; the episode was omitted from 'most … subsequent editions', see xxvii, 201 nn.; see also Cleland's *Memoirs of a Coxcomb* (1751) ed. Hal Gladfelder (Peterborough, Ont.: Broadview Press, 2005), 103, 106; Tobias Smollett, *The Adventures of Peregrine Pickle*, ed. James L. Clifford, revised Paul-Gabriel Boucé (Oxford: Oxford University Press, 1983), 242, ch. xlix (this passage was removed in the second edition, see 789 n. 4). *Peregrine Pickle* was published in February 1751 and *Amelia* in December (though dated 1752).
29. See Cleland, *Memoirs of a Woman of Pleasure*, ed. Sabor, 201 n. 159.
30. Ian McEwan, *The Child in Time* (1987; London: Picador, 1988), 8–9, 192–3. See also Hilary Mantel, *The Giant, O'Brien*, ch. 8 (London: Fourth Estate, 1998), 120.
31. Swift, *A Proposal for Giving Badges to the Beggars* (1737), in Davis, ed., *Prose Writings*, vol. XIII, 134.
32. Yeats, 'In Memory of Major Robert Gregory' (1918), vi.

# 12

## CHARLES A. KNIGHT

# Fielding's afterlife

One might envision Fielding's afterlife as 'A Journey from This World to the Next' that travels through the Elysian field of novelists, where Fielding is greeted by his successors.[1] The writers who welcome him are diverse: Smollett, Haywood, and Sterne; Burney and Austen; Scott and Byron; Dickens and Thackeray; Trollope and Meredith. European followers include Stendhal among the French, Pushkin and Gogol among the Russians. International modernists greet him as a precursor: Brecht, Mann, and Musil; Proust, Gide, and Joyce. These are joined by the comic novelists Evelyn Waugh, Kingsley Amis, Muriel Spark, Fay Weldon, David Lodge, Malcolm Bradbury, P. G. Wodehouse, and Tom Sharpe, as well as by the late modernist and post-modernist writers Gombrowicz, Kundera, Rushdie, Fowles, Coover, and Barth. They recognize in Fielding five images that identify his spirit as a novelist and that they have inherited: Fielding the self-conscious narrator, Fielding the ironist, Fielding the comic novelist, Fielding the creator of deep narrative patterns, and Fielding the immoralist.

### Fielding the narrator

Henry Fielding and Samuel Richardson are traditionally regarded as progenitors of the English novel, and one of the implications of this dual ancestry is the delineation of two quite different kinds of novel. The Richardsonian novel purports to be lifelike, told by the participants or from the participants' point of view, with little or no narrative intrusion to deflect from a direct relationship between readers and characters. In Fielding's kind of novel the readers' primary relationship is to the narrator, through whose eyes they see the characters and the action. The result, for naïve readers, may be a certain restiveness with the narrator's judgement, but the main effect is to throw the emphasis on plot rather than on the inner life of the characters. The image of Fielding the narrator is fixed by Samuel Johnson's famous distinction between Richardson and Fielding: 'that there was as great a difference between them as between a man who knew how a watch was made, and a man who could tell the hour by looking on the dial-plate'.[2] A history of the afterlife of Fielding could be constructed by this contrast with Richardson, but the contrast oversimplifies both novelists.

Erasing the distinction between showing and telling is a major function of contemporary criticism, which sees language and the use of language as action. The narrated novel that is Fielding's bequest operates on two levels of complexity: complexity of plot made possible by the sacrifice of depth psychology, and complexity of narration that restores in another way the ambiguity that derives from the absence of a controlling narrator in Richardson's novels. The contrast of telling to showing obscures the narrator's flexible and mutable relations to his readers and his material. The narrator may claim to be telling a story that has some independent authority, either because it actually happened or because it derives from a quasi-independent source (as with the narration of *Don Quixote*); or the narrator may admit his own authority, as Thackeray does when, at the end of *Vanity Fair* (1847–8), he puts his puppets back in their box. Fielding may assert a tyrannic role as the creator of his text or its genre. He may pontificate about the novel or about life. He may describe characters with evident irony or questionable uncertainty. He may summarize the background of scenes, or he may disappear from the scene altogether, leaving characters to their own discourse. The intrusive narrator can speak with a variety of voices that the illusion of realism limits and can do so without relinquishing responsibility for the text and its ambiguities. Fielding's antagonism towards Richardson's *Pamela* may lie in the fact that the text, and hence its moral uncertainties, belong to Pamela rather than to Richardson. Fielding's direct and indirect attacks on Richardson in *Shamela*, *Jonathan Wild*, and *Joseph Andrews* imply that the realistic, unnarrated novel is illusionistic, even pretentious. In the narrated novel realistic elements remain, but they are filtered through a narrative consciousness, creating possibilities of narrative interpretation even when the narrator is silent.

Characters such as Pamela can be saved from being victims of the ironic interpretation of readers by becoming the target of the author's ironies. Distance between the narrator and his characters allows the space for complex analysis, as in the case of George Meredith's *The Egoist*.[3] Meredith admired Fielding as a comic writer, and for Meredith comedy requires a distance from which pretension, contradiction, and absurdity can become apparent to the reader as well as the narrator. Perceptions of Willoughby Patterne, the novel's comic centre, are the focal point of *The Egoist* (1879, rev. 1897), which develops a lively counterplay among his self-perceptions, the perceptions of his mostly female admirers, those of his disillusioned fiancée Clara Middleton, those of the narrator, and those of readers. Fielding's and Meredith's narrators achieve this distance in part by revealing the character's inner thoughts as they are witnessed rather than as they are thought. A key to this comic use of narrative intrusion is the narrator's insistent generalizing – both by applying general principles to the characters' thoughts and by deducing principles from them. As a result characters tend to become typical as well as individual. This procedure is particularly useful in observing the ratiocination of the characters – the ways they convince themselves of ideas they know are false. Willoughby is insistent on his superiority and on his individuality, even his uniqueness. His sense of superiority requires that he be admired, and that need for admiration requires that he subordinate his inner self to the self that is admired by society. Hence by the end of the novel the egoist has essentially lost his ego. What Meredith primarily learned from Fielding was the use of the distant and ironic narrator as a lens through which to look at character.

But because the Fielding narrator looks at far more than character, and because his tendency is to move towards generality and the experience of readers, he often erases the distinction between fictional and expository writing. The result is the embedded essay, which may be distinct and defined, as in the case of the prefatory chapters of *Joseph Andrews* and *Tom Jones*, or may be a topical excursion of several paragraphs. Scott creates awkward narrative surrogates who sometimes take responsibility for essayistic intrusions, but otherwise he and other nineteenth-century authors seem as comfortable as Fielding in writing expository digressions. Gogol's digressions, such as the discussion of naming characters at the beginning of Chapter 9 of *Dead Souls* (1842–55), seem close to Fielding in their whimsy and their insistence on the novel as the author's creation. In later novels, such as Joyce's *Portrait of the Artist as a Young Man* (1914–15) or Musil's *Man without Qualities* (1930–43), the intrusive essay may be assigned to the central character rather than the narrator. In some post-modern novels, Kundera's *The Book of Laughter and Forgetting* (1979, rev. 1985), for example, essays and fictions are the products of the same consciousness, and the author is the admitted inventor of the story. If Fielding did not introduce the embedded essay as an element of fiction, he certainly authorized its use by later novelists. In doing so he incorporated the function of the epic to record and transmit a range of cultural knowledge.

The self-conscious novelist need not, of course, write directly about novels or the novel he is composing, but such self-criticism naturally accompanies the movement from novelist to essayist. The essays that open the eighteen books of *Tom Jones* are unusual, even among self-conscious novelists. They reflect Fielding's sense that he is an early practitioner of fictional history and that he can take advantage of that position to address, sometimes directly but often playfully, the ways he should be read. He does this both for the narrative elements of his novel and, as with the discussion of Black George in the first chapter of Book VII, for the principles by which characters can be judged. Fielding's Prefaces have not been widely imitated among major novelists; their modern equivalents seem to be book tours, journal articles, and interviews in the *Partisan Review*. They nonetheless call attention to the novelist's need to redefine the genre in terms of a particular text. The extraordinary power that Fielding claims as a narrator seems to rob him of the right to claim that he is only showing life as it is. But his power as a narrator is both justified and limited by his claim that, as he put it in the Preface to *Joseph Andrews*, 'every thing is copied from the Book of Nature'.[4] The Book of Nature is read by the same people who read *Joseph Andrews*, and Fielding's evocation of it throws the responsibility for meaning back on his readers. It is perhaps because he is aware of the responsibility of readers that Fielding is so talkative as a narrator.

Although the narrator of *Tom Jones* is remembered as a filtering and directing consciousness, he shifts voices and tones – at times ironic, at times mock-heroic, at times sympathetic. He generalizes about aesthetic and moral points; he summarizes characters and events; but he also presents scenes and dialogue with a dramatic immediacy. This shifting narrative voice contributes to the novel's lively pace. It is a principal legacy to Jane Austen, who complicates it and extends it with a free indirect discourse that allows her simultaneously to present and to comment upon the consciousness of characters. She is closest to the self-conscious Fielding in the opening and closing chapters of *Northanger Abbey* (1818) and in her defence of novelists in Chapter 5 of the first volume. Her more significant debt to Fielding lies in the shifting multiplicity of narrative voices that enables complex perspectives. Jo Alyson Parker's comparison of Fielding and Austen emphasizes their use of the inheritance plot, their strategies to establish authority, and Austen's gendered rewriting of Fielding.[5]

## Fielding the ironist

The shifting of narrative voices is a prime means by which the novelist creates irony – through dislocating shifts between authorial summary and authorial comment, between the speech of the characters and the voice of the narrator. In *Jonathan Wild*, *Joseph Andrews*, and *Tom Jones* irony is often signalled by a mock-heroic tone, but even where that tone is not evident, an indirect but apparent disjunction between the material of the novel and the narrator's emotional response or moral evaluation is frequent in Fielding, sometimes obvious and sometimes subtle. The ubiquity of such narrative irony in Fielding surely stimulated the ironies of later comic novelists such as Frances Burney and Jane Austen, especially in their depiction of naïve or deluded characters.

In addition to the narrative irony created by the distance between the tone and meaning of the narrator's language, verbal irony emphasizes the culturally significant misinterpretation of a key term – usually signalled by the difference between the original or commonly understood meaning of the term and its meaning as used in contemporary society. Fielding canvasses such language in the 'modern glossary' he provides in *Covent-Garden Journal*, No. 4, and he uses the contradictions implicit in the social use of language to telling effect in the cases of 'greatness' in *Jonathan Wild* and 'prudence' in *Tom Jones*. Such dislocating irony calls into question the capacity of language to render meaning precisely, especially when language is used by self-serving individuals or by a culture where values are askew.

Both narrative and verbal ironies are talkative, but irony can also function as narrative silence when a harsh judgement is appropriate. Once the narrator has established his ironic voice, it is difficult to know when he is not being ironic. The Heartfrees seem to function as good and naïve alternatives to the evil Jonathan Wild, but readers may be inclined to read them as ironic characters, so that Heartfree's unquestioning trust seems almost culpable, and Mrs Heartfree's protestations of chastity seem vain. At the same time Jonathan seems a feckless as well as evil hero, and readers may find him likeable.[6] The Chaplinesque failures of his pretensions to power often resemble our own predicaments.

The most immediate successor to *Jonathan Wild* was Smollett's *The Adventures of Ferdinand Count Fathom* (1753). Less extensively than Fielding, Smollett parodies history books, and Fathom, like Wild, is a caricature of a hero. Like Wild, Fathom is contrasted to notable good characters, here his childhood friend and companion Renaldo Count de Melvil. Fathom is marginally more successful as a conman and decidedly more successful as a seducer than Wild, but he avoids the hanging that is Wild's fate, to make a distracting appearance in Smollett's later *Humphry Clinker* (1771). Smollett's irony is less insistent and less telling than Fielding's, and he has greater difficulty in making his story interesting. Thus Fathom seems unforgivable not because he is evil but because he is boring. The problem may be mitigated when the ironic centre is a flawed first-person narrator rather than an omniscient author.

The narrator of *Jonathan Wild* finds it difficult to sustain ironic sympathy for his hero; Thackeray's *Barry Lyndon* (1844), clearly modelled on *Jonathan Wild*, suffers greater problems of ironic control. For the first two-thirds of the novel, its hero is an amoral Irishman whose excuses and evasions are enter-taining. Once he marries, he becomes an unsympathetic, irresponsible, and abusive husband. *Barry Lyndon* is narrated by its hero in his unhappy old age, and hence major sources of irony are the distance between the past and its present consequences and Lyndon's unawareness of the moral implica-tions of the connection. *Barry Lyndon*, like *Jonathan Wild*, is based on a historical character, and Barry becomes a stereotypical Irishman. Just as Lyndon is unwilling to make moral judgements about his own actions, he is unwilling to see that his actions have unfortunate consequences. Although he is certainly on the make throughout, his ambition is not as sharply defined as that of Wild; Lyndon seems lazy, but Wild is hyperactive. In both novels the irony satirizes society generally by implying that what the characters do is what others do. Like *Jonathan Wild*, *Barry Lyndon* is unpleasant, despite the interests of irony, and both are secondary efforts by their authors. Nonetheless, the tradition of ironically represented rogues continues to the present.

Brecht's *Threepenny Novel* (1934) is a bleaker version of his well-known play. As Claude Rawson has suggested, Brecht may also have used Fielding's ironic equation of the powerful and the criminal in his play *The Resistible Rise of Arturo Ui* in which Adolf Hitler is equated with a gangster.[7] Rawson further notes the Wildian elements of Alfred Jarry's *Ubu* plays (*Ubu Roi*, 1896), of Charlie Chaplin's *The Great Dictator* (1940), of Barbara Garson's *MacBird* (1966), and of Philip Roth's *Our Gang (Starring Tricky and His Friends)* (1971), to which I would emphatically add Salman Rushdie's *Shame* (1983), in which the fictional equivalents of Bhutto and General Zia repre-sent more broadly the battle between secular corruption and religious fanati-cism, and Robert Coover's *The Public Burning* (1977), in which Richard Nixon expatiates with pleasure on the execution of the Rosenbergs. Fielding's ironic accomplishment is to have taken, as Gay did in the *Beggar's Opera* (1728), the historical figure of Wild and suggested a com-parison to the political Robert Walpole, who is then elevated, by virtue of parody, to the level of such canonical heroes as Alexander and Caesar.

A modern extension of Fielding's ironic interests is *Ferdydurke* (1938) by Witold Gombrowicz. Gombrowicz sees identity as imposed more or less arbitrarily by external figures. The narrator and central character is himself an author; outsiders see his character as childish, and therefore he behaves in childish ways. The irony of narrators who do not say what they mean or how they feel is echoed by the ironic disjunction between personal and social readings of identity. Irony, from Fielding to Gombrowicz, engages a problem endemic in the novel but illustrated particularly by Jane Austen. There is a triple disjunction of perception: the central character, whose perceptions the reader often but not always shares, mistakenly perceives a situation which may well be misperceived in different ways by still other characters, but it is, in turn, ironically presented by the narrator, who may shift among the novel's multiple planes of perception. A central topic of the ironic novel is the ubiquity of misperception.

## Fielding the comic novelist

A central cause of misperception is deceptive presentation. In his Preface to *Joseph Andrews* Fielding sees affectation as 'the only source of the true Ridiculous' (7), and irony uncovers the vanity and hypocrisy that for Fielding constitute the ridiculous. But the comic epic contrasts to comic drama in other respects: 'its Action being more extended and comprehensive; containing a much larger Circle of Incidents, and introducing a greater Variety of Characters' (4). It differs from romance in its 'light and ridiculous' fable and action, its introduction of characters from low life, and its 'ludicrous' sentiments and diction. Fielding's variety of characters and incidents implies a variety of discourse. Despite the controlling force of narrative consciousness, the novels include the diversity of voices and perspectives that Bakhtin famously describes as 'the social diversity of speech types' or 'heteroglossia'.[8] The comic novel is characterized by variety, by pace, and by its exploration of social contradictions; what Fielding particularly added to it was its breadth and complexity of plot and the structures that organize that plot. Fielding's comic novel reveals the absurdities of society, flowing from the vanities and hypocrisies that make it up. It presents a formal struggle between the chaotic diversity and recalcitrant grit of its material on one hand and, on the other, the structural order that reveals the intelligent design of its godlike creator. What differentiates the comic novel from the picaresque is the manifestation of a structuring principle that may be aesthetic, consisting of correspondences, symmetries, and balances, or may be thematic, as in the case of Fielding's foundling plot and depiction of social victimization.

Comic structure is driven by the force of causality, whose significance varies from novel to novel and reader to reader. Causality may be merely random, as in the case of Smollett's *Roderick Random* (1748), it may be providential, as in the case of *Amelia*, or it may be paranoiac, as in the case of Pynchon's *Gravity's Rainbow* (1973). It becomes most significant when it operates below the level of presentation, becoming one of the silences of the narrator. Charles Dickens's *Great Expectations* (1860–1), like *David Copperfield* (1849–50), resembles *Tom Jones* so closely as to seem modelled on Fielding's masterpiece.[9] (Dickens, after all, named one of his sons after Fielding.) A dominant image in *Great Expectations* is the chain, and characters are variously chained to each other and to the consequences of their actions, but the chain of causality remains invisible to the reader and to Pip the narrator until Magwitch appears on Pip's stairs and the links begin to join.

Causality in *Great Expectations* implies the inner connections that join all human beings, but it has a different significance in modern novels self-consciously modelled on Fielding, such as André Gide's *The Counterfeiters* (*Les Faux-Monnayeurs*) (1926) and John Barth's *The Sot-Weed Factor* (1967).[10] Gide revisited Fielding during a dry point in the composition of his novel. 'The translation of *Tom Jones*, the proofs of which Dent has just sent me, is most mediocre. I decline to write the introduction . . . I find myself again confronted with my *Faux-Monnayeurs*, but this brief plunge into Fielding has enlightened me as to the insufficiencies of my book. I am wondering whether I shouldn't expand the text, intrude myself (in spite of what Martin du Gard says), make comments. I have lost touch.'[11] If Gide felt disoriented in writing the novel, readers have felt disoriented in reading it. Gide uses several narrators: an authorial narrator outside the text, who presents the action and on at least one occasion (Part II, ch. 7) evaluates the characters and their situations, perhaps not reliably, and a fictional quasi-narrator inside the text. Edouard is a novelist writing a novel with the same title as Gide's, in which he introduces characters based on the people he encounters. Some of Gide's novel consists of straightforward narrative, some of Edouard's journal, and some of letters written by various characters. (The writing, reading, exchange, and stealing of letters is a significant theme in the novel.) As if this were not enough, Edouard's young friend Bernard, realizing that Edouard will not actually write 'The Counterfeiters', suggests that he will write it himself. The intervention of the narrator in Part II is important in reinforcing the unreliability of Edouard as narrator and actor. Gide's narrative manipulation constantly undercuts both characters and narrators. But the problem that Edouard sets for himself as author becomes the problem that Gide too faces: how to write a novel in an uncertain world. That problem then brings us to the major theme shared by Gide and Fielding: the relationship of appearance to reality. Gide's characters do not say what they mean or act as they intend. They repeatedly misconceive the actions and motives of other characters and even of themselves. Such complexities are appropriate to a novel peopled by adolescents who try out various roles in an effort to discover or create their identities. For older adults the appearance-reality gap is apparent in hypocrisy. But sometimes hypocrisy itself seems the defensive strategy of good characters. There are actual counterfeiters in the novel, but counterfeiting becomes an image of deliberate falseness, as it applies to both art and behaviour.

Fielding's certainties also dissolve in John Barth's *The Sot-Weed Factor*, a novel equal to *Tom Jones* in length, complexity, and pacing, if not in narrative distance. In his foreword to the Anchor edition, Barth speaks of intending to write a twentieth-century novel in eighteenth-century style: 'The style would echo that of the big eighteenth-century comic novelists, especially Henry Fielding.' He sought to write 'a story at least as complicated, and if possible as energetically entertaining, as Fielding's *Tom Jones*'.[12] Primary among the themes and devices shared by the novels is the idea that appearances are not reality and that maturity is a matter of reading appearances with appropriate scepticism. At question is the nature of the reality that lies behind the veneer of appearances. For Barth reality consists of a series of performances played one within another, and the task of perception is not to distinguish between deceit or false appearance and reality, as in the case of Fielding, but to recognize the meaning of performance. The possibility that one may be mistaken in one's perceptions of the most important things is the stuff of tragedy. The comic vision makes it endurable by seeing it both as a revelation of the limits of social order and as a recognition that allows personal development. Despite the different epistemological positions of Fielding and of his modern and post-modern successors, they share the acceptable disorientation of the comic vision.

## Fielding's deep narratives

Fielding has an important role in the transmitting of deep narrative patterns that represent basic situations of the human condition and elicit nearly universal identification on the part of readers. Because these patterns are quite resonant, they recur over time and thus often seem the common property of cultures rather than the original creations of individual authors. The self-conscious use and transmission of such narrative patterns nonetheless seem an important element of authorial influence. Two patterns in particular help to characterize the importance of Fielding for subsequent novelists: the identification of the foundling and the victimization of the hapless individual by repressive social forces and institutions. Such patterns ultimately stand for the search of the hero for his appropriate place in society, and to represent that search they have to identify the criteria by which his place may be deemed appropriate as well as the qualities that allow him to earn it or that hinder him from doing so.

A basic narrative pattern employed by Fielding is the foundling myth – the story of the young man separated from his father by death, illegitimacy, or abduction. In the case of *Amelia* the foundling figure is not Booth but his wife Amelia. Although Booth shares with Jones an expulsion from an Edenic paradise, he is a more serious sinner than Tom. But Amelia is the disinherited figure, and the discovery of her mother's will fortuitously resolves the plot. The foundling plot is connected to the issue of inheritance in all three of Fielding's major novels, and the quest for the father is directly connected to the quest for a spouse in *Joseph Andrews* and *Tom Jones*. The conjunction of quests gives urgency and direction to the hero's search for a place in society. Fielding conjoins the aristocratic myth of worth inherited at birth with the genuinely bourgeois novel in which individual effort must struggle to achieve modest success. Badly off as Tom Jones may be, he does not actually work to survive, in contrast to the more decidedly middle-class novels of the nineteenth century, Dickens's *Great Expectations* and Thackeray's *Pendennis* (1848–9), in which work becomes the foundling's salvation.

Godwin's *Caleb Williams* (1794) focuses on an intense relationship between the orphaned hero and his master, whom he may see as a father or even as a lover. But the strong linear movement of the novel leads to Caleb's discovery of his master's dangerous secret and his consequent flight from persecution. In Scott's *Redgauntlet* (1824), a novel that seems to draw from most of its great eighteenth-century precursors, the orphaned Darcy Latimer has a decidedly mysterious past, and his efforts to unravel it lead to a complex of adventures that take him and his friend Alan Fairfield through cultural conflicts of religion, class, and nation. The foundling pattern recurs repeatedly in Dickens: *Oliver Twist* (1838), *Nicholas Nickleby* (1838–9), *Martin Chuzzlewit* (1843–4), and *Bleak House* (1852–3), but most significantly in *David Copperfield* and *Great Expectations*. Since the foundling lacks a protective father, he moves in a world where discernment of friends and enemies is crucial, where the possibilities of alternative outcomes, from hanging to triumph, are manifold, and where the discovery of parentage, vocation, or marriage signals his accommodation to society. The adolescent quest for parentage is, of course, a notable element of Joyce's *Ulysses* and of Gide's *The Counterfeiters* as well.

Robert Alter has written sensitively about the narrative features that Stendhal learned from Fielding.[13] But *The Charterhouse of Parma* shares structural characteristics of the foundling plot as well. These include the hero's search for a father or bride, and a symmetrical structure in which events and characters significantly repeat and correspond. Fabrizio, like Tom, grows up in an isolated environment filled with boyhood adventures. He leaves home, although not, like Tom, rejected. Both go towards an important battle in which they do not take part. Both have significant affairs with women. In both novels there is the threat of incest: Tom with Jenny Jones; Fabrizio (more remotely) with Sanséverina. Both are attacked by men whom they kill (or, in Tom's case, seem to kill), and both are imprisoned.

Tom loves Sophia from early in the novel; Fabrizio wonders for much of the novel whether he is capable of love, but becomes infatuated with Clelia. But both the linear plot and the marriage plot are unfulfilled in *Charterhouse*. While Tom and Sophia reject the evils of the city and return to the country, Fabrizio joins the rigor and isolation of the Carthusians. Fabrizio retains an outlaw status that threatens him throughout much of the novel; Tom's status as outlaw or prisoner is briefer and more local. Fabrizio's meditative loneliness is appropriate to his final Carthusian vocation; Tom's generous affability is rewarded by his marriage and his place in a community. *Charterhouse* contains repeated or echoing events: Fabrizio's flight from Waterloo (and his killing of a Prussian soldier) is echoed by his flight after his killing of Giletti; Count Mosca's convenient alliance with the corrupt liberal Judge Rassi parallels Sanséverina's arrangement with the radical poet Palla. *Charterhouse* presents fairly obvious contrasting characters: Sanséverina with Clelia; Mosca with Fabrizio. *Tom Jones* lacks the complex and ironic treatment of court politics in *Charterhouse*, but its significant treatment of the foundling pattern offers the capacity to see the hero both as a developing character and as a figure who moves through a hostile and threatening social world.

The delineation of that social world, then, is the second resonant narrative pattern that Fielding passed on to his successors. It is implicit in the foundling plot, where the hero's difficult journey becomes a device for revealing and judging society. But in *Amelia*, Fielding adds an important and striking element to the novel's social exposition: indirectly expressed authorial anger. In the opening chapters the innocent Captain Booth is arrested and sent to Newgate by the corrupt and illiterate Justice Thrasher. There he encounters a series of figures – some disgusting, some innocent, some violent, many corrupt. The sequence has an impact that is unprecedented in English fiction. Its power derives in part from its careful narration, which moves from the eccentric or horrifying characters Booth meets to Booth's reactions and to the concerned voice of the narrator himself. The naïve reactions of Booth are contrasted to the more knowledgeable information he receives from his acquaintance Robinson. These encounters define the apparent hopelessness of his plight and, more generally, the helplessness of the innocent in a society unable to distinguish between innocence and guilt. The scene resembles the tour of Newgate a century later that Wemmick gives to Pip, but Pip is not an inmate and does not know the connections to Newgate that will haunt him later. The novels of Dickens are filled with set pieces describing the horrific effects of social injustice – the workhouse and Jacob's Island of *Oliver Twist*, Tom-all-Alone's in *Bleak House*, Coketown in *Hard Times* (1854), the Marshalsea in *Little Dorrit* (1855–7). Descriptions of the conditions of workers and their families in Elizabeth Gaskell's *Mary Barton* (1848) and other novels on the condition of England repeat the same point as Fielding – that individuals at the bottom of society are victimized by outside forces that they cannot control. The same point is made by Engels in *The Condition of the Working Class in England* (1845) and is surely a direct response to the perception of injustice rather than a result of literary influence. But Fielding's recognition that fiction could function not only to record social injustice but to stimulate emotional reactions to it was an important precedent.

### Fielding the immoralist

Although for the past half-century it has been usual to think of Fielding as a moral author, he has spent most of his afterlife in the biographical purgatory to which he was sent by the scandalous and unsubstantiated tales of Arthur Murphy's preface to Fielding's collected works (1762). On the literary side, Samuel Johnson's important consideration of modern fiction in *Rambler*, No. 4 has generally been seen as directed against *Tom Jones*. Johnson argues that since fiction is a highly realistic, emotionally powerful medium, read in particular by the young, it has a strong obligation to represent not the total spectrum of chaotic reality but those elements that lead to good behaviour. 'In narratives, where historical veracity has no place, I cannot discover why there should not be exhibited the most perfect idea of virtue; of virtue not angelical, nor above probability, for what we cannot credit we shall never imitate, but the highest and purest that humanity can reach, which, exercised in such trials as the various revolutions of things shall bring upon it, may, by conquering some calamities, and enduring others, teach us what we may hope, and what we can perform.'[14] *Tom Jones* falls far short of this standard.

Although the authority of Johnson and Murphy may account for considerable coolness towards Fielding in the late eighteenth century, there was pronounced squeamishness in the nineteenth century. William Makepeace Thackeray is a good example of the ambivalence of novelists. Thackeray had used, adapted, and imitated Fielding. The connections between *Jonathan Wild* and *Barry Lyndon* were noted at the time. *Vanity Fair* draws on *Amelia* for its central characters: George Osborne is a feckless echo of Booth, properly dispatched fairly early in the novel; faithful Dobbin resembles Sergeant Atkinson, Becky Sharp ably fills the place of Miss Matthews, and Amelia Sedley closely resembles Amelia Booth, Thackeray's favourite heroine.[15] *Pendennis* is a novel of development similar in some respects to *Tom Jones*, and in his Preface Thackeray cites Fielding as an exemplar in his effort to portray his hero with all his faults: 'Since the author of *Tom Jones* was buried, no writer of fiction among us has been permitted to depict to his utmost power a Man. We must drape him, and give him a certain conventional simper.' Notwithstanding the apology, Arthur Pendennis is considerably less faulty and more anaemic than either Jones or Booth. In 1840, Thackeray reviewed an edition of Fielding, and, though noting that he must be read with caution, claimed that 'those who have a mind to forgive a little coarseness for the sake of one of the honestest, manliest, kindest companions in all the world cannot, as we fancy, find a better than Fielding'.[16] Thackeray repeats his praise of Fielding in his 1851 lecture on 'Hogarth, Smollett and Fielding', but adds serious moral objections to Tom Jones: 'I can't say that I think Mr Jones a virtuous character; I can't say but that I think Fielding's evident liking and admiration for Mr Jones shows that the great humourist's moral sense was blunted by his life, and that here, in Art and Ethics, there is a great error.'[17] In Chapter 4 of *The Newcomes*, Colonel Newcome articulates much the same position, with emphasis on Fielding's failure to observe class distinctions: 'If Mr Fielding was a gentleman by birth, he ought to have known better; and so much the worse for him that he did not.'[18] Thackeray had difficulty reconciling the honest, charming companion with the author who could depict the immoral rascal Tom Jones in a sympathetic light.

But Fielding's alleged immorality is one of his greatest contributions to the history of fiction. He became the literary authority for withholding moral judgement about his characters. His novels assert that the complexity of his characters' motives, the extent of human irrationality, and the gaps between appearance and reality make judgement difficult and unreliable. What irritated the nineteenth century particularly was his failure to punish his offensive heroes. But the silence of the talky narrator about ultimate moral judgements, especially moral judgements of attractive characters, shifts the function of the novel away from exemplary moral instruction and towards the comic perception of human complexity and contradiction. Fielding was, of course, deeply concerned about moral behaviour, but the comic epic he developed freed the novel both to consider moral issues more openly and to withhold moral judgement. He freed the novel from being the servant of conventional morality.

Fielding's afterlife takes several forms. Some novelists – Dickens, Thackeray, Barth, for example – acknowledge his influence directly. Others, such as Stendhal and Gide, acknowledge it privately but manifest it nonetheless. Some, such as Frances Burney and Jane Austen, seem constrained by his unsavoury reputation from associating with him too closely, but borrow significant elements of his comic and ironic narrative. Some elements of his legacy were not original with him but became part of his novelistic identity. Thus some later writers borrowed his original material, while others used characteristics he passed on from earlier novelists, Cervantes especially. Fielding's afterlife extends indirectly to authors who may not have read him and did not consciously imitate him. Fielding's self-conscious narration, his combination of novels with the essay, his authorial ironies, his elaboration of epic archetypes, his affection for characters that are not exemplary – all these are constituents of the kind of novel that Fielding passed on to later novelists. These later novelists wrote out of different cultures and different values, and their debts to Fielding sometimes reveal their differences from him. But the ways in which these novelists used, shaped, sharpened, and altered Fielding's comic epic in prose help to define the nature of his accomplishments. Such continual refashioning is the best assurance of a long and prosperous afterlife.

## NOTES

1. The major work on Fielding's literary reputation is still Frederick T. Blanchard, *Fielding the Novelist: A Study in Historical Criticism* (New Haven: Yale University Press, 1926); a more selective but modern list is provided in Robert Alter, *Partial Magic: The Novel as a Self-Conscious Genre* (Berkeley: University of California Press, 1975); see also the last chapter of Alter's *Fielding and the Nature of the Novel* (Cambridge, MA: Harvard University Press, 1968), 179–202, and Claude Rawson, ed., *Henry Fielding: A Critical Anthology* (Harmondsworth: Penguin, 1973).
2. James Boswell, *Life of Johnson*, ed. G. B. Hill, rev. L. F. Powell, 6 vols. (Oxford: Clarendon Press, 1934), vol. II, 49.
3. Maaja A. Stewart develops this point in 'Techniques of Intellectual Comedy in Meredith and Fielding', *Genre* 8 (1975), 233–49.
4. Fielding, *Joseph Andrews*, ed. Martin C. Battestin (Oxford: Clarendon Press, and Middletown, CT: Wesleyan University Press, 1967), 10.
5. Jo Alyson Parker, *The Author's Inheritance: Henry Fielding, Jane Austen, and the Establishment of the Novel* (DeKalb: Northern Illinois University Press, 1998).
6. Claude Rawson in *Henry Fielding and the Augustan Ideal under Stress* (London: Routledge and Kegan Paul, 1972), 101–36.
7. Ibid., 171–227, and Rawson's preface to Henry Fielding, *Jonathan Wild*, ed. Hugh Amory, Claude Rawson, and Linda Bree (Oxford: Oxford University Press, 2003), xxiv–xxvi.
8. M. M. Bakhtin, *The Dialogic Imagination*, ed. Michael Holquist, trans. Caryl Emerson and Michael Holquist (Austin: University of Texas Press, 1981), 263.
9. Dickens's debts to Fielding as narrator, social critic, and constructor of plots and character are weighed in Andrew Sanders, *Dickens and the Spirit of the Age* (Oxford: Clarendon Press, 1999), 172–85, and Helen Small, 'The Debt to Society: Dickens, Fielding, and the Genealogy of the Novel', in *The Victorians and the Eighteenth Century: Reassessing the Tradition*, ed. Francis O'Gorman and Katherine Turner (Aldershot, Hampshire: Ashgate, 2004), 14–40.

10. See William B. Coley, 'Gide and Fielding', *Comparative Literature* 11:1 (Winter 1959), 1–15.
11. André Gide, 'Journal of *The Counterfeiters*', trans. Justin O'Brien, in *The Counterfeiters*, trans. Dorothy Bussy (New York: Vintage, 1973), 441–2.
12. John Barth, *The Sot-Weed Factor* (New York: Anchor Books, 1987), unpaginated.
13. Robert Alter, 'Stendhal, Fielding, and the Fiction of Discrimination', *Providence* 3:1 (Fall 1995), 32–49.
14. Samuel Johnson, *Rambler*, No. 4; in *Yale Edition of the Works of Samuel Johnson*, ed. W. J. Bate and Albrecht B. Strauss (New Haven: Yale University Press, 1969), vol. III, 24.
15. Winslow Rogers, 'Thackeray and Fielding's *Amelia*', *Criticism* 19 (1979), 141–59, concentrates particularly on the possible influence of Fielding on Thackeray's narration and provides a survey of earlier comment on the Thackeray–Fielding connection.
16. Quoted in Claude Rawson, ed., *Henry Fielding: A Critical Anthology* (Harmondsworth: Penguin, 1973), 263.
17. Quoted in ibid., 278.
18. William Makepeace Thackeray, *The Newcomes*, 2 vols. (London: Dent, 1910), vol. I, 43.

*Editions*

The Wesleyan Edition of the works of Henry Fielding, edited by William B. Coley and others, includes the following volumes (Oxford: Clarendon Press, 1967–).

*Joseph Andrews*, ed. Martin C. Battestin, textual intro. Fredson Bowers, 1967
*Miscellanies*, vol. I, ed. Henry Knight Miller, textual intro. Fredson Bowers, 1972
*The History of Tom Jones: A Foundling*, ed. Martin C. Battestin and Fredson Bowers (2 vols.), 1974, subsequently reissued as a one-volume paperback
'*The Jacobite's Journal' and Related Writings*, ed. W. B. Coley, 1974
*Amelia*, ed. Martin C. Battestin, 1983
'*The True Patriot' and Related Writings*, ed. W. B. Coley, 1987
'*An Enquiry into the Causes of the Late Increase of Robbers', and Related Writings*, ed. Malvin R. Zirker, textual intro. Fredson Bowers, 1988
'*The Covent-Garden Journal' and 'A Plan of the Universal Register-Office'*, ed. Bertrand A. Goldgar, 1988
*Miscellanies*, vol. II, intro. and commentary Bertrand A. Goldgar, text ed. Hugh Amory, 1993 (includes *Journey from this World to the Next*)
*Miscellanies*, vol. III, intro. and commentary Bertrand A. Goldgar, text ed. Hugh Amory (*Jonathan Wild*), 1997
*Contributions to 'The Champion' and Related Writings*, ed. W. B. Coley, 2003
*Plays*, vol. I, 1728–31, ed. Thomas Lockwood, 2004
*Plays*, vol. II, 1731–4, ed. Thomas Lockwood, forthcoming 2007
'*The Journal of a Voyage to Lisbon', 'Shamela', and Occasional Writings*, ed. Martin C. Battestin with the late Sheridon W. Baher, Jr, and Hugh Amory, forthcoming 2008

Of the novels, *Shamela* and *Joseph Andrews* (often published together, as in the Riverside edition, ed. Martin C. Battestin, 1961; Norton Critical Edition, ed. Homer Goldberg, 1987; Everyman edition, introduction by Claude Rawson, notes by A. R. Humphreys, 1998; and Oxford World's Classics edition, ed. Douglas Brooks-Davies, revised Thomas Keymer, 1999) are widely available. However, an older edition of *Shamela* (Augustan Reprints 37, Los Angeles: William Andrews Clark Memorial Library, 1956) is of interest both as a facsimile of the original and for the introduction by Ian Watt. There are many editions of *Tom Jones* in print (notably the Norton Critical Edition, ed. Sheridan Baker, 1973, 2nd edn 1995; Everyman, introduction by Claude Rawson, 1991; and the Penguin edition, ed. Thomas Keymer and Alice Wakeley, 2005). *Jonathan Wild*, text ed. Hugh Amory, introduction by Claude Rawson, notes by Linda Bree, was published by Oxford World's Classics in 2003. There is currently no paperback edition of *Amelia* in print; an edition edited by Linda Bree (Peterborough, Ont.: Broadview Press) is forthcoming.

Individual plays available in reputable modern editions include:

*The Author's Farce*, ed. Charles B. Woods (Lincoln: University of Nebraska Press, 1966; London: Edward Arnold, 1967)

*The Tragedy of Tragedies*, with its earlier version, *Tom Thumb*, ed. L. J. Morrissey (Edinburgh: Oliver and Boyd, 1970)

*The Grub-Street Opera*, ed. Edgar V. Roberts (Lincoln: University of Nebraska Press, 1968; London: Edward Arnold, 1969); ed. L. J. Morrissey (Edinburgh: Oliver and Boyd, 1973)

*The Covent-Garden Tragedy*, ed. O. M. Brack, William Kupersmith, and Curt A. Zimansky (Iowa City: University of Iowa Press, 1973)

*'The Historical Register for the Year 1736' and 'Eurydice Hissed'*, ed. William W. Appleton (Lincoln: University of Nebraska Press, 1967)

*The Covent-Garden Tragedy, Tom Thumb, and Pasquin* are all included in *Burlesque Plays of the Eighteenth Century*, ed. Simon Trussler (Oxford: Oxford University Press, 1969)

Useful editions of the non-fictional prose are *The Journal of a Voyage to Lisbon*, ed. Tom Keymer (Harmondsworth: Penguin, 1996), and a volume of Fielding's critical writings, *The Criticism of Henry Fielding*, ed. Ioan Williams (London: Routledge, 1970)

Battestin, Martin C., and Clive T. Probyn, eds., *The Correspondence of Henry and Sarah Fielding* (Oxford: Clarendon Press, 1993)

*Collections of early criticism (including Henry Fielding's own)*

Paulson, Ronald, and Thomas Lockwood, eds., *Henry Fielding: The Critical Heritage* (London: Routledge and Kegan Paul, 1969)

Rawson, Claude, ed., *Henry Fielding: A Critical Anthology* (Harmondsworth: Penguin, 1973)

*Bibliographical and related studies*

Hahn, H. George, *Henry Fielding: An Annotated Bibliography* (Metuchen, NJ: Scarecrow Press, 1979)

Morrissey, L. J., *Henry Fielding: A Reference Guide* (Boston: G. K. Hall, 1980)

Ribble, Frederick G., and Anne G. Ribble, *Fielding's Library: An Annotated Catalogue* (Charlottesville: Bibliographical Society of the University of Virginia, 1996)

Stoler, John A., and Richard D. Fulton, *Henry Fielding: An Annotated Bibliography of Twentieth-Century Criticism, 1900–1977* (New York: Garland, 1980)

## Biographical studies

Battestin, Martin C., with Ruthe R. Battestin, *Henry Fielding: A Life* (London and New York: Routledge, 1989, reprinted 1993) – fullest current biography, with much new information, some of it speculative, and insecure attributions of anonymous work. Important, but to be used with caution.

Cross, Wilbur L., *The History of Henry Fielding*, 3 vols. (New Haven: Yale University Press, 1918) – the first modern biography, still readable

Dudden, F. Homes, *Henry Fielding: His Life, Works, and Times*, 2 vols. (Oxford: Clarendon Press, 1952) – criticized by some Fielding biographers, but contains useful information

Pagliaro, Harold, *Henry Fielding: A Literary Life* (Basingstoke: Macmillan, 1998) – useful short account

Paulson, Ronald, *The Life of Henry Fielding* (Oxford: Blackwell, 2000) – a biography focused on the writings and their context, notably useful for account of William Hogarth's importance to Fielding

Rogers, Pat, *Henry Fielding: A Biography* (London: Paul Elek, 1979) – the best short biography

Thomas, Donald, *Henry Fielding* (London: Weidenfeld, 1990) – a helpful and vivid biography, with local feeling for Fielding's Somerset and Bath

## Critical studies of Fielding and his work

Alter, Robert, *Fielding and the Nature of the Novel* (Cambridge, MA: Harvard University Press, 1968)

Bell, Ian A., *Henry Fielding: Authorship and Authority* (London: Longman, 1994)

Bender, John, *Imagining the Penitentiary: Fiction and the Architecture of Mind in Eighteenth-Century England* (Chicago: University of Chicago Press, 1987) – discussion of *Amelia*

Bertelsen, Lance, *Henry Fielding at Work: Magistrate, Businessman, Writer* (Basingstoke: Palgrave, 2000)

Blanchard, Frederic T., *Fielding the Novelist: A Study in Historical Criticism* (New Haven: Yale University Press, 1926) – important study of Fielding's reputation

Campbell, Jill, *Natural Masques: Gender and Identity in Fielding's Plays and Novels* (Stanford: Stanford University Press, 1995)

Castle, Terry, *Masquerade and Civilization: The Carnivalesque in Eighteenth-Century English Culture and Fiction* (London: Methuen, 1986) – discussion of *Amelia*

Cleary, Thomas, *Henry Fielding: Political Writer* (Waterloo, Ont.: Wilfrid Laurier University Press, 1984)

Donaldson, Ian, *The World Upside-Down: Comedy and Society from Jonson to Fielding* (Oxford: Clarendon Press, 1970)

Empson, William, 'Tom Jones', in *Using Biography* (London: Chatto and Windus, 1984)

Ehrenpreis, Irvin, *Fielding: 'Tom Jones'* (London: Arnold, 1964)

Harrison, Bernard, *Henry Fielding's 'Tom Jones'* (London: Sussex University Press, 1975)

Hatfield, Glenn W., *Henry Fielding and the Language of Irony* (Chicago: University of Chicago Press, 1968)

Hume, Robert D., *Henry Fielding and the London Theatre 1728–1737* (Oxford: Clarendon Press, 1987)

Hunter, J. Paul, *Occasional Form: Henry Fielding and the Chains of Circumstance* (Baltimore: Johns Hopkins University Press, 1975)

Hutchens, Eleanor, *Irony in 'Tom Jones'* (University, AL: University of Alabama Press, 1965

Irwin, William Robert, *The Making of 'Jonathan Wild': A Study in the Literary Method of Henry Fielding* (New York: Columbia University Press, 1941)

Keymer, Tom and Peter Sabor, *'Pamela' in the Marketplace: Literary Controversy and Print Culture in Eighteenth-Century Britain and Ireland* (Cambridge: Cambridge University Press, 2005)

Liesenfeld, Vincent J., *The Licensing Act of 1737* (Madison: University of Wisconsin Press, 1984)

Lewis, Peter, *Fielding's Burlesque Drama: Its Place in the Tradition* (Edinburgh: Edinburgh University Press, 1987)

Mace, Nancy A., *Henry Fielding's Novels and the Classical Tradition* (Newark: University of Delaware Press, 1996)

McRea, Brian, *Henry Fielding and the Politics of Mid-Eighteenth-Century England* (Athens: University of Georgia Press, 1981)

Miller, Henry Knight, *Essays on Fielding's Miscellanies: A Commentary on Volume One* (Princeton: Princeton University Press, 1961)

O'Brien, John, *Harlequin Britain: Pantomime and Entertainment, 1690–1760* (Baltimore: Johns Hopkins University Press, 2004)

Paulson, Ronald, *Henry Fielding: A Collection of Critical Essays* (Englewood Cliffs, NJ: Prentice Hall, 1962)

Paulson, Ronald, and Thomas, Lockwood, *Fielding: The Critical Heritage* (London: Routledge, 1969)

Potter, Tiffany, *Honest Sins: Georgian Libertinism and the Plays and Novels of Henry Fielding* (Montreal and Kingston, Ont.: McGill-Queen's University Press, 1999)

Preston, John, *The Created Self: The Reader's Role in Eighteenth-Century Fiction* (London: Heinemann, 1970)

Price, Martin, *To the Palace of Wisdom: Studies in Order and Energy from Dryden to Blake* (Garden City, NY: Anchor Books, 1965)

Rawson, Claude, *Henry Fielding and the Augustan Ideal under Stress* (London: Routledge and Kegan Paul, 1972; corrected paperback edition, Atlantic Highlands NJ: Humanities Press, 1991)

*Order from Confusion Sprung: Studies in Eighteenth-Century Literature from Swift to Cowper* (London: Allen and Unwin, 1985; corrected paperback edition, Atlantic Highlands NJ: Humanities Press, 1992)

*Satire and Sentiment, 1660–1830: Stress Points in the English Augustan Tradition* (Cambridge: Cambridge University Press, 1994; new edition, New Haven and London: Yale University Press, 2000) – discussions of Fielding include comic epic in prose

Rawson, Claude, ed., *Henry Fielding: A Critical Anthology* (Harmondsworth: Penguin, 1973) – critical discussion, 1730–1968, including Fielding's own

*Henry Fielding, Novelist, Playwright, Journalist, Magistrate (1707–1754): A Volume for Two Anniversaries* (Newark: University of Delaware Press, forthcoming 2007)

Richetti, John, *The English Novel in History 1700–1780* (London: Routledge, 1999)

Richetti, John, ed., *The Cambridge Companion to the Eighteenth-Century Novel* (Cambridge: Cambridge University Press, 1996)

Rivero, Albert J., *The Plays of Henry Fielding: A Critical Study of His Dramatic Career* (Charlottesville: University Press of Virginia, 1989)

Rivero, Albert J., ed., *Critical Essays on Henry Fielding* (New York: G. K. Hall, 1998)

Rinehart, Hollis, 'The Role of Walpole in Fielding's *Jonathan Wild*', *English Studies in Canada* (Winter 1979), 420–31

Rosengarten, Richard A., *Henry Fielding and the Narration of Providence: Divine Design and the Incursions of Evil* (Basingstone: Palgrave, 2000)

Simpson, K. G., ed., *Henry Fielding: Justice Observed* (London: Vision, 1985)

Smallwood, Angela J., *Fielding and the Woman Question: The Novels of Henry Fielding and Feminist Debate, 1700–1750* (Hemel Hempstead: Harvester Wheatsheaf, 1989)

Stevenson, John Allen, *The Real History of Tom Jones* (Basingstoke: Palgrave, 2005)

Varey, Simon, *Henry Fielding* (Cambridge: Cambridge University Press, 1986)

*Joseph Andrews: A Satire of Modern Times* (Boston: Twayne, 1990)

Watt, Ian, *The Rise of the Novel: Studies in Defoe, Richardson and Fielding* (London: Chatto and Windus, 1957)

West, Rebecca, *The Court and the Castle: A Study of the Interactions of Political and Religious Ideas in Imaginative Literature* (London: Macmillan, 1958) – essay on Fielding, 'The Great Optimist', with discussion of *Amelia*

Zirker, Malvin J., Jr, *Fielding's Social Pamphlets: A Study of 'An Enquiry into the Causes of the Late Increase of Robbers' and 'A Proposal for Making an Effectual Provision for the Poor'* (Berkeley: University of California Press, 1966)

## Useful background works

Beattie, J. M., *Crime and the Courts in England 1660–1800* (Princeton: Princeton University Press, 1986)

*Policing and Punishment in London, 1660–1750: Urban Crime and the Limits of Terror* (Oxford: Oxford University Press, 2001)

Brewer, John, *The Pleasures of the Imagination: English Culture in the Eighteenth Century* (London: HarperCollins, 1997)

Charke, Charlotte, *A Narrative of the Life of Mrs. Charlotte Charke* (1755; reprinted Gainesville, FL: Scholars' Facsimiles and Reprints, 1969)

Cibber, Colley, *An Apology for the Life of Mr. Colley Cibber* (1740), ed. W. W. Lowe (1889; reprinted New York: AMS Press, 1968); ed. B. R. S. Fone (Ann Arbor: University of Michigan Press, 1968)

Cockburn, J. S., ed., *Crime in England 1550–1800* (London: Methuen, 1977)

Dillon, Patrick, *The Much-Lamented Death of Madam Geneva: The Eighteenth-Century Gin Craze* (London: Review, 2002)

George, M. Dorothy, *London Life in the Eighteenth Century* (New York: 1925; reprinted New York: Capricorn Books, 1965)

Goldgar, Bertrand A., *Walpole and the Wits: The Relation of Politics to Literature, 1722–1742* (Lincoln: University of Nebraska Press, 1976)

Grundy, Isobel, *Lady Mary Wortley Montagu: Comet of the Enlightenment* (Oxford: Clarendon Press, 1999)

Harris, Michael, *London Newspapers in the Age of Walpole* (London and Toronto: Associated University Presses, 1987)

Hay, Douglas, et al., *Albion's Fatal Tree: Crime and Society in Eighteenth-Century England* (London: Allen Lane, 1975; Harmondsworth: Penguin, 1977, reprinted 1988)

Hudson, Nicholas, *Samuel Johnson and the Making of Modern England* (Cambridge: Cambridge University Press, 2003)

Hunter, J. Paul, *Before Novels: The Cultural Contexts of Eighteenth-Century Fiction* (New York: Norton, 1990)

Linebaugh, Peter, *The London Hanged: Crime and Civil Society in the Eighteenth Century* (Cambridge: Cambridge University Press, 1992)

McKeon, Michael, *The Origins of the English Novel, 1600–1740* (Baltimore: Johns Hopkins University Press, 1987)

McLynn, Frank, *Crime and Punishment in Eighteenth-Century England* (Oxford: Oxford University Press, 1991)

Ogborn, Miles, *Spaces of Modernity: London's Geographies 1680–1780* (New York: Guilford Press, 1998)

Paulson, Ronald, *Satire and the Novel in Eighteenth-Century England* (New Haven: Yale University Press, 1967)

Plumb, J. H., *Sir Robert Walpole*, 2 vols. (London: Cresset Press, 1956–60)

Pringle, Patrick, *Hue and Cry: The Story of Henry and John Fielding and their Bow Street Runners* (New York: Morrow, c. 1955)

Sharpe, J. A., *Crime in Early Modern England 1550–1750* (London: Longman, 1984)

Stern, Tiffany, *Rehearsal from Shakespeare to Sheridan* (Oxford: Oxford University Press, 2000)

Watt, Ian, *The Rise of the Novel: Studies in Defoe, Richardson and Fielding* (London: Chatto and Windus, 1957)

# INDEX

Jarry, Alfred
  *Ubu Roi*, 180
Johnson, Samuel, 80, 97, 106, 109, 123, 125,
    140, 147, 162, 175, 186, 189
  *Rasselas*, 62
Joyce, James, 167, 175
  *Portrait of the Artist as a Young Man*, 177
  *Ulysses*, 166, 184
Julius Caesar, 68, 70, 180

Kelly, John
  *Pamela's Conduct in High Life*, 55
Keymer, Thomas, 48, 173
Koon, H., 135
Kreissman, Bernard, 48
Kundera, Milan, 175, 177

*Ladies Magazine*, 106
Lattimore, Richmond, 158, 173
Le Sage, Alain-René, 129
Leavis, F. R., 80, 92
Lennox, Charlotte, 125, 132, 133
  *Female Quixote*, 131
Licensing Act, 2, 10, 17, 18, 19, 35, 73, 112
Lincoln's Inn Fields, 22, 23, 35
Linebaugh, Peter, 151
Lisbon, 122
Lockwood, Thomas, 19, 27, 35, 36, 37,
    113–14, 120, 121
Lodge, David, 175
*London Daily Advertiser*, 96, 119
*London Magazine*, 96, 97, 106
Louis XIV, 83
Lucian, 5
Lyttelton, George, Lord, 5, 10, 12, 13, 111,
    114, 116

Mace, Nancy, 107
Macklin, Charles, 8
Madam Geneva, 141 (see also gin)
Mallet, David, 63
Manley, Delarivier, 129, 131
  *New Atalantis*, 129
Mann, Thomas, 175
Mantel, Hilary, 174
Marlborough, John Churchill, Duke of, 3
Marriage Act, 81
Martyn, Benjamin
  *Timoleon*, 27
McEwan, Ian
  *Child in Time*, 171, 174
Meredith, George, 175, 176–7
Metropolitan Police, 17

Michie, Allen, 108
Middleton, Conyers, 39
Millar, Andrew, 37, 94, 98, 106, 117, 118
Milton, John, 109, 168
  *Paradise Lost*, 70, 71
  *Paradise Regained*, 55
*Mist's Weekly Journal*, 110, 111
Molière, Jean-Baptiste Poquelin
  *L'Avare*, 8, 29
  *Le Médecin malgré lui*, 8, 29
Montagu, Lady Mary Wortley, 7, 15, 16, 21,
    22, 23, 125–6, 132, 139, 151, 173
*Monthly Review*, 96, 106, 130
Moore, Lucy, 77
Moore, Robert Etheridge, 123, 134
Morgan, Fidelis, 135
Murphy, Arthur, 9, 13, 14, 15, 18, 20, 36, 98,
    106, 107, 186
Musil, Robert, 175, 177

Newgate, 68, 70, 75, 78, 95–6, 99, 146,
    150, 153, 154, 164–5, 166, 167,
    173, 185
Nixon, Richard, 180
Nourse, John, 110
Novak, Maximillian E., 65, 77

*Ordinary of Newgate his Account, Of the
  Behaviour, Confession, and dying
  Words of the Malefactors, who were
  Executed on Monday the 24th of this
  Instant May, at Tyburn, The*, 78
Otway, Thomas
  *Marius*, 27

Parnell, Thomas, 163
Paulson, Ronald, 26, 48, 78, 100, 107, 135
Pelham, Henry, 114, 115, 116, 148
Penlez, Bosavern, 14, 143, 144–6, 150
Pilkington, Laetitia, 37, 173
Piozzi, Hester Lynch, 107
Pirandello, Luigi, 26
Pitt, William, Lord Chatham, 5
Plato, 53
Pope, Alexander, 1, 8, 18, 24, 27, 28, 54, 109,
    112, 126, 154, 160, 162, 163, 166
  *Dunciad*, 7, 27, 28, 66, 109, 124, 129, 130,
    144, 160, 163–4, 166, 173
  Fielding's mock-epic attack on, 125
  *Epistle to a Lady*, 154
  *Epistle to Dr Arbuthnot*, 158
  *First Satire of the Second Book of Horace*,
    126, 174

# Cambridge Companions to...

## AUTHORS